Revelation in Indian Thought

T. R. V. Murti

REVELATION IN INDIAN THOUGHT

A Festschrift
in Honour of Professor T. R. V. Murti

Edited by

Harold Coward
and
Krishna Sivaraman

DHARMA PUBLISHING

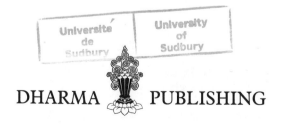

ISBN: 0-913546-52-6
Library of Congress Catalog Card Number: 77-71192

Typeset in Fototronic Plantin
Printed by Dharma Press, Emeryville, California
9 8 7 6 5 4 3 2 1

Contents

Editors' Introduction vii

About the Authors ix

Academic Biography of T. R. V. Murti xii
by Harold G. Coward

STUDIES IN THE PHILOSOPHY OF LANGUAGE

Ṛgveda 10.71 on the Origin of Language 3
by Frits Staal

Some Perspectives on Indian Philosophy of Language 15
by J. G. Arapura

The Word as a Category of Revelation 45
by Krishna Sivaraman

Bhartṛhari's Dhvani: A Central Notion in Indian Aesthetics 65
by Harold G. Coward

Man Carries the Power of All Things in his Mouth:
Jacob Boehme's Ideas on Word and Language 87
by Klaus Klostermaier

STUDIES IN BUDDHISM

The Problem of Self in Buddhist Philosophy 99
by Hajime Nakamura

Trikāya in Buddhist Philosophy—Tibetan and Chinese Hua-Yen Interpretation 119
by Herbert V. Guenther

Insight and Paradox in Buddhist Thought 141
by A. K. Chattarjee

Saṃskāra-Duḥkhatā and the Jaina Concept of Suffering 153
by P. Jaini

STUDIES EAST AND WEST

Nietzsche and Nāgārjuna: The Origins and Issue of Scepticism 159
by Mervyn Sprung

The Unspeakable in Metaphysics 171
by R. K. Tripathi

Religious Diversity and Movements of Religious Life and Thought 185
by Robert Lawson Slater

Complete Bibliography of the Writings of Professor T. R. V. Murti 191

Editors' Introduction

Putting together a *Festschrift* so that it is more than just a series of disconnected papers is a difficult challenge. The editors have attempted to give this volume continuity by grouping the papers around the three themes that have occupied much of Professor Murti's scholarship and teaching. They are: (1) Studies in the Philosophy of Language, (2) Studies in Buddhism, and (3) Studies, East and West. Although T. R. V. Murti is probably best known as a published scholar in Buddhism, it is really the study of Language that, in the final analysis, seems closest to his heart. But whether his teaching and writing is focused on Buddhism or Language, Professor Murti's constant drive is to bridge the gap between East and West. It is the sincere hope of the Editors that this collection of essays will in some small way share in Professor Murti's search for truth in these three areas–and thus be a fitting tribute to him.

Having successfully grouped the papers together according to theme, the Festschrift editors' next problem is to find a title suitable for both the contents of the volume and the person being honored. In this case, the title came spontaneously from the content of Professor Murti's own teaching and scholarship. Whatever T. R. V. has done or said, as teacher or writer, has clearly been directed towards one end–the revelation of reality. Thus the title "Revelation in Indian Thought" seemed exactly right for a

Festschrift volume in honour of T. R. V. Murti, and, when taken in its broadest sense, seemed an accurate description of most of the papers included.

But a collection of papers and an appropriate title do not themselves a *Festschrift* make. Acknowledgement must be made of the considerable contribution made by staff members in the Department of Religious Studies, The University of Calgary—especially Penny Rusk and Carolina Maloney, who spent many long secretarial hours on the book. Professor Leslie Kawamura must also be thanked for his constant encouragement and helpfulness. Judy Robertson and her staff at the Dharma Press were most co-operative from the start, and always found a path through difficulties in a spirit befitting the Press' name. And, finally, it was the generosity of the University of Calgary in providing a grant that enabled the publication of this volume to go ahead. To all of the above the editors express their sincere thanks.

February 7th, 1977.

HAROLD G. COWARD

KRISHNA SIVARAMAN

The University of Calgary
Calgary, Alberta, Canada

About the Authors

JOHN G. ARAPURA is Professor of Religion at McMaster University, Hamilton, Ontario, Canada. He holds a Ph.D. from Columbia University and was a Fellow of the Indian Institute of Philosophy, Amalner, Maharashtra, India for two years. Before joining McMaster University he was Chairman of the Department of South Asian Studies at the Hartford Seminary, Hartford, Connecticut. He is the author of *Radhakrishnan and Integral Experience* (1966), *Religion as Anxiety and Tranquility* (1972), and numerous articles on language and comparative religion.

A. K. CHATTARJEE, Reader in Philosophy, Banaras Hindu University, formerly Professor of Philosophy, Agra College, Agra University, Author of *The Yogacara Idealism* (1975), *Facets of Buddhism* (1975), *Readings on Yogacara Buddhism* (1971), and of several articles published in *Anviksiki* (Banaras), *Indian Philosophical Annual* (Madras), and other Indian Journals.

HAROLD COWARD is Associate Professor and Head of the Department of Religious Studies at the University of Calgary, Calgary, Alberta, Canada. He holds a Ph.D. in Indian Philosophy and Religion from McMaster University. In 1972, he was a visiting scholar at Banaras Hindu University, Varanasi, India. His essays and reviews have appeared in *The Philo-*

sophical Quarterly (India), *The Journal of the American Academy of Religion*, *The Journal for the Scientific Study of Religion*, and *Studies in Religion*. He is the author of *Bhartṛhari* (1976) and editor of *Mystics and Scholars* (1977).

HERBERT GUENTHER is Professor and Head of the Department of Far Eastern Studies at the University of Saskatchewan. He studied in Munich, Vienna, India, and Tibet and has taught at Vienna University, Lucknow University, the Sanskrit University, and the International School of America before assuming his position at the University of Saskatchewan. His many books include *Das Seelenproblem im alteren Buddhismus*, *Yuganaddha—The Tantric Way of Life*, *Tibetan Buddhism without Mystification*, *Buddhist Philosophy in Theory and Practice*, and *Kindly Bent to Ease Us, I, II* and *III*.

PADMANABH S. JAINI is Professor of Buddhist Studies at the University of California, Berkeley. He holds a Ph.D. from the University of London, and taught in Banaras and London for several years. He is the editor of the *Abhidharmadīpa* (1959) and the author of several articles on comparative studies in Buddhism and Jainism.

KLAUS KLOSTERMAIER is Professor of Religious Studies at the University of Manitoba, Winnipeg, Manitoba, Canada. He holds a Dr. Phil. in Philosophy from the Gregorian University, Rome and a Ph.D. in Ancient Indian History and Culture from Bombay University, and studied and taught in India for nine years. He is the author of *Hinduismus* (1965), *Hindu and Christian in Vrindaban* (1970), *Mahatma Gandhi: Freiheit ohne Gewalt* (1968), *Salvation, Liberation, Self-realization* (1974), and numerous articles in Orientalist and Philosophical and Religious Studies Journals.

HAJIME NAKAMURA is Emeritus Professor, Tokyo University. He received his D.Litt. from Tokyo University and has studied and taught in such places as Banaras Hindu University, University of Hawaii, Harvard University and Hong Kong University. He is author of *Ways of Thinking of Eastern Peoples* (1960), *The New Buddhist Dictionary* (1961), and numerous other articles.

KRISHNA SIVARAMAN has degrees from Annamalai, Madras and Banaras Hindu Universities, and was a Post Doctoral Fellow at the Center for the

Study of World Religions at Harvard University during 1963-64. He has been a teacher on the faculty of Banaras Hindu University and is currently at McMaster University, Hamilton, Canada, as Associate Professor of Religious Studies. Author of *Saivism in Philosophical Perspective* (1972), and of several papers published in *Anviksiki* (Banaras), *Indian Philosophical Annual* (Madras), *Religion and Society* (Bangalore) and other journals.

ROBERT LAWSON SLATER, Emeritus Professor of World Religions, Harvard University was formerly Director of the Center for the Study of World Religions, Harvard University and has been Visiting Professor at Banaras Hindu University. Publications include *Paradox and Nirvana: A Study of Religious Ultimates with special reference to Burmese Buddhism* (1951) and *World Religions and World Community* (1963).

MERVYN SPRUNG is Professor of Philosophy at Brock University, St. Catherines, Ontario, Canada. He holds a Ph.D. from Berlin, and his published articles have appeared in various Philosophy and Religious Studies journals. He is the editor of *The Problem of Two Truths in Buddhism and Vedānta* (1973).

FRITS STAAL is Professor of Philosophy and South Asian Languages, University of California at Berkeley. He studied at Amsterdam and Madras and held lecturing positions in American, Dutch, English, Indian and Japanese Universities, and is author of *Advaita and Neo-platonism* (1961), *Nambudiri Veda Recitation* (1961), *Word Order in Sanskrit and Universal Grammar* (1967), *A Reader on the Sanskrit Grammarians* (1972), *Exploring Mysticism* (1975), and numerous articles.

R. K. TRIPATHI is Professor of Philosophy, Banaras Hindu University, sometime Director, Center of Advanced Study in Philosophy, Banaras Hindu University, Professor and Head of the Dept. of Philosophy, Kasividyapit, Varanasi. He is author of *Spinoza in the Light of the Vedanta* (1971), *Problems of Philosophy and Religion*, and many Learned articles in *Anviksiki* (Banaras), *Indian Philosophical Annual* (Madras), and *Philosophy East and West* (Honolulu).

Academic Biography of Professor T. R. V. Murti

Harold G. Coward

TIRUPATTUR RAMESESHAYYER VENKATACHALA MURTI was born on the 15th of June, 1902, in a South Indian middle class Brahmin family. He was educated first at Tiruppattur and later at Tirucchinapalli where early undergraduate study was undertaken at the then Bishop Heber College. His college studies were interrupted when at a young age he joined the nationalist movement started by Mahatma Gandhi. Part of the independence movement requirement was a boycott of colleges, courts and other public offices, as these were conducted under British auspices. Leaving college, he and his brother walked some two thousand miles to North India, where Murti entered the second stage of his educational career. His one year stay at the Nationalist eudcational center of Gurukul Kangri at Haradwar can be described as a period of apprenticeship for his subsequent Sanskritic studies.

After a gap of several years spent in the cause of Gandhi's Nationalist Movement (which included, among other things, being jailed for five months), Murti, in 1925, joined the Banaras Hindu University, the all-India Nationalist Movement University started by one of the foremost Hindu nationalist leaders of the times. Banaras was the renowned seat of Hindu classical learning, providing a forum for top ranking scholars and teachers in fields of Sanskritic Studies and Sanskrit Grammar. This was especially true of the Banaras Sanskrit College. Banaras Hindu University, however, even though begun as a part of the Nationalist Movement against the British, followed the traditional British style of university education with English as the medium of higher learning and research. The presence of both the Sanskrit College and the Hindu University side by side in Banaras allowed Murti the unique and for him formative experience of simultaneously pursuing classical Sanskrit training and Western style University study—a pattern which he has continued to follow. In 1927 Murti received a B.A. with honours in Sanskrit and Philosophy from the Banaras Hindu University, and in 1929 an M.A., mainly in Western Philosophy. Also in 1929, from the Sanskrit College where he studied under such teachers at Balakrishna Misra, Kaliprasad Misra and Devanarayan Tiwari, Murti was awarded *Śāstri* (the classical Sanskrit equivalent to a B.A.) with specialization in Vedānta; in 1941 he was awarded *Āchārya* (the classical Sanskrit equivalent to an M.A.) with specialization in Vyākarana or Grammar. All of the above degrees were achieved with 1st class standing. In 1948 the D.Litt. degree (the highest degree of Banaras Hindu University) was awarded to Professor Murti for his thesis entitled "The Mādhyamika Dialectic."

A unique aspect of the above survey of Murti's academic training is its dual character. Murti mastered the classical punditic system involving the studying of Sanskrit texts line by line—until great depths of understanding were reached—and then committing these texts—every inflection and every syllable—to memory. Not only were the basic texts thus learned, but also the important commentaries. Murti demonstrated equal excellence in the modern, Western system of education with its impulse toward critical examination and free exploration. Both these influences have been continuously present in Murti as a teacher and research scholar. His ability to achieve distinction in both Classical Indian and Modern Western scholarship, and his ability to bring these two traditions into academic dialogue, has helped to establish a model for a new generation of Indian scholarship. This dual background also qualified Professor Murti for important service on the "Sanskrit Commission" which was constituted during the period 1955-60 by the Indian government to review the scope and future of Sanskrit *vis-a-vis* higher education in India.

Another landmark in Murti's career—of formative significance toward his role as the 'thinker' of Indian Philosophy—was his seven year stay, from 1929-36, at the Institute of Philosophy at Amalner, near Bombay. He was initially a Fellow and subsequently a member of the Faculty. The Institute was the only institution of its kind founded with the express object of promoting creative philosophical thinking in keeping with the spirit of Vedānta. The *Philosophical Quarterly* was its official organ; it was the only journal of its kind during the Thirties, Forties and the Fifties of this century which embodied original Indian philosophical writing. Many of Murti's writings appeared first in this journal. Murti has himself acknowledged the debt he owes to the Institute for furnishing him a good basic training for his vocation as a scholar. Contemporary Indian philosophers such as Rashvihari Das, D. M. Datta and N. V. Banergee were also associated with the Institute during Murti's stay, however, he was principally influenced by the original and profound Indian philosopher K. C. Bhattacharya. Murti has consistently acknowledged that K. C. Bhattacharya was the teacher who influenced his most, especially in the creative relating of classical German philosophy to the key issues of Advaita Vedānta. Murti's own later philosophical writings, quickened as they are by his first hand acquaintance with Mahāyāna Buddhism, depart considerably from Bhattacharya's perspectives; yet, one can see continuity between the two especially in their interpretation of Advaita Vedānta, Sāṇkhya and Jaina systems of thought.

In 1936 Murti was appointed Assistant Professor of Philosophy in the Banaras Hindu University at the special initiative of its founder Pandit Madan Mohan Malavya, who saw in Murti the requisite potential for a regeneration of Indian Philosophy in keeping with both the Classical Sanskrit tradition and the stringent expectations of modern academia. Evidence that Murti lived up to this expectation is in the fact that he became the first Professor of Philosophy who was also completely at home in Sanskrit. Radhakrishnan, the great Indian philosopher and statesman, was then Vice-Chancellor of the University, and Murti had close intellectual contacts with him. Radhakrishnan continued to be his well wisher and always extended his full support to Murti. It was Radhakrishnan's discovery of Murti as a major talent that was responsible for his introduction to the international audience. Murti deputized for Radhakrishnan as the Spalding Professor of Eastern Religion and Ethics at Oxford in 1949–50.

In 1949 Murti was invited to be the first Professor of Philosophy at the University of Ceylon. He had by then achieved recognition for his excellent scholarship in the area of Buddhism, and his three year stay at the University of Ceylon resulted in the inauguration of a full-fledged Department of Philosophy oriented towards Indian Philosophy and Buddhism.

At the special invitation of the then Vice-Chancellor of Banaras Hindu University, Murti returned to Banaras in 1953 and occupied the very prestigious Sayaji Rao Gaekwad chair as Professor of Indian Civilization and Culture, succeeding Radhakrishnan. During his eventual life as Professor at Banaras, he also held the following visiting appointments: Lecturer at the Hebrew University, Jerusalem, in 1958; Professor of Philosophy, Stanford and Yale Universities, 1960–61; and Professor of World Religions, Center for the Study of World Religions, Harvard University, 1963. In 1964 he attended, as a Panel Member, the 4th East West Philosophers' Conference held at Honolulu, and in 1965 participated in the 11th Congress of the International Association for the History of Religions held at Claremont, California. In due recognition of his special expertise and international reputation, in 1962 Murti was appointed Vice-Chancellor of the Sanskrit University, Banaras.

Centers of Advanced Study in Philosophy were created in three University centers in India thanks to the happy circumstance that the President of India was the philosopher statesman Radhakrishnan. Murti was made Director of the center at Banaras. In addition to this recognition from within academia, Murti was selected by the Government of India to receive the *Padma Bhushan* (award of Distinction).

The sincere concern to communicate the teachings of Indian Philosophy to the West, evident throughout Murti's career, reasserted itself following his retirement from Banaras Hindu University. In 1968 he was appointed Visiting Professor at both Brock and McMaster Universities in Canada. From 1969–72 he continued as Visiting Professor at McMaster University, Hamilton, Ontario.

With regard to scholarly publication, Murti has a distinguished record. His study of the Mādhyamika System entitled *The Central Philosophy of Buddhism*, first published in 1955 with a second edition in 1960, has achieved world-wide recognition as a standard and authoritative work on the subject. As Edward Conze put it in his review of the book, "The rare combination of philological accuracy with philosophical profundity and spiritual zest make this one of the most outstanding publications on Buddhism which we have seen for some time."[1] Conze's assessment of Murti's book is not an isolated opinion but one which has been repeated by the leading Buddhist scholars from 1955 right up to the present. The *Central Philosophy of Buddhism* is certainly one of the most important philosophical books to come out of India in this century. In addition to this major book, Murti was joint author of another entitled *Ajñāna* on the theory of ignorance in Vedānta. He has also published some forty-five articles in leading journals of philosophy throughout the world.

In more recent years Murti's interest has turned from Mādhyamika

Buddhism and Vedānta to the topic of language in Indian philosophy. His article entitled "Some Thoughts on the Philosophy of Language in the Indian Context," first given as his Presidential Address at the 37th Session of the Indian Philosophical Congress in 1963, and recently published in the *Journal of Indian Philosophy*, has sparked a scholarly reassessment of the place of language in Indian thought–as evidenced in the essays by Sivaraman and Coward included in this volume. Murti's other area of important scholarly research is that of Advaita Vedānta. Perhaps his most important article in this regard is the paper entitled "Tatastha and Svarūpa Lakṣanā of Brahman in Advaita" written for the K. C. Bhattacharyya Memorial volume.

In addition to his own writing Murti has made significant editorial contributions. He was General Editor for the Darsana (Philosophy) Research Series and responsible for publishing some six volumes. In his capacity as Director of the Center of Advanced Study in Philosophy at Banaras, Murti inaugurated publication of the All-India Seminar Proceedings, which related to different themes of Indian Philosophy. In this regard he conducted systematic textual seminars analyzing difficult and often intractable Advaita Vedānta texts like *Vivaraṇa*, *Citsukhi* and *Advaita Siddhi.* He also continued to lead in the study of Bhartṛhari's writings and Kashmir Śaiva texts. As many as thirty-five doctoral dissertations were written during this period under his immediate supervision; among them are many which have been acclaimed as major publications in Indian Philosophy. Many of his students are now professors of philosophy or religious studies in Indian and Western universities.

Those who were privileged to hear or study with Professor Murti know him to be a rare and gifted teacher. He can make archaic Sanskrit texts come alive from the musty corridors of time in which they are framed. Through his explanation and insight, the issues that these old texts grapple with are 'lifted' out of the past to speak powerfully to the problems of today. Through him one gains a respect for and understanding of tradition, not as static authoritative doctrine, but as the source from which flows a continuous stream of thought and culture. From him one also learns to be open to all philosophical viewpoints, and to make every effort to understand each position in its own terms.

Murti's relationship with his students was challenging, demanding and yet forgiving, loving, and supporting in a most initmate and indescribable way. He communicated an unspoken criterion of excellence which drove one never to be satisfied with anything less than the very best effort–and even then to realize the weakness and inadequacy in what was being presented. But this high requirement for academic excellence was never directed toward any shallow or surface intellectual achievement, its goal was always the student's own spiritual awakening and self-understanding. The student who came into contact with Professor Murti could have the rare experience of perceiving that such a forbidding challenge could also become a most exciting opportunity. It is in gratitude for the intellectual and spiritual opportunity given by Professor T. R. V. Murti to so many, that this *Festschrift* is presented.

1. Edward Conze, "A Review of the Central Philosophy of Buddhism by T. R. V. Murti" in the *Journal of the Royal Asiatic Society*, April 1956.

Revelation in Indian Thought

Ṛgveda 10.71 on the Origin of Language

Frits Staal

Introduction

Professor Murti's fame is derived in the first place from his book *The Central Philosophy of Buddhism*, which stands unequalled for its combination of textual knowledge and philosophical acumen. His pre-eminence among Indian philosophers is due not only to his authorship of this work, but also to his knowledge of Western and Indian philosophy, his mastery of Sanskrit, and his familiarity with the Hindu Śāstra literature, in particular with grammar and the philosophy of language.

In "Some Thoughts on the Indian Philosophy of Language"[1], Murti describes the two principal Indian traditions which deal with language. According to one tradition (represented by the Cārvāka and by early Buddhism) language is conventional and arbitrary. According to the other (represented by the Vedānta, Mīmāṃsā, Sāṃkhya-Yoga, the school of grammar and Kashmir Śaivism), language is of divine or transcendental origin. The latter tradition has a spiritual dimension on which Murti dwells at some length; it also expresses a fact about language, which the former tradition ignores or neglects: viz., that there are features of language which are independent of sound.

The place and significance of this doctrine in Indian philosophy and in philosophy in general is clearly brought out by Murti: "That language is underived and that the word is a form and is thus distinct from its material embodiment, sound, are established by the Mīmāṃsā theory of the Eternality of the Word (Śabda-nityatva-vāda)" (Murti 1963, xi–xii). And: "The eternality of Words as propounded by the schools of Mīmāṃsā and Grammar is the Indian counterpart of the (Platonic) doctrine of Ideas" (p. xiii).

Since the permanent embodiment of language is considered to be the Vedas, the doctrine of the permanence of language takes us back to them. Murti quotes several Vedic passages which refer to language. He also refers to a verse of the *Ṛgveda*, which "tells us that the ignorant man seeing and hearing speech in its overt manifest forms does not know its real nature" (p. viii). The following pages aim at an interpretation of *Ṛgveda* 10.71, from which the verse referred to here has been taken.

Before embarking upon an interpretation of ideas on language which are at least 3,000 years old, I shall briefly rehearse some contemporary ideas on language. This is not because I am convinced that these ideas are necessarily correct (after all, the Cārvāka and early Buddhist view of language, which is demonstrably false, has long been rampant among Western linguists); but because these contemporary views provide us with a better terminology than does ordinary language, and any contemporary interpretation is likely to be in these terms.

Most contemporary Western linguists and many philosophers look upon language as a system which relates two domains to each other: sound and meaning. Both domains are structured domains, i.e., domains characterized by regularities which can be formally represented by rules. The structured domain of sound is the subject of phonology; the structured domain of meaning is the subject of semantics. The relationship between these two domains can be approached from different perspectives. For example, the sounds of language can be thought of as conveying or expressing meaning. What is important in the present context is that the relationships between sound and meaning constitute again a structured domain. This domain is the subject of syntax. To what extent semantics, syntax and phonology are distinct or dependent on each other, and whether there are other sciences which have to be taken into account (e.g., pragmatics), is a matter of controversy, but this is inessential in the context of this paper.

Text and Translation of Ṛgveda 10.71

Bṛhaspate prathamaṃ vāco agraṃ yat prairata nāmadheyaṃ dadhānāḥ /
yad eṣāṃ śreṣṭhaṃ yad aripram āsīt preṇā tad eṣāṃ nihitaṃ guhaviḥ ⟨1⟩

saktum iva titaünā punanto yatra dhīrā manasā vācam akrata /
atrā sakhāyaḥ sakhyāni jānate bhadraiṣāṃ lakṣmīr nihitādhi vāci ⟨2⟩

yajñena vācaḥ padavīyam āyan tām anv avindann ṛṣiṣu praviṣṭām /
tām ābhṛtyā vy adadhuḥ purutrā tāṃ sapta rebhā abhi saṃ navante ⟨3⟩

uta tvaḥ paśyan na dadarśa vācam uta tvaḥ śṛṇvan na śṛṇoty enām /
uto tvasmai tanvaṃ vi sasre jāyeva patya uśatī suvāsāḥ ⟨4⟩

uta tvaṃ sakhye sthirapītam āhur nainaṃ hinvanty api vājineṣu /
adhenvā carati māyayaiṣa vācaṃ śuśruvāñ aphalām apuṣpām ⟨5⟩

yas tityāja sacividaṃ sakhāyaṃ na tasya vācy api bhāgo asti /
yad īṃ śṛṇoty alakaṃ śṛṇoti nahi praveda sukṛtasya panthām ⟨6⟩

akṣanvantaḥ karṇavantaḥ sakhāyo manojaveṣv asamā babhūvuḥ /
ādaghnāsa upakakṣāsa u tve hradā iva snātvā u tve dadṛśre ⟨7⟩

hṛdā taṣṭeṣu manaso javeṣu yad brāhmaṇāḥ saṃyajante sakhāyaḥ /
atrāha tvaṃ vi jahur vedyābhir ohabrahmāṇo vi caranty u tve ⟨8⟩

ime ye nārvāṅ na paraś caranti na brāhmaṇāso na sutekarāsaḥ /
ta ete vācam abhipadya pāpayā sirīs tantraṃ tanvate aprajajñayaḥ ⟨9⟩

sarve nandanti yaśasāgatena sabhāsāhena sakhyā sakhāyaḥ /
kilbiṣaspṛt pituṣaṇir hy eṣām araṃ hito bhavati vājināya ⟨10⟩

ṛcāṃ tvaḥ poṣam āste pupuṣvān gāyatraṃ tvo gāyati śakvarīṣu /
brahmā tvo vadati jātavidyāṃ yajñasya mātrāṃ vi mimīta u tvaḥ ⟨11⟩

Bṛhaspati! When they came forth to establish the first beginning of language, setting up names, what had been hidden in them as their best and purest good became manifest through love. ⟨1⟩

Where the sages fashioned language with their thought, filtering it like parched grain through a sieve, friends recognized their friendship. Their beauty is marked on the language. ⟨2⟩

They traced the course of language through ritual; they found it embodied in the seers. They gained access to it and distributed it widely; the seven chanters cheered them. ⟨3⟩

Many who look do not see language, many who listen do not hear it. It reveals itself like a loving and well adorned wife to her husband. ⟨4⟩

Many, they say, have grown rigid in this friendship; they are not sent to the contests. Such a one goes with the power of a milkless cow, for he has heard language which is fruitless and flowerless. ⟨5⟩

He who abandons a friend who knows with him has no share in the language. If indeed he hears, he hears in vain, for he does not know the path of good action. ⟨6⟩

Though all the friends have eyes and ears, their mental intuitions are uneven. Some are like shallow ponds, which reach up to the mouth or armpit, others are like ponds which are fit for bathing. ⟨7⟩

When mind's intuitions are shaped in the heart, when brahmins perform rites together as friends, some are wittingly eliminated, others emerge on account of the manifest excellence of the power of language. ⟨8⟩

Those who do not improve or progress, who are not real brahmins, who do not take part in the Soma libation, they use language in wrong fashion; they weave flowing waters without understanding. ⟨9⟩

All rejoice about the friend who emerges famous and victorious in the assembly. He dismisses harm, he bestows food. He is fit for the contest. ⟨10⟩

One sits down multiplying the wealth of verse. One chants a chant in the *Śakvarī* meter. One sets forth the newly-born knowledge. One lays out the measure of the rites. ⟨11⟩[2]

Remarks on Translation

The following comments on terminology and specific phrases could have been increased almost indefinitely, but I have tried to keep references to other Vedic and non-Vedic passages to a minimum.

The most important term, *vāc*, which occurs seven times in this hymn, is generally translated as 'speech' (Geldner: *Rede*, Renou: *parole*). I have translated it here as 'language' (as sometimes Renou: *langue*). The reason is that 'speech' is ambiguous: it is sometimes synonymous with 'language'; but generally it stresses the vocal, auditory and phonological properties of language, viz., sound. It is moreover specifically applicable to unique occurrences, i.e., to what philosophers call a *token*, as against 'language', which stands for the *type*. Since *Ṛgveda* 10.71 discusses, among other things, the place of sound in the whole of language, the translation 'speech' would beg the question.

Elsewhere in the *Ṛgveda, vāc* is used of animals (especially birds), of fire, of Soma, and of rain and thunder. At first sight such uses may seem to stress sound. But this is due to the fact that *we* may not think of meaning in such contexts. The Vedic Indians and poets generally refer without hesitation to the language of animals and of natural phenomena. Another indication that *vāc* might mean 'language' is the fact that the common word for 'language' in later Sanskrit, *bhāṣya*, does not occur in the *Ṛgveda*.

There is one occurrence in the hymn of the important word *brāhman* (in verse 8) which I have translated as 'power of language'. There has been much discussion of this term and several special studies have been devoted to it (notably by Gonda, Renou and Thieme). It is now generally accepted that *brāhman*, among other things, is close to *vāc* in meaning. In contexts like the present, the rendering 'power of speech' would be uncontroversial. I have changed this into 'power of language' to be in line with the translation of *vāc*.

The word *agra* in the first verse, which I translate 'beginning', can also mean 'most excellent'. Gonda translates it as 'foremost' in: "the first and foremost part of speech." The combination with *prathama* 'first' makes it clear, however, that a beginning is referred to, whence 'first beginning' (Geldner: *erster Anfang*) seems preferable.

The term *nāmadheya* in *nāmadheyaṃ dhā* 'to set up names' does not occur elsewhere in the *Ṛgveda* but is increasingly common in later times. The same holds for *preman* 'love', though the verb *prī* "love; be pleased; please" occurs frequently in the *Ṛgveda*.

Gonda translates *bhadrā lakṣmīḥ* as "auspicious 'sign' (prognostication of luck and prosperity)." Renou takes *bhadrā* as 'beautiful' rather than 'auspicious': " 'de bon augure', mais aussi et d'abord 'beau' (esthétiquement)." Gonda has adopted the characterization of *lakṣmī* arrived at in his study on Viṣṇuism as "an object the very existence or presence of which means something." On this interpretation, everything is bound to be *lakṣmī*. I have preferred 'beauty' as a single translation for both words because it is simple, makes sense, is sufficiently ambiguous and complements "best and purest good" in the previous verse.

I have translated as 'ritual' or 'rite' the word *yajña* which occurs twice and is generally translated as 'sacrifice'. The verb *yaj*, which occurs once with the prefix *sam*, has been accordingly rendered as 'to preform rites (together)'. The phrase *yajñena vācaḥ padavīyam āyan* has been translated by Gonda as: "by means of worship (the sacrifice) they (another group, the 'historical seers', or 'second generation', being interested in the liturgical function of speech) went the way of Speech." In a footnote, Gonda contrasts these 'first seers' with the 'human seers': "appearing on the scene when the sacrifice has been instituted, see *Ṛgveda* 10.130.6, cf. also 150.4." There undoubtedly is such a distinction in the *Ṛgveda*, and yet the meaning of the phrase is not made any clearer. A more literal translation would be: "through ['by means of', 'with'] ritual they followed the traces of language." This indicates that ritual enabled the sages to trace language, which still requires an explanation.

The verb *nu* is used for cheering, singing, and also for the roaring of cattle; *abhi-sam-nu* which occurs in verse 3 means 'to cheer together'.

In verse 5, *sthirapīta* is derived from *sthira* 'firm, fixed' and *pīta* 'drunk' (from *pā*) or 'swollen, fat' (from *pī, pi*). The latter meaning is preferable because *pī/pi* is elsewhere used of *dhī* 'inspiration, intuition' (Gonda 1963, p. 126; Renou 1967, p. 141). Renou also refers to *Śatapatha-brāhmaṇa* 4.6.9.7, where a priest first sits down controlling his language (i.e., speechless) and swelling it, and subsequently performs rites with that controlled and swollen language. In the Soma rituals, Soma is made to swell (*āpyāyana*) by sprinkling it with water and with language. In *Ṛgveda* 10.71, *sthirapīta* is used in a negative sense, and seems to indicate that the swelling is fixed, checked or arrested. Hence 'grown rigid' in my translation.

In verses 7 and 8, *manaso java* 'mind's intuition' and the compound *manojava* 'mental intuition' refer to the velocity or speed of mind. Renou (1955, p. 23) compares this with improvisation in the poetic contests of classical, post-Vedic times. However, it should be borne in mind that courtly associations are anachronistic and that the Vedic contests were not merely poetic contests. In the same verses there is an untranslatable play on the words *hrada* 'pond' and *hṛd* 'heart'.

In the last verse, the verb *puṣ* means 'rear, nourish, grow, increase, multiply' and *poṣa* is the accompanying or resulting 'growth, wealth, abundance'. The verb *mā* 'measure' (and analogously the noun *mātrā*) means, according to Grassmann, not 'measure how big something is' but 'determine by measurement how big something should be'. Grassmann was not only author of the dictionary of the *Ṛgveda*, but also a linguist and mathematician (in fact, one of the founders of multi-dimensional geometry). Hence *mātrāṃ vi-mā* 'to lay out the measure'.

Interpretation

Throughout *Ṛgveda* 10.71, a contrast is made between two forms of language:

language is hidden;	language is manifest;
it is hidden in the sages and embodied in the seers;	it is widely distributed by the sages;

it is looked at and listened to (without understanding);	it is seen and heard (with understanding);
it is fruitless and flowerless;	it reveals itself;
it is used in wrong fashion, without understanding;	
it is hidden from shallow intuitions;	it is reached by deep intuitions.

When the hidden becomes manifest, language originates. This is the 'newly born knowledge' (verse 11), from which the hymn derives its name, *jñāna-sūkta* 'hymn of knowledge'. Gonda has quoted *Bṛhaddevatā* 7.109, where Bṛhaspati praised that knowledge "which is immortal light and by union with which one attains to *brahma*." The person who sets forth the newly born knowledge is in fact the Brahman priest, as we shall see.

That language consists of different levels—in fact, four quarters, three of them hidden and one manifest and spoken by men—is mentioned in *Ṛgveda* 1.164.45. The grammarian Patañjali quotes this verse in the Introduction to his *Mahābhāṣya*. He interprets the four quarters as the parts of speech—nouns, verbs, preverbs and particles. Patañjali has enough common sense to refrain from drawing the conclusion that, on this interpretation, men should use only one of the parts of speech, presumably particles. Even so, he gives the same interpretation to the four horns of a bull when quoting *Ṛgveda* 4.58.3. Patañjali also quotes *Ṛgveda* 10.71.4 and 2, taking 'friends' to mean *vaiyākaraṇāḥ* 'grammarians'. It is worth noting that Murti, who has followed Patañjali in quoting these Ṛgvedic passages, has not followed Patañjali's grammatical zeal in interpreting them.

The main idea of the hymn is that language originated when hidden knowledge became manifest, i.e., when meaning was attached to sound. This applies, as the hymn explicitly states, to the origin of language, i.e., of *all* language. Those who like the word 'sacred' may think of language at its origin as 'sacred language', but 'sacred' should be used here in the unrestrictive and not in the restrictive sense. The hymn deals with the origin of language, which may be called sacred language, but not with the origin of 'sacred language' as a part of language (like 'academic language' or 'vulgar language').

This interpretation makes sense of most parts of the hymn. It explains why the origin of language is dealt with in a 'hymn of knowledge'. It also suggests that, when language came into being, sound was already available. Other verses support this. Various things are referred to as *preceding* the origin of language. One of these is presupposed in the phrase: 'The seven chanters cheered them' (verse 3). This cheering could not have been in language without circularity. Cheering obviously involves sound, as does the chant in the *Śakvarī* meter referred to in the last verse. Such cheering and such chants, like *Sāmaveda* chants, consist of meaningless syllables (*stobha*) and are similar to lullabies which precede the origin of language, for language involves meaning.

That meaningless sound preceded meaningful language is in accordance with the idea that language, when merely regarded as sound, is listened to and looked at without understanding meaning. Only when meaning is attached to it is language heard, seen and understood. So language originated when the domain of meaning, which was hidden, was recognized and attached to the domain of sound, which was already publicly available. The domain of sound was a structured or rule-governed domain, for it possessed meter (like lullabies, wordless songs and music generally).

Just as sound can be conceived of as the body of language, meaning is its soul or self. In later speculation this is couched in terms which are similar to the Ṛgvedic expressions. In the Upaniṣads and the Advaita Vedānta, the self is 'hidden in a cave'. "The self can be viewed as the essence or the reality of the body (*nihitaṃ guhāyām*)" (Murti 1958, p. 144). This self which becomes conscious is *brāhman*, the meaning or power of language, the good and beautiful essence which is marked on sound and turns it into language.

The 'setting up of names', *nāmadheya*, constitutes an important feature, but is not all of the origin of language. The *Ṛgveda* is therefore ahead of Adam's naming activity in *Genesis* 2.19-20. The reason is that language does not consist merely of names, or sequences of names, but possesses a structure into which nouns are introduced together with other parts of speech. (The implications of this are only beginning to be understood by Western philosophers.) The beginning of language (*vācārambhana*) and the setting up of names (*nāmadheya*) remain distinct in later texts. In *Chāndogyopaniṣad* 6.1, for example, we meet three times with the phrase: *vācārambhanaṃ vikāro nāmadheyam*. In the first context, the discussion centers on the analysis of a piece of clay: essentially it consists of clay, but its distinctiveness is due to language (*vācārambhana*), it is a modification (*vikāra*), a set-up (*nāmadheya*). The truth (*satya*) is that it is only clay.

The basic distinction between language and naming explains a development which would otherwise remain paradoxical. Following the Upaniṣads, several later philosophical systems, Buddhist and Jaina as well as Hindu, consider the realm of name and form (*nāmarūpa*), sometimes identified as mind and body, as a reality of lower level which is transcended by the absolute. But how can this be consistent with the Vedic notion, accepted by many of the Hindu systems, that language is eternal? The answer lies precisely in the distinction between language and naming. While language expresses the self of man, naming differentiates the multitude of things. The distinction between language and naming is therefore essential to the *ātmavāda*. In the *nairātmya* tradition, where man does not have a self, there is no need for a transcendental origin of language, and language reduces to naming. All of this fits in well with the perspective of Murti's *Central Philosophy of Buddhism*.

Just as a domain of structured sound preceded the origin of language, the formerly hidden and unconscious domain of meaning which was attached to sound is also a structured domain. It would not be possible otherwise to refer to its various features which are reocgnized as the best and purest good, friendship, beauty, and mental intuitions shaped in the heart. We are thus entitled to say that for language to originate, structured domains of sound and meaning had to be connected. Such a process cannot be understood without the help of semantics and phonology. But where did syntax come from?

There is another domain which clearly precedes the origin of language according to *Ṛgveda* 10.71: the domain of ritual. This fact seems to contradict Gonda's assumption, that the 'liturgical function of speech' was of later origin. Gonda's view holds good historically, in the sense that ritual increased in the later Vedic period, but it is inconsistent with the perspective of the hymn. Ritual was available to the sages before they found language, for it assisted them in "tracing the course of language." The performance of rites is therefore on a par with the shaping of mental intuitions in the heart, and the laying out of the measure of the rites is on a par with the newly born knowledge.

The simplest hypothesis which makes sense of these various puzzling expressions is the assumption that a structured domain of ritual preceded the origin of language just as did structured domains of sound and (unconscious) meaning. In simple terms this means that men already sang, danced and performed rites before they spoke; and that they already had a self, of which, however, they were unaware. This is further supported by the fact that animals do sing and perform rites, but do not speak. The "tracing of the course of language through the ritual" is thus seen to refer to syntax: it is the syntactic structure of language which has a ritual origin. This hypothesis is further supported by the remarkable similarities which exist between the syntax of language and ritual syntax.[4] Verse 3 of the hymn, therefore, means that the sages related sound and meaning to each other through the structured domain of syntax, which was ritual in origin and remained so in character. For syntax does not depend on phonology, nor does it perform a semantic function.

The final verse corroborates this by the manner in which it refers to ritual. The one who sits down multiplying the wealth of verse is the Hotā priest of the *Ṛgveda*, who recites *śastra* recitations which consist entirely of Ṛgvedic verse. Such 'multiplying' of verse precedes language in its full-fledged, meaningful form, for it does not require any meaning. This is in accordance with the contemporary view that the generative power of language resides in syntax, and is accounted for by recursive rules which syntax and ritual have in common. The one who chants a chant in the *Śakvarī* meter is the Udgātā priest of the *Sāmaveda*, who chants *stotra* chants which largely consist of wordless and meaningless but structured melodies (*aniruktagāna*). The one who sets forth the newly born knowledge is the Brahman priest, later attached to the *Atharvaveda*, who knows the meaning but who as a rule does not utter a sound. The one who lays out the measure of the ritual is the Adhvaryu priest of the *Yajurveda*, who lays out the sacrificial enclosure and the altars, makes all measurements and performs the manual tasks which the rites require.

Taken as a whole, the final verse illustrates the relationship between language and ritual. This in turn makes sense in the context of a statement on the origin of language only if ritual plays an important part. Without this assumption it is difficult to explain the presence of this verse. Geldner tried to explain it by saying: "Der Schluss gibt die Verteilung der sakralen Rede auf die vier Hauptpriester an" ("The end indicates the distribution of sacred speech among the four principal priests"). But the verse does nothing of the sort. This is most obvious in the case of the Adhvaryu: what feature of language does *he* inherit? The real significance is different. When language originated, sounds were already multiplied according to recursive rules, and chants without words were already sung. Then meanings were attached to sounds, following the complex structures of ritual. Thus sounds were ritually brought to life, just as in later times a *yantra*, a bronze image or a piece of clay is animated by *prāṇapratiṣṭhā* rites. Where the rites were ignored, language ceased to develop and became rigid. Where they were performed, *brāhman* was found and language flourished. Thus language incorporates ritual structures in its syntax. Ritual, on the other hand, does not place great emphasis on celebrating or re-enacting myths, prehistory, or the creation of man or of the universe, nor does it have to reflect social structure. Its primary function is to contribute to the origin and development of language.

Finally a comment may be made on verse 6, which says that a person who does not know 'the path of good action' (*sukṛtasya panthā*) does not understand language. This is complemented by verse 9, where 'weaving water' corresponds to our 'writing in sand'. Is this a warning, a piece of moralizing, or a magical belief inconsistent with the telling of lies and other abuses of language? Or are we to believe that language was originally employed only by good persons and for good purposes? It seems more likely that we witness here a reflexion of the widespread ancient belief that language, knowledge, truth and goodness are all closely related. We find variations of this in the notion of *satyāgraha* 'holding to the truth', which survived as a program until Gandhi's time. We find it moreover in Socrates' conviction, which puzzled Augustine and many others, that the man who knows the good, is good. And we also find it in the Upaniṣadic and Vedāntic doctrine that he who knows Brahman, becomes Brahman (*brahman veda brahmaiva bhavati*: Murti 1963, p. xxx).

Notes

1. Professor Murti's Presidential Address to the 1963 session of the Indian Philosophical Congress.

2. This translation is a slightly modified version of a translation which I published recently (Staal 1975, p. 322), of which an earlier draft was improved by Leonard Nathan and which was made after consulting Brown 1968, p. 397, Geldner 1951, 3.248–250; Gonda 1959, pp. 137, 146; Gonda 1965, pp. 164ff; Renou 1955, pp. 22–23; Renou 1967, pp. 141–142; Schmidt 1968, p. 124; and Thieme 1952, p. 124—to which Gonda 1963, pp. 107–109 should be added.

3. The interpretation and supplements and may be supplemented by: (Staal 1975, pp. 319–24; Staal, *Ritual Syntax*, forthcoming.

4. Staal, *Ritual Syntax*, forthcoming.

Bibliography

Brown, W. N. "The Creative Role of the Goddess Vāc in the Rig Veda," *Pratidānam: Festschrift F. B. J. Kuiper* (The Hague, 1968) pp. 393–97.

Geldner, K. F. (transl.) *Der Rig-Veda*, Cambridge, Mass., 1951.

Gonda, J. *Four Studies in the Language of the Veda*, The Hague, 1959.

Gonda, J. *The Vision of the Vedic Poets*, The Hague, 1963.

Gonda, J. *Change and Continuity in Indian Religion*, The Hague, 1965.

Grassmann, H. *Wörterbuch zum Rig-Veda*, Wiesbaden, 1955.
Murti, T. R. V. *The Central Philosophy of Buddhism*, London, 1955.
Murti, T. R. V. "The Two Definitions of Brahman in the Advaita (Taṭastha-lakṣaṇa and Svarūpa-lakṣaṇa)" *Krishna Chandra Bhattacharyya Memorial Volume* (Amalner, 1958) pp. 135-50.
Murti, T. R. V. "Some Thoughts on the Indian Philosophy of Language," *Presidential Address, Indian Philosophical Congress*, 37th Session (Chandigarh, 1963) pp. i-xxxi.
Renou, L. "Les pouvoirs de la parole dans le Ṛgveda," *Etudes védiques et pāṇinéennes* Vol. 1, (Paris, 1955) pp. 1-27.
Renou, L. *Etudes védiques et pāṇinéennes*, Vol. 16, Paris, 1967.
Schmidt, H. P. *Bṛhaspati und Indra*, Wiesbaden, 1968.
Staal, Frits. "The Concept of Metalanguage and its Indian Background," *Journal of Indian Philosophy* (1975) Vol. 3, pp. 315-54.
Staal, Frits. "Ritual Syntax," forthcoming.
Thieme, P. "Brāhman," *Zeitschrift der deutschen morgenländischen Gesellschaft* (1952) Vol. 102, pp. 91-129.

Some Perspectives on Indian Philosophy of Language

J. G. Arapura

The Mystery of Language

The vocation of philosophy is to bring to light everything that lies hidden. No doubt all human, intellectual inquiry has this character. But philosophy as a means of bringing to light has a special feature in that, while it brings out phenomena from their hiding places, it also simultaneously, by the same act, brings us into the light of knowledge. Here then the subject and the object, the thinker and that which is thought are inextricably bound together.

The fact that in every kind of knowledge self-knowledge is involved is what makes philosophy different from all other scientific quests. Knowing the self is not merely knowing it in reference to particular situations–as it relates to objects sought to be discovered or known so that one may be able to critically grasp those situations for the purpose of an accurate knowledge of the objects concerned–it is knowing it quite apart from all such projections which come and go. Such knowledge of the self is not a by-product but rather something directly aimed at. This directing of knowledge to the self in and through the knowledge of objects is undoubtedly a central quality of philosophical thought. Therefore, when we are to think philosophically, our mind, which of its own accord goes forward to the objects and assumes their form (*citta-vṛtti*) has got to be stopped (*nirodha*) so that there results a retraction of the mind to itself and finally to the self resulting in *samādhi*. Genuine thought is thus a spontaneous activity of the mind culminating in a self-absorptive non-activity. However, the realm of objective reality, far from being surrendered, is fully appropriated and brought to the synthesizing centre of all apperception where alone it becomes knowledge—which is possible because all this takes place in the light of consciousness. But although everything must be brought to consciousness in order to be lighted, consciousness in its every-day operation is also shaded by dark areas, so that thought must also seek ways to lighten consciousness. The function of thought is much more than delivering all things over to consciousness. Thought, then, is to be viewed as the grasping of consciousness by itself so that while it lightens all things it simultaneously expurgates any darkness that there is within it. Thought must therefore be regarded as a supreme activity and a supreme non-activity such being the condition for consciousness to grasp itself. This aspect of apparent polarity between being both motion and the opposite of it is true of light—and thought is light.

Language is a mystery which belongs with consciousness. Being a mystery, it is hidden and it also brings all things to light. The philosopher Hamann rightly describes language as a mystery and a revelation.

A mystery is something hidden but not something unknown. A mystery is that hidden thing which we feel an irresistible call to uncover. There should be no other reason for us to want to know it than its own inherent challenge. As such, its very existence is not external to our consciousness. The quest to know it is really nothing other than acting in obedience to the inner command of consciousness. The habitation of all mystery is consciousness. Language inhabits consciousness like all other mysteries, no doubt, but does so even more because consciousness *becomes* language—like no other mystery.

'Consciousness *becomes* language' means that in the same way language reveals the presence of consciousness, consciousness in turn conceals the essence of language. But somewhere at some unfathomable depths they are one. Our life is guided by specific—and sometimes isolated—injunctions which originate in our consciousness and then float up to the surface of our awareness, expressed through concrete verbal modes; taking the form of mental moods these injunctions remain poised also for translation into action. All our learning is a way of coming to a knowledge of this. The master under whom we learn is language. In learning, language turns our face to that unfathomable depth from which all manifested truths come floating up. Learning, however, is only activity, only motion. Furthermore, it is always under the control of specific truths which happen to have floated up to the surface awareness and to have been embodied in concrete language. On the contrary, thought surpasses the limitations of activity, and motion, and surpasses also the accidental character of the truths grasping our minds. While the learner remains outside what he learns, the thinker is never outside. In thought not only is our face turned towards the unfathomable depths, but we make them our habitual dwelling-place. Learning is awakening while thinking is living in wakefulness itself.

At their depths, indeed language and consciousness belong together, constituting a single mystery. Therefore, the searching of the depths of the one is the searching of the depths of the other as well.

The nature of language is the object of diverse kinds of inquiry. Apart from the science of linguistics (which has several branches), philosophy, psychology, poetry, and anthropology have all, with their respective interests and assumptions delved deeply into the phenomenon of language. There is an enormous diversity of language describing language and it is fairly accurate to say that no other topic has commanded the attention of so many disciplines. No one can speak for all of them; indeed, no one can even speak for philosophy, as philosophers themselves speak diversely. Unfortunately, the proliferation of words about language is not always conducive to light and wisdom. On the contrary, much that is spoken and written seems to be inimical to the coming of light. Multiplication of quantity only produces false enlightenment–in other words, a thickening of darkness, to which, particularly in our modern age, we have become hapless heirs. The great wealth of our intellectual life does not necessarily make us truly rich. Learning unguided by genuine thinking cannot in the long run help us to turn our faces in the right direction.

The Human Phenomenon of Language

Language is the most characteristically human of all phenomena. The unity of man and language is the most striking of all human facts; it is a unity which cannot be dissolved. The fact that man alone has language is immensely significent. This significance cannot be ignored or circumvented by developing specious arguments about the way man came to possess the faculty of speech or the way machines can be programmed to produce imitative or even non-imitative speech. The relationship where man dwells in speech and speech dwells in man is unique. There are no third parties to which this relationship can be extended, although in its imagination mankind has fancied the gods and spirits, on the one hand, and the non-human animals, on the other, to have the power of speech. Our mythologies and our animal fables, however, only reinforce the unique relation between man and language while adding an element of pathos to it. The gift of language is bestowed upon man alone, and he pays a heavy price for it; as the world of man becomes lighted by speech, man is shut off by silence from the heavens and from nature.

On account of this altogether unique relationship Aristotle felt it necessary to define man as that being which has *Logos* (*Logos* originally meant language: the connotation of reason came afterwards, on which rested the later definitions of man as *animal rationale*).[1] As a definition it speaks not only about the possession of language by man but also about its non-possession by the rest of the animal kingdom. Language, accordingly, provides a basis for distinction between man and the rest of the animal world.

On that basis the philosopher Descartes pushed the distinction to the extreme. Language, he felt, pointed to the existence of mind in man. In this respect animals appeared to Descartes to be little better than automata, although—as he conceded—they did have sensation and feeling.[2] In a letter to Henry More he writes as follows:

> But the principal argument, to my mind, which may convince us that the brutes are devoid of reason, is that, although among those of the same species, some are more perfect than others, as among men, which is particularly noticeable in horses and dogs, some of which have more capacity than others to retain what is taught them, and although all of them make us clearly understand their natural movements of anger, of fear, of hunger, and others of like kind, either by the voice or by other bodily motions, it has never yet been observed that any animal has arrived at such a degree as to make use of true language; that is to say as to be able to indicate to us by the voice, or by other signs, anything which could be referred to thought alone; for the word is the sole sign and the only certain mark of the presence of thought hidden and wrapped up in the body; now all men, the most stupid and the most foolish, those even who are deprived of the organs of speech, make use of signs, whereas the brutes never do anything of the kind; which may be taken for the true distinction between man and brute.[3]

J. G. Herder tried to substantiate Descartes' theory by means of some tests and like Descartes argued "that human language is different in kind from exclamations of passion and that cannot be attributed to superior organs of articulation, nor obviously, can it have its origins in imitation or in its 'agreement' to form language."[4]

Man and language are bound to each other in an indissoluble way. But this binding can lead in one of two directions, viz., either towards a philosophy of man *or* towards a philosophy of language. In the post-Cartesian West it led largely in the direction of a clearer and surer apprehension of man rather than of language as such. In fact a quest for a rigorous definition of language itself leads one towards a reduction of language to human language and finally and inevitably to man; this has invariably happened. The belonging together of *consciousness* and language must appear to be exclusively identical with the binding of *man* and language, as man would seem to be the measure of consciousness. The Biblical notion of the domination of man over nature left no alternative to equating consciousness with man—omitting from this field the Divine consciousness for the time being. The class of conscious beings and the class of human beings became one and the same. This was inevitable because both theological pre-supposition and empirical knowledge precluded the possibility of leaving the class of conscious beings unenclosed and unbounded. Consciousness was apprehended as what takes place between an 'I' and a 'Thou', as their being revealed together in mutual encounter. Language was both the medium for the operation of the 'I-Thou' consciousness and at the same time its constriction to the world of human beings. If the 'I-Thou' world were extended beyond human beings, it would also be necessary to extend language and therefore consciousness likewise—which could be done only by way of a hypothesizing act or mystical ecstasy, and both these were excluded. In this atmosphere consideration of language always pointed back to man.

It was within this framework that Descartes did his thinking on language and on consciousness. Thus he interpreted consciousness as self-consciousness expressed by the proposition, "I think, therefore I am," which became the ground of ultimate certainty upon which all things, including language, could be considered. This gave an orientation to modern philosophy and science from which they have never been able to turn away. There have been, of course, other variations of the binding together of consciousness, language and man operating in the self-same framework. One of the most interesting of these variations, having special significance for language quest, is the Romantic one associated with the names of Herder and Wilhelm von Humboldt, who, in the words of Professor H. G. Gadamer (the eminent German philosopher), "saw the original human character of language as the primordial linguisticality of man and worked out the fundamental significance of this phenomenon for man's view of the world."[5] Over against this view of language as a gift a man exclusively and a human possession, there is also a view—neglected in modern thought—according to which, as Professor Gadamer points out, language is the language of things. The task of the philosophy of language now would seem to be to go to the depths without being exclusively trapped in either alternative, a task well indeed performed by Gadamer and Heidegger.

Characteristics of Ancient Indian Thought on Language

At this point we must turn our attention to the Indian tradition in linguistic thought, which goes back to the *Ṛgveda* itself. Without moving from language to a definition of man on the one hand, and to things (and the world), on the other, the ancient Indians insisted on pondering the mystery of language as such and seem to have done so in a unique way. However, consciousness, not constricted as human consciousness, and the world, not limited to the enumerable things, did become the conceptual partner with language as the illuminator.

One of the most interesting features of ancient Indian thought on the subject of language is that it understood language both in its phenomenal and metaphysical aspects, and fully studied each aspect scientifically and philosophically. These aspects were also joined together into a single, homogeneous field where warranted. Detailed scientific study of phonetics, semantics, etymology, etc., were at appropriate points integrated with philosophical contemplation of language (and consciousness) as of Reality. The skill and penetration that went into these gigantic intellectual efforts—stretching over countless centuries—recalls a similar but different tradition in the West, which particularly in our own day, thanks to the great German philosophers, seems poised for some momentous developments.

Because there was scrupulous concern for the phenomenal, there never was any temptation to down-grade the position of language as human language or to disregard the objects of the world to which language was bound. Grammarians like Gārgya (and later Pāṇini) and etymologists like Yāska were clearly concerned with human speech, with language in the empirical world; but they always kept an aperture in their systems open to the metaphysical inquiry, so that in the Śābdika and Vedānta-Mīmāṃsā philosophies the two could be fully integrated without having to break holes in any enclosing walls. This feature of diverse traditions of thought, developed with an eye to one another, is unique and is a source of genuine intellectual blessing.

In traditional Indian thought the effort to understand a given phenomenon and the contemplation of it as a mystery do not preclude each other. This dual character seems to have been maintained by all the sciences which have come out of the Vedas. The Vedas themselves, far from being a record of human thought, seem to furnish a ground upon which all human thinking—both the efforts to analyze and the contemplation of mysteries—can take place.

Language in the Ṛgveda

Although, undoubtedly, the *Ṛgveda* is the original framework for thinking about any subject, we cannot claim that language is a very prominent theme in it. But then in the *Ṛgveda's* role as the ground and framework of all thinking, there exists no need to thematize anything at all. The 'theme' of language, however, is articulated in the *Ṛgveda* in three ways, (1) as the goddess Vāc, (2) as *vac* and (3) in the symbolism of the cows. Obviously, these are by no means totally different from one another.

In one place,[6] we read of the goddess Vāc as personified speech describing herself: she is all-encompassing; she accompanies all the gods; she particularly supports Mitra-Varuṇa, Indra, Agni, and the Aśvins; she bends Rudra's bows against the sceptic. Elsewhere, she is called the gatherer of prayers,[7] and celebrated in other ways. In the *Śatapatha Brāhmaṇa*,[8] she is identified with Sarasvatī, who is known (in the post-Vedic literature) as the goddess of learning, wisdom and inspiration. It is Sarasvatī, in her turn, who is reported in the *Vājasanayī Saṃhitā* 19.12 to have imparted vigour to Indra through speech (*vācā*), obviously linking inspiration and wisdom with power.

But speech symbolized by the cows seems to play an even more important role in the *Ṛgveda*. In the cow symbol we encounter a brooding sense of the mystery of language. Ancient texts on etymology and interpretation inform us that cows are to be regarded as standing for language. In the *Nighaṇṭu* we notice that 'cow' (*gowḥ*) and *vāc* are etymological synonyms.[9]

Indra's special association with the cows is well-known. His epic battle with the Dānava and his releasing of the waters, which are likened to the cows, is sung in some *mantras.*[10] Agni and even more particularly Bṛhaspati are associated with Indra in these exploits, and of the several accounts of this association, two are particularly fascinating.[11] Indra's cows are stolen by the demons, and so Bṛhaspati joins the search to recover them. Bṛhaspati storms the stronghold of Vala the chief of the demons and, gathering to himself the cows, frees them. It is sung:

> Bṛhaspatiramata hi tyadāsām nāma svarīṇām sadane guhā yat
> āṇdeva bhittvā śakunasya garbham—udusriyāḥ parvatasya tmanājat.[12]

> That secret name borne by the lowing cattle within the cave Bṛhaspati discovered
> And drave, himself, the bright kane from the mountain, like a bird's young after the eggs' disclosure.[13]

Bṛhaspati has discovered that the cows had been kept bound in the cave of *Anṛta*, falsehood or chaos that is, (*guhā tiṣṭantīranṛtasya setau*) as he had been seeking light amidst darkness (*jyotiricchannudusrā*).[14] In a prayer to Bṛhaspati, it is declared that wise men's giving names to objects was the first and earliest of speech's utterances, and "all that was excellent and spotless and treasured within them was disclosed through their affections." Here it is sung:

> Bṛhaspate pradhamam vāco agram yat prairata nāmadheyam dadhānāḥ
> yadeṣām śreṣṭham yadaripramāsītpreṇa tadeṣām nihitam gūhaviḥ[15]

> When Bṛhaspati, giving names to objects, sent out Vāk's first and earliest utterances,
> All that was excellent and spotless, treasured within them, was disclosed through their affection.

It is significant that the search for the cows and the quest for light are often linked with each other, and finding the cows is dispelling darkness.[16] And inasmuch as cows symbolize language, the darkness hiding them—they being kept bound in the cave—had to be shattered by the appearing of light.

Like Bṛhaspati, Soma is also associated with speech; he is called Vācaspati, Lord of Speech:[17] We also read that the cows had called out to him (Soma) with a thousand streams (*tam gavo abhyanūṣata sahasradhāramakṣitam*),[18] in response to which he was sent to the skies. This explains his being called Vācaspati.

Thus although thematized only briefly and in conjunction with other themes, we are, in a highly symbolic manner, summoned in these texts to a quest after the mystery of language. Language must be discovered and brought to light. But the quest to which we are ultimately summoned is not after phenomenon as such, but after the one hidden Reality behind all phenomena, in the revelation of which language seems to have a special place because it is the medium of all knowledge. The question is, is the knowledge of language, the medium of knowledge, in some pre-eminent sense an inseparable aspect of the knowing of Reality? In the search for an answer to this question the obvious place to look is the Upaniṣads.

Language in the Upaniṣads

The Upaniṣads bring language to light—in some very significant ways—by explicitly linking language with consciousness, with the phenomenal world and with Brahman. The range of concepts about language is truly enormous.

Speech is often spoken of as being on a par with other faculties; yet as the instrument of understanding it eventually assumes a unique position, which brings it to its source, Brahman itself. As a faculty, along with other faculties, it is a medium of creation or becoming. One most interesting passage is in *Aitareya Upaniṣad*, Chapter 1, where we read of the creation of the Cosmic Person, which begins with the statement: *ātmā vā idam eka evāgra āsīt, nānyat kiṃ cana misat. sa aikṣata lokān nu srjā iti.*[19] (Atman indeed was all this, one only, in the beginning. Nothing else whatsoever winked. He desired "let me now create the worlds.") He created the worlds, the elements and then the person (*puruṣa*) to whom he gave shape.

He brooded over him, the person (*tam abhyatapat*); thus brooding he gave him mouth and produced speech from mouth and from speech fire (*mukhād vāg, vāco 'gniḥ*). But this was followed by the creation of other faculties and senses; the distinction is that speech is the first, a position that is normally maintained throughout the Upaniṣads. Speech is the first faculty to be created in the person. In the creative process the order of source and product are reversible. Thus for instance, if fire (*agni*) is said to have come from speech, it is also said in the next section that fire (*agni*), having become speech, entered the mouth, (*agnir vāg bhūtvā mukham praviśat*).[20]

Phenomenally it is essential to polarize the indivisible Ātman as creator and the created person (*puruṣa*), although the word *puruṣa* in its primary sense does not admit the attribute of createdness. Here *puruṣa* represents becoming; in becoming, speech is the first of the 'created' faculties essential to personhood. But speech must always lead to the Ātman. Purely in terms of becoming, insofar as a polarization is maintained, speech leads to the Ātman, as it is itself not the final source of light. Thus we read in the *Bṛhadaraṇyaka Upaniṣad: astam iti āditye. . . . śāntāyām vāci, kim jyotir evāyam puruṣa iti, ātmaivāyam jyotiṣāste,* etc.[21] (When the sun has set and speech has become silent, what indeed is this person's light here? Ātman indeed becomes his light, etc.)

All the human faculties are the means by which Brahman manifests itself, *etad vai dīpyate yad vācā vadati.*[22] This Brahman indeed shines forth, when one speaks with speech): so we read in the *Kauṣītaki Upaniṣad*. However, since here a different theme is pursued—the distinction between life and death—it is *prāṇa* (life-breath) which gets the primacy.[23] But, among the faculties through which Brahman (Ātman) shines forth, speech still remains the first.

Yet language must be understood not only in the becoming aspect of the person, but also in the being aspect of Brahman or Ātman. Thus we are told that speech is Brahman (*vāgvai brahmeti*).[24] Speech is *virāt.*[25] Speech is also everything. It is the world (*vāgeva ayam lokah*),[26] it is the gods (*devāh*),[27] it is *agni*,[28] and so on. It is the *Ṛgveda*,[29] it is the one source of all the Vedas.[30]

The *Māṇḍūkya Upaniṣad* gives the most complete expression of language, having worked out an identification of language with Ātman, at four levels, through the symbol of AUM. The *Chāndogya Upaniṣad* discusses the four quarters of Brahman in a different way—speech appears as but one, the other three being breath, the eye and the ear,[31] *Agni* (fire), air, the sun and the directions also are coordinated with them. The symbol of AUM had been employed by several of the previous Upaniṣads, chiefly be the *Chāndogya, Taittirīya* and *Maitrī*. But the *Māṇḍūkya*, the special AUM Upaniṣad, pulls all these diffuse ideas together and works out a thorough systematic correlation of them all by producing, so to say, the final symbolic equation whereby language, consciousness (the psyche), and the Cosmos are all coordinated under the supreme word-symbol. The *Māṇḍūkya Upaniṣad* begins this grand, systematic project with the introduction: *aum iti etat akṣaram idam sarvam, tasyopavyākhyānam* etc., (AUM, this syllable is all this. [Here is] an explanation of it, etc.). *Sarvam etat brahma, ayam ātmā brahma, so'yam ātmā catuṣ-pāt* (All this is indeed Brahman. This Ātman is Brahman. This Ātman is four-quartered.)

Historically speaking Vidusekhara Bhattacaraya's thesis (*Āgamaśāstra of Gauḍapāda*) may be plausible—not, however, for the reasons of Buddhist influence, and not with a view to arguing that the Upaniṣad is a work based on the *Kārikās* known by that name.[32] Be that as it may, its highly systematic character in respect of the use of a highly complex linguistic symbol for achieving a three-way co-ordination of language with the psyche, and the cosmos, and all finally with Brahman, must suggest a later date than most of the other major Upaniṣads. The conception of the mental states and the levels of the cosmos represented by the *vaiśvānara, taijasa* and *prajña* quarters and their integration with the three letters and leaving the fourth (*turīya*) in a transcendent state of purity, unity, and homogeneity in all three respects, viz., the psyche, the cosmos, and language, does bring the whole theme of language to an unequivocal clarity and completeness.

A long trail in the quest for the mystery of language finally reached this high point. It cannot possibly be said that human consciousness (even I-thou) or the phenomenal world has been left out of consideration in the interests of an obsessive mysticism.

The Diversity of Later Systematic Developments and the Lessons We Can Learn from Them.

The lessons which the Vedic texts and the Upaniṣads teach us are several: (1) language is a mystery that must be sought after; (2) language and consciousness, constitute a single mystery; (3) while we seek to bring language to light we learn that language brings itself to light and brings everything else to light—because it is light; (4) language is the framework in which our entire knowledge of Reality—and the self-revelation of Reality as well—is made possible, as the *Māṇḍūkya Upaniṣad* finally works it out by means of a great symbolic equation.

But the question is, can these truths be idealized and absolutized in such a way as to say that language simply is the Reality as expressed by the doctrine of *Śabdabrahman*? Is this not going too far, and perhaps unintentionally contributing to the misunderstanding of the very truths underlying such an effort?

Bhartṛhari's *Vākyapadīya* is undoubtedly one of the greatest landmarks in man's quest for the mystery of language and is the finest and the most comprehensive expression of the principles we have mentioned, but the question still remains: by making literal the equation: Reality (Brahman) = Language, does this not encourage some kind or reductionism, not intended even by the *Māṇḍūkya Upaniṣad*, not to say the rest of the Upaniṣads and the Vedic Mantras, and perhaps not intended by Bhartṛhari himself? No truer words than the following have been ever spoken in respect of language:

> pratyastamitabhedāya yadvāco rūpamuttamaṃ yadasminneva tamasi jyotiḥ śuddham vivartate.

vaikṛtam samatikrāntā mūrtivyāparadarśanam vyatītyālokatamasī prakāśam yamupāsate yatra vāco nimittāni cinhānīvākṣarasmṛte śabda purvena yogena bhāsante pratibimbavat.
adharvṇāmangīrasām sāmnāmṛgyajusya ca yasminnuccāvacā varṇāḥ pṛthaksthitiparigrahāḥ.[33]

The most excellent form of speech, which being undifferentiated is light pure, that appears in this darkness as differentiated.
Which those who have surpassed the multiform world perceive as an idol and worship (though) they have gone beyond the (opposition between) light and darkness.
Wherein the instrumentalities of speech, signs as it were of the letter-text (referring to AUM or even to the *Māṇḍūkya Upaniṣad*), put forth a reflection by union with pre-existing Word.
(This is) grasped in separate states of its existence as the Atharva, Sāma, Yajus and Ṛk and as the letter-sounds which constitute them.

This is Supreme Brahman, which it is said in the next *kārikā*, quite literally, is attained by the discipline of grammar. (*tadvyākaraṇamāgamya param brahma adhigamyate.* It is claimed that language is the gateway to *mokṣa* (*tadvāram apavargasya*),[34] etc.

This doctrine of Bhartṛhari–and some of the Grammarians–has had its share of critics, including the Advaitins. But most of the criticisms have been directed at its theory of meaning, *sphoṭa*, rather than its broader metaphysical implications.

At the root of it all is the question as to how one understands the difference between the symbolic and the literal. If one conceives language itself as being essentially symbolic in character, realism can somehow be maintained with regard to given aspects of it. On the contrary, within the literal, the symbolic has no place. Once we arrive at the literal equation Reality = Language, no aspect of it can any longer be held as symbolic. The pursuit of, and meditation on, language becomes a literal technique for *mokṣa*.

There are ways in which Reality = Language can be regarded as real, that is, insofar as the objective is understanding. Reality, when understood, expresses itself by re-enacting the whole order of projection and creative manifestation. Since the means of understanding is language, it can be maintained unequivocally that language, as the means of recounting, of re-enactment in understanding, is literally the medium as well as the source of projection and manifestation. At this point Language and Reality meet and merge, but we must always keep in mind that the reason for this is understanding. Of course understanding must itself be based on language, but other than in terms of understanding's own need to re-enact to itself through language the projective and creative order, there is no justification for literally reifying language.

Likewise also is the belonging together of consciousness and language. The *Vākyapadīya* has apparently turned it all into a literal and simple equation. Gaurinath Sastri, a modern exponent of this great text, seems to sum it up correctly: "The Ultimate Reality is the Absolute Consciousness, and consciousness and word being identical, it is the Absolute Word. In the system of Bhartṛhari consciousness and word are interchangeable terms. This makes for the difference from the Vedānta, though both of them are at one with regard to the unitary character of the Absolute."[35] Mr. Sastri also points out the reasons why the whole order of creative production of the world in the *Śābdika* system of Bhartṛhari based on the concept of the powers of the word–dynamic as in Kashmir Śaivism–is so different from the Advaita order which is based on the principle of *anirvacanīya* (the indefinable). Now *anirvacanīya* concerns language as much as anything else, fundamentally because there are questions which cannot be answered by 'yes' or 'no', and yet can be answered, in a way, by both. All this reveals the paradoxical character in which language, the foundation of all understanding and thought, has to be seen.

The uniqueness of Śaṇkara's position is that he could legitimately say both 'yes' and 'no' at the same time to some important propositions, as they must be subsumed under *anirvacanīya*, and yet could also say neither. In his *Bhāṣya* on the *Brahma sūtra*[36] he rejected the *sphoṭa-vāda* associated with Śabdabrahman and took this stand with the Pūrva-Mīmāṃsakas (whom he elsewhere opposed for other reasons concerning the Word). Śaṇkara rejected the *sphoṭa* because of its metaphysical implications. He saw a derivative order of entities from names leading to species names, implying the genesis of species as a real consequence of *sphoṭa*, according to which "it would not be contrary to say that Gods, etc., are born of eternal words." The notion of actual origin of entities from words would be an error of realism pertaining to language which must be avoided.

On the other hand, the co-ordination of language, consciousness, and the world, if not to be pushed to an extreme of positive identity, is essential. On the other side of the ledger is the Pūrva-Mīmāṃsā. Although it accepts the belonging together of language and consciousness to the extent that it understands language primarily in terms of *vidhi* (injunction) and *artha-vāda* (calculated to create a liking for *vidhi* in one's consciousness),[37] its view has a limiting effect on consciousness for it is understood as 'act'. There is a unity of consciousness and language at the very depth of both. In this Bhartṛhari is right, although this unity is not to be thought of as a simple metaphysical identity—for it must come up to the surface of our awareness and must be expressed comprehensively in language. This unity can be expressed only by the term *jñāna*; it is not to be conceived of narrowly and limitedly as activity (*karma*), or, for that matter, speaking in a different context, *bhakti*. This was the issue that Śaṇkara took with the Pūrva-Mīmāṃsakas.

Language is the means by which we can plunge into the depth of our own consciousness. *Jñāna*, then, as an object of philosophical pursuit, has a certain reflexivity which comes to us as self-knowledge attendant on the pursuit of the mystery of language.

Language and Transcendence

Language is a mystery that has to be brought to light. But side by side with this proposition we must state that language itself is the light. The result of these two propositions is the truth that language is a kind of self-concealing light. In order to uncover it we are summoned to understand its belonging together with consciousness, which is itself a self-concealing light. These two are again co-ordinated with the world, which left to itself is darkness. In their coordination these three give us a glimmer of light which beckons us to reach out to a depth—or height—which is the source of all illumination, that is, the self-shining light.

Philosophy is the reaching out towards the light. But then such reaching out itself must be understood as nothing but the shining of the light *appearing* to put on the visage of human achievement. This only shows that the concealing cover cannot be actually removed: it is only rendered transparent. The cover remains.

We say that the mystery of language is to be discovered, but putting it this way is itself a way of veiling the Word by words. Language hides in itself, and this hiding is co-ordinated with its concealment in the structures of the world—and in the layers of consciousness. Language must, therefore, be sought primarily in its own hiding places. So discovering the mystery of language—as a task of philosophy—is only one of two poles in a dialectical whole. The other pole is letting language discover all that is hidden—including itself.

Language itself has a mission which must be set alongside philosophy's mission. It is language that makes all thought possible. It is because of this that most of the major traditions of Indian philosophy considered language as self-shining light. The doctrine of *pratibhā*, (along with some synonyms), as Mahamahopadhyaya Gopinath Kaviraj makes it clear,[38] surely stands for this. Kashmir Śaivism calls it by such expressive words as *sphurattā* (self-illumination), *vimarśa* (self-manifestation), etc. Parallels of this idea run all across the board in Indian religious philosophies; it is most certainly a central notion in Vedānta as well.[39] The notion of *paśyantī*, the highest level of language–subject to the debate whether *parā-vāk* may be accorded this status–must be taken to stand for the transcendence of the self-shining light.

When we say that the mission of language is to discover or to reveal, it also means that it has the mission to lead us to Being. We may call this the primary religious function of language but this in no way should be understood as standing apart from philosophy's task of bringing language to light. As philosophy must bring to light hidden things in their entirety, it would not leave something so essential to language as its religious function unaccounted for, and hide in some obscurantism of its own willful making.

Levels of language: signification of the highest

Any attempt to look deeply into language will show that it exists at different levels. The *Māṇḍūkya Upaniṣad* gives four; the *Vākyapadīya* and the Grammatical Philosophy may give three or four, according to various interpretations. Even if we look at these systems from the outside, we can still see these levels; it is even possible to speak of four levels which do not correspond to any of the traditional classifications. We can think of our everyday talk as one level, language as a force in life and in the affairs of the world as another, and language in terms of its logical structure as a third. But perhaps these are not levels in the strict sense of the word–for they comprehend one another and in fact belong together as the whole of language as we know it. These levels are applicable to every department of our lives, society, business, politics, art, love, religion, etc. Nothing is excluded. But either separately or all together, they do not tell us anything about the transcendent. And the transcendant would seem to be that which sustains the integrity and wholeness of language as it functions, or at least ought to function, in our lives.

If we speak of the transcendent, we should recognize that the language in which it is expressed–functioning co-ordinately with consciousness (which level by level corresponds to it–alone gives us a clue to it. Hence transcendence of language and transcendence of consciousness become co-eval with the transcendent as such. Language's identity with the transcendent may be essentially symbolic, but then symbol, by definition, represents and participates in reality.[40]

The existence of parallel structures of language, consciousness (or the self), and the world is an insight of traditional Indian ontology. The only possibility of establishing Being is by means of their co-ordination. But then we also realize that traditional ontologies also function within a fundamentally mystical framework with an emphasis on "realization" or even *mokṣa*. Elaborate techniques of realization (*sādhana*) have become appurtenant to such an ontology. In certain systems like the Tantric there arose cultic techniques with a highly esoteric flavor classically represented by *mantra-śāstra*. In these systems, although philosophy is not suppressed, it has become an activity of mere exposition auxiliary to the cult—which by definition is secret, and inaccessible to the 'outsider'.[41] Kashmir Śaivism shares most of these tantric characteristics. However, Vedānta and the Philosophy of Grammar, in spite of the fact that their doctrines encourage mysticism still retain to a large extent the independence of their ontology thus making it accessible to philosophy.

Gaurinath Sastri is among the scholars who are painfully aware of this predilection to mysticism—particularly in the Philosophy of Grammar. He observes thus: "It may seem that the conclusion that word and consciousness are identical is inspired by the exigencies of religious mysticism, and that the arguments employed to validate it have been conceived *a priori* and the linguistic forms and phenomena have been so twisted as to fit into the architectonic plan in order to bolster up a mystical doctrine conceived independently and *a priori*." Mr. Sastri is confident that the ontology in question can be unhinged from mysticism and demonstrated on purely 'logical' grounds. Hence he continues: "It is imperative that the plausibility of this impression should be examined in all its bearings in order to convince ourselves of the logical validity (or otherwise) of the grammarian's [Bhartṛhari's] metaphysical stand. This can be achieved by the critical scrutiny of the nature of word as it comes within our ken in ordinary experience."[42] While the legitimacy of this perception, underlying which there exists a wholly commendable concern for an open metaphysics of the transcendence of the Word, must no doubt be accepted, it may be that another way to proceed would be to envisage a more general ontology of language, without disturbing the integrity that language maintains with consciousness, allowing both mysticism and an alternative way of transcendence to be held together as equal possibilities.

The demand for such a general ontology does not come from the need to satisfy the conceptual thrust of the mind, but rather from the need to take account of, and comprehend, alternatives which address themselves to the same goal, in the same respect (the concern for transcendence), but nevertheless do so differently. The general is only in that sense general. The phrases 'same goal' and 'in the same respect' must be emphasized—for they indicate the concern for transcendence as well as for maintaining the integrity of language with consciousness. Mysticism, as the highest form of self-activity/self-non-activity of the language-consciousness complex, has a genuine counter-part in another kind of thinking—that is, existential thinking or even sheer ontological thinking—which may very well be the result of some modern men's inability to participate in traditional religion and mysticism. In the latter, the view of transcendence becomes different from the way mysticism understands it, yet is nevertheless an authentic approach to transcendence.

This modern alternative also recognizes the validity of distinguishing the essential transcendent level of language (and consciousness)—corresponding to the transcendence of Being—from the levels at which we ordinarily apprehend language. It is represented most impressively by that modern movement in philosophy centred around the name of Martin Heidegger.

Although this modern philosophy depicts a totally different kind of transcendence from the traditional Indian philosophies, there are some interesting similarities, particularly with regard to the conception of the mission of language and the vital question of 'signification' as central to that mission. Indian philosophies understand the 'essence of language' to be *vāk, śabda-brahman* (or *sphoṭa*) the *vimarśa* (or *sphurattā*) of God etc. (according to the system in question), and they understand consciousness to be eternal and non-temporal (and hence the Word too is eternal and non-temporal). The eternity and unity of the Word are co-ordinated with the eternity and unity of Consciousness. The Heideggerian philosophy does not at all understand the 'essence of language' in this way: in the place of eternal consciousness there is Dasein, so temporal, so worldly, that, from the Indian point of view it calls for an inverted 'mysticism' of the Word and Being.

Yet these two ways of understanding the 'essence of language' seem to be able to stand together in resisting certain minunderstandings about language and in the commitment to expurgate the inauthentic from language. The Upaniṣadic analysis of language, (understanding the self [consciousness] and the world in a co-ordinated way) has its counter-part in Heidegger as he says that "to work out in advance the ontologico-existential whole of the structure of discourse on the basis of Dasein"[43] is a decisive step to be taken if one has to grasp the "essence of language". He criticizes certain attempts to grasp that essence that have used, as clues, the ideas of 'expression', 'symbolic form' communication as 'assertion', of the 'making known' of experiences, of the 'patterning' of life. He adds, "Even if one were to put these various fragmentary definitions together in Syncretistic fashion, nothing would be achieved in the way of a fully adequate definition of 'language'.[44]

Heidegger presses forward to a doctrine of signification, which he believes will not result from a Romantic quest for an original language or from a descriptive, comparative study of languages, but from finding its roots in Dasein. So he writes: "A doctrine of signification will not emerge automatically even if we make a comprehensive comparison of as many languages as possible, and those which are most exotic. To accept, let us say, the philosophical horizon within which W. von Humboldt made language a problem, would be no less inadequate. The doctrine of signification is rooted in the ontology of Dasein. Whether it prospers or decays depends on the fate of this ontology."[45]

Signification is associated with meaning; it always carries meaning. The two are distinguished thus: meaning is what "can be articulated in interpretation, and thus even more primordially in discourse," while signification is what is derived by the breaking up of the "totality of significations [Bedeutungsganze] which is what [actually] "gets articulated as such in discursive Articulation."[46] Thus although meaning is more primordial to discourse, signification is more immediate in the existential. But this calls our attention to the fact that it is not discursive primordiality but existential immediacy that should get primacy in a philosophy which seeks a radical new starting point. In this way even meaning must be re-constituted. Coupled with this is the fact (for Heidegger who speaks solely in terms of the West) that the handed-down structures of discourse primarily consist of assertions. Heidegger explains:

> The Greeks had no word for 'language'; they understood this phenomenon 'in the first instance' as discourse. But because the *Logos* came into their philosophical ken primarily as assertion, *this* was the kind of *logos* which they took as their clue for working out the basic structures of the forms of discourse and its components. Grammar sought its foundation in the 'logic' of this *logos*. But this logic was based upon the ontology of the present-at-hand. The basic stock of 'categories of signification' which passed over into the subsequent science of language, and which in principle is still accepted as the standard today, is oriented towards discourse as assertion. But if on the contrary we take this phenomenon to have in principle the primordiality and breadth of an *existentiale*, then there emerges the neces-

> sity of re-establishing the science of language of foundations which are ontologically more primodial. The task of liberating grammar from logic requires *beforehand* a *positive* understanding of the basic *apriori* structure of discourse in general as an *existentiale*.[47]

Dasien is described as Being-in-the-world and with respect to that it is stated: "Discoursing or talking is the way in which we articulate 'significantly' the intelligibility of Being-in-the-world."[48] The expressibility (and along with it the understanding) of Being-in-the-world creates a further predicament for signification through language, as one makes a distinction between 'Being-in' and 'Being-outside' with respect to it (viz., Being-in-the-world). This shows that a kind of language other than assertive (which expresses understanding, which in turn pre-supposes a Being-outside position with respect to Dasien's Being-in-the-world) becomes necessary. Such a language exists. Heidegger clarifies it thus: "Being-in and its state-of-mind [mood] are made known in discourse and indicated in language by intonation, modulation, the tempo of talk, 'the way of speaking'. Continuing, he writes, "In 'poetical' discourse, the communication of the existential possibilities of one's state of mind can become an aim in itself, and this amounts to a disclosing of existence."[49]

In the Indian traditions of the ontology of Language, although surely the self and consciousness are conceived in an almost antithetical way to what has been described as Dasein's Being-in-the-world, a frameword of *Logos* (*vāk*) exists where assertive discourse and its logical structure—in spite of their having developed to the highest degree—have not captured monopoly over language. The most striking example comes from the *Chāndogya Upaniṣad*, which has set forth a profound philosophy of language as Chant (based on meditation upon the *Udgītha*, the *Sāmaveda*, etc.), as invocation and such like, and in a way that expresses the centrality of the Self and its non-duality. This Upaniṣad begins with the statement: *aum iti akṣaram udgītham upāsīta, aum iti hṛd gāyati*, etc. (AUM. One should meditate on the syllable, the *udgītha*, for one heartily chants it as AUM, etc.), thus giving an immediate explanation of this mysterious symbol which sums up language. In AUM, that which is sundered in phenomenal language is reunited; the division between the assertion on the one hand and invocation, chant, prayer, expression of wish, etc., on the other hand, is overcome. It restores the unity of language by recognizing it for what it is. Śaṇkara, commenting on this passage, states that this symbol is a representation of the Supreme Self—like the image and such like—and that what is learnt from all the Vedānta texts is that AUM, being the name and form of the Supreme Self, is the best means of meditating upon it (*arcādivat parasyātmanaḥ pratīkam sampadyate; evam nāmatvena pratīkatvena ca paramātmopāsana-sādhanam śreṣṭham iti sarva-vedānteṣu avagatam*).

AUM is the heart of all signification, the very origin of language. What AUM discloses is not primarily the individual human being's (Dasein's) Being-in-the-world and state of mind, but rather the Supreme Self—while indicating a path by which the individual human being in his actual phenomenal and existential condition can reach it. This is language's primary mission.

A Misadventure in the Quest for the Essence and Origin of Language in the Indian Tradition.

F. Max Müller did very great service to the cause of Vedic and Vedantic studies in his day and we have rightly not forgotten him. But the inadequate presuppositions, directly taken from Romantic Linguistics and Philology (from W. von Humboldt particularly), having frozen into a dogma, have contributed to a kind of misadventure in the quest for the origins of Indian religious perceptions embodied in the ancient language and literature. The perusal of traditional texts themselves would call for a different approach to the question. Lessons learnt from contemporary philosophical investigations should make it possible for us to appreciate the traditional views of language as an envoy and plenipotentiary of the Supreme Reality and as a light unto our feet as we journey on to our highest goal.

True to his Romantic predilections, Max Müller entertained certain presuppositions. "The earliest work of art, wrought by the human mind," he wrote, "more ancient than any literary document and prior even to the first whisperings of tradition, the human language forms an uninterrupted chain from the first dawn of history down to our own times."[50] Language, as he argues, "still bears the impress of the earliest thoughts of man, obliterated, it may be, buried under new thoughts, yet here and there still recoverable in their sharp, original outlines."[51] To pursue language to its origins would really be the task set for researchers on language. For Müller the essence of language is expression. To express oneself is a natural instinct and hence language is a product of instinct, and as such belongs to the realm of nature. He believed that with the aid of Comparative Philology, we could go back to the original form of human consciousness, the *primum cognitum*.

This hypothesis has even influenced the project of recovering the 'original' signification of the names of deities. For instance, physically perceived objects like the dawn or the spoken word itself, due to a primeval transformation which took place in the pilgrimage of language became divine, mythological beings. Thus *EOS* (dawn), for instance, [corresponding to USA] becomes a goddess and eventually the wife of Tithonos; and *fatum* becomes the Goddess of Fate.

It is well known that Müller applied this method to the study of religion in general and to Vedic religion in particular, in his book *Lectures on the Origin of Religion as Illustrated by the Vedas*. He pointed a direction in which many students of Vedic religion have since walked. It is, no doubt, to be agreed that the problem of the origin of religion must be resolved by drawing from insights into the essence of language; the essence of language likewise must be considered in conjunction with consciousness. Müller, after a study of names common in Aryan languages, claimed that these names had originally an expressive power, and that the discovery of them would alone explain the mythological language and "render intelligible that phase of the human mind which gave birth to the extra-ordinary stories of gods and heroes, of gorgons and chimeras—of things that no human eye had ever seen, and no human mind in a healthy state could have ever conceived."[52]

When in our quest for the essence of language, instead of considering the mystery of signification we emphasize a concern for 'origin', the question arises whether we are not moving the whole matter out of the only ground, i.e., consciousness, where certainty is possible. Can 'origin' itself be traced back through a presumedly straight path of convergence of all human (or even Indo-Aryan) languages to some primeval self-revealing splendour of physical consciousness? Or is it not rather the case that we must pursue the problem of the power of signification—which lies in the corroborative evidence it furnishes for the purpose of exegeting the essence of language in consciousness—as it is always at hand although it conceals itself from clear view? At least the *Chāndogya Upaniṣad* (as also others), in its own words and in the words of its interpreters like Śaṇkara, appear to think so. Accordingly, physical brilliance and all nature-mediated sensations, all being part of object-awareness, are merely a refraction of consciousness's mediation of its essence to itself.

The concept of brilliance is to be considered first. Explicating the terms *devas* and *asuras*, (*Chāndogya Upaniṣad* 1.2.1.) Śaṇkara writes:

> The term '*deva*' is derived from the root '*div*', to shine; hence the word '*devas*' stand for such functionings of the sense-organs as are illuminated

> (regulated) by the scriptures; opposed to these are '*asuras*' etymologically explained as '*aśuṣuramaṇah*',[53] delighting in the spheres of all their own natural life, and 'inclinations' as appertaining to all objects of sense; hence the term stands for those natural functions of the sense organs which are of the nature of darkness (ignorance).[54]

If the *asuras* stand for darkness or ignorance, the *devas* stand for light and knowledge, and it is in respect of the struggle between the two, mentioned in many places in the Brāhmanas and also in the Upaniṣads (see *Bṛhadāraṇyaka* 1.3.1; *Chāndogya* 1.2.1), the word of words, the *udgītha* becomes the primary symbol of meditation (being the primary weapon of the devas). Concerning the deities (*adhidaivatam*) the *Chāndogya Upaniṣad* 1.3.1 states, *ya evāsau tapati tam udgītham upāsītadyan vā eṣa prajābhya udgāyati* (He who glows yonder one should meditate as the *udgītha*). The Sun is the obvious physical expression of such glowing or shining. In explanation of this passage, Śaṇkara writes:

> *On rising, He* [*the Sun*] *dispels, for the sake of living beings, the darkness*—of Night—and also the danger arising from that Darkness.—One who knows the Sun as endowed with these qualities *becomes the dispeller*—destroyer *of danger*—i.e., the danger to the Self, of being born and dying;—as also *of Darkness*, in the shape of ignorance,—which is the source of that danger.[55]

The *devas* shine because they know the most secret essence (*rasaḥ*) of speech, which is the *udgītha*, the chant of chants. Man (*puruṣa*) stands located in the world as the essence of all that constitutes it; he is himself in need of an essential goal, which comes from the light of the highest form of speech.

Now it is clear that it is not the primitive experience of Nature—for instance, the brilliance and glory of the sun—which suggested to man the idea of the gods; rather it was the light of speech which already constituted his essential being. The Vedic and Vedantic explication of the phenomenon is different indeed from the hypothesis of Max Müller; and the former accords well with the understanding of the particular modern philosophy which we have sought to utilize to the permissible extent. Hence it is understandable why the *Vākyapadīya* starts out with this statement:

> anādi nidhinam brahma śabdatatvam yadakṣaram
> vivartate arthabhāvena prakṛyā jagato yataḥ

> That one which has no beginning and no end, Brahman, of which the principle is the Word, projects itself into objects; [hence] from it comes the world's creation.

Language, Transcendence and 'Religion'

Therefore, when we pursue the primoridal essence of language we must be led to the primordial essence of human, phenomenal consciousness. This has brought us to our final theme, namely the relation between language, transcendence, and 'religion'. When we are searching for the close relationship among them we are led to the conclusion that our interest hovers around not the problem of *religious language* but that of potentiality for religion in primoridal language.

What is called religious language—usually the subject of much analytical study particularly in philosophy—is simply incomprehensible unless we recognize as inclination towards 'religion' in primordial language. This is our point of departure. The distinction between religious language and non-religious language is a derivative one, which comes into being owing to the essential character of self-forgetfulness built into the primordial language. Self-forgetfulness is a necessary protection against self-awareness, its scorching radiation and its infinite de-ontic power. No one can stand the terror of self-awareness. One's mind turns to the terror that Arjuna experienced in the *Viśvarūpa-darśana* as a fitting paradigm.

We have no warrant to call this primoridal language *religious* language in the manner of religious or theological propositions. We know that that language is not at all a language of assertion, for there is nothing to assert. There may be something to cry out or turn one's face away from in terror, and hence invoke. In Heidegger's words here one expresses the uncanniness—unhomelikeness?—(*unheimlich-keit*) of existence (*Sein und Zeit*, section 188, *Being and Time*, p. 233) and the sense of being-not-at-home (*das nichtzuhause-sein*).

We should recognize (1) that there is a state of dislocation into which self-awareness throws the human self and (2) that there is an act of self-re-location spontaneously succeeding the knowledge of the former. As Heidegger makes clear, being-in-the-world is not that which one flees—as if by fleeing it one falls into dislocation—rather the contrary. Because not-being-at home is more primoridal, Being-in-the-world is never being-at-home-in-the-world. If any one wants an argument to prove the fact of man's dislocation, he is only resorting to sophistry in order to set aside an existential problem.

Nature is alienated from Being; the world is Being alienated from itself. History is alienated from Nature and Being. Likewise, Nature and history are alienated from themselves. The human self is the measure of all such alienations. Man has to bear all these burdens plus the burden of

God's existence and non-existence as well. All this because of man's self-awareness. But the involvement of the human self is such that the fact of dislocation is apprehended not only in itself but in the possibility of its being overcome. But how do we interpret this syndrome of dislocation and its being overcome? The fact is, we don't and we don't have to, because it has interpreted itself. The self-interpretation, self-expression, of this peculiar human syndrome is what is historically called 'religion'. Our task is simply to understand the terms in which it has and does take place. The word 'religion' is itself not at issue; and why quarrel over it?

Names, particularly names of gods and goddesses, are linguistic entities which arise in the context of the function of language in re-housing what is found dislocated–namely the human self. Names do not necessarily stand for substantive entities and simply cannot be understood apart from the significatory function of language.

We must still pay heed to the parting of ways that history exhibits. There are two opposite orientations which arise from the *potentiality for religion*. One of these orientations never manifests itself as religion; rather it refuses to be religion. It hovers on the brink of religion, and its self-sustaining dynamics is a form of radical existential scepticism which draws its substance from the actual religions and reverses the direction of what it draws; it becomes itself in history by its resistance to religion. The modern age of anxiety and *scepsis* reveals this to us. The reconstruction of *Logos* as language follows this pattern; whether the great Greek tradition of *Logos* was actually such is a moot question. It does, however, indeed entail a rejection of the main Western (Platonic and post-Plantonic) tradition, as Heidegger argues, and, one would think, all similar high metaphysical traditions of the world as well.

The other orientation manifests itself definitely as religion; there is a continuing tradition through which the significatory level of language has maintained a religio-metaphysical form. Here the essence of language that we are looking for is truly found; although by muffling the sceptical, 'modern' outlook, it provides a metaphysical version, a *gnosis* version, of signification.

The most powerful and unbroken expression of the latter tradition is found in the Vedānta. In this respect there is nothing anywhere more striking than the paradigm of the AUM symbol presented in the *Māṇḍūkya Upaniṣad*. It expresses the primordial role of language in this tradition, although because its approach is essentially mystical, it speaks from the end of re-location (of ultimate unity with Brahman or Ātman), and allows no irremovable anxiety to persist in language and consciousness. Śaṇkara in his introduction to the *Māṇḍūkyapaniṣad-bhāṣya* writes:

> AUM is the substratum of the entire illusion of the world of the word (*vākprapañca*) having for its contents such distortions (*vikalpas*) as *prāṇa* etc. imagined in the Ātman. And AUM is verily of the same essential character as the Ātman; for it is the name for the Ātman. All *vikalpas* such as *prāṇa* etc. having Ātman for the substratum and denoted by words—which are but modification of AUM—cannot exist without names. This is supported by such Śruti passages as 'The modification being only a name arising from speech', 'All this related to It (Brahman) is held together by the cord of speech and strands of names. All these (are rendered possible) by names . . .

This primoridal structure of *vikalpa* (and of *māyā-avidyā*) is revealed to us through the counter-positing reality of the primary word (divine names etc., included), symbolically represented by the all-comprehending AUM. As had become obvious in the *Māṇḍūkya*, in the *Vākyapadīya*, as well as in all Vedānta—indeed as in all mystical tradition of *Logos* or Vāk—the word is identified either actually or symbolically with metaphysical Reality. This is not the case in the modern existentialist view, where an alternative, a radically different conception of Being, reigns. However, as the mystical word, AUM brings about awareness of itself as of that which it counter-posits: namely the *vikalpa* structures.

However within the framework of the mystical and metaphysical tradition, *Vāk* as AUM identifies itself with the human self in its state of dislocation and not-being-at-home. It does not abandon man in the extremities of the *vikalpa* structures; rather it grasps him and carries him forward to the place of overcoming. Hence it is declared to be the best support (*ālambanam*) and man is summoned to meditate on it (*aumityatmānām yunjīta*). That is the mission of language.

Here then we have the greatest paradigm of the religious and mystical orientation in the potentiality for religion in primordial language. There is clearly a discourse form to it, but the discourse is not primarily assertion or a system of assertions. It has a primary form of invocation, of chant; it is also benediction, glorification, divine adoration. But it also incorporates assertion without which language cannot function.

The language of AUM as analysed in the *Māṇḍūkya* shows that it is essentially *directional* in mode, that it is really a *path for man* to follow. Its ontological essence (or Being) is itself a *direction*, a movement. It is like an arrow discharged from below; yet at the same time it is a self-launching missile that comes from beyond the highest flight of the human spirit. It is a messenger and guide. And also, it is the face of Reality turned towards man. It is a healer that heals, viz., the metaphysical breach between man and Being. Nevertheless, AUM or *Vāk* is not religious language; rather, it is that from which certain religious languages have come.

But in all cases we have to distinguish between the potentiality for religion present in the language of signification (the essence of language), and actual languages with religious and theological meaning. Actual theological language has to have logical form and logical meaning. It is inevitable that in logical form and meaning there should be diversity, and what obtains in one theological language cannot be easily harmonized with what obtains in another. The meaning problem is acute. Here signification itself has to stand in the service of meaning rather than clearly above it, for there is a chance that no actual religious language that claims to stand above logical meaning can do so without contradicting it. And all actual religions, except those that go to the fringes of occultism, will try to avoid contradicting logical meaning because they are aware of the peril of disorder. The problem of grasping what is beyond meaning is fraught with intense danger. The irrational for its own sake must at all costs be avoided in religious language. Thus St. Paul warns the Corinthians against the practice of *glossolalia* (speaking in tongues as it is called): "I had rather speak five words with my understanding" "than ten thousand words in an *unknown* tongue,"[56] as he believes that "God is not the author of confusion but of peace."

Religious language itself is derivative and it must have a normally propositional form. It could take the form of injunction and prohibition (*vidhi* and *niṣedha*) as in the Pūrva-Mīmāṃsā; or the form of commandments as in Old Testament; or laws as in the Old Testament and the *Dharma-śāstras*, etc.

The forms of religious language are always human, cultural, historical. Here we have the religions in the plural. The languages in which we apprehend the transcendent also vary; here there is no common meaning—essence to which we can reduce these different individualities.

But we must never forget that religious languages are what they are because of the essential character of language, (where lies signification) because it infuses itself into them and gathers itself from them. But existentially speaking, language bespeaks itself before it bespeaks God, revelation, scripture, or *śruti*. That is the existential ground of transcendent unity, a unity which can never be translated into logical meaning structures; upon it and because of it religious languages can significantly differ; and also that which is non-religious can differ from that which is religious.

Language itself holds that unity; in its keeping is transcendence. Ultimately language must and does speak for itself. What we speak is an imitation of it, but the authenticity of what we speak is measured by how we imitate it; with understanding, or without it. The statement concerning meditation on the *udgītha*, etc., is intended to direct us into authenticity, at least as a constant reminder.

Notes and References

1. The author's mind became clear on this point through participating in the seminars of Prof. H. G. Gadamer.
2. This theme was developed in *Discourse on Method*, see *The Philosophical Works of Descartes*, trans. E. S. Haldane and G. R. T. Ross, Vol. 1, pp. 116–17.
3. See *The Descartes-More Correspondence*. The part relating to this theme is translated by L. C. Rosenfield (L. Cohen), in the *Annals of Science*, vol. 1, No. 1 (1936); here quoted from Noam Chomsky, *Cartesian Linguistics*, New York and London, Harper & Row, 1966, p. 6.
4. Ibid. pp. 13–14.
5. From a privately circulated seminar paper.
6. *Ṛgveda* 10.125.
7. *Vāgdevī brahmasaṃcitā, Atharvaveda* 19.9.3b.
8. *Śatapatha Brāhmaṇa* 9.3.4.17.
9. *Nighaṇṭu* 5.5
10. *Ṛgveda* 1.61.10.
11. Ibid. 10.67,68.
12. Ibid. 10.68.6,7.
13. Note: The English rendering of the above text and the one to follow are taken from R. T. H. Griffith's translation of the *Ṛgveda*.
14. *Ṛgveda* 10.67.4.
15. Ibid. 10.71.1.
16. Ibid. 10.68.4,9; 9.97.39.
17. Ibid. 9.26.2,4; 9.101.5, 6.
18. Ibid. 9.26.2.
19. *Aitareya Upaniṣad* 1.1.1.
20. Ibid. 1.3.4.
21. *Bṛhadāraṇyaka Upaniṣad* 4.3.6.
22. *Kauṣītakī Upaniṣad* 2.13.
23. Ibid. 2.14.
24. *Bṛhadāraṇyaka Upaniṣad* 4.1.2.
25. *Chāndogya Upaniṣad* 1.13.2.

26. *Bṛhadāraṇyaka Upaniṣad* 1.5.4.
27. Ibid. 1.5.6.
28. Ibid. 3.2.14.
29. Ibid. 1.5.5; *Chāndogya Upaniṣad* 1.7.1.
30. *Bṛhadāraṇyaka Upaniṣad* 2.4.11.
31. *Chāndogya Upaniṣad* 3.18. 2-6.
32. The *Māḍḍūkya's* conception of language may be regarded as the very antithesis of the Buddhist view of language (*śabda, sadda*) viz., that it is an action (*Kathāvattu*, 12.3) or that it is a physical vibration (ibid. 9.9-11). See trans. by S. L. Aung and C. A. F. Rhys Davids of this text, section entitled "Points of Controversy".
33. *Vākyapadīya* 1.18-21.
34. Ibid. 1.14.
35. Gaurinath Sastri, *The Philosophy of Word and Meaning*, Calcutta, Sanskrit College, 1959, p. 24.
36. See *Brahma Sūtra* 1.3.28.
37. See *Śābara Bhāṣya* on Jaimini's *Mīmāṃsā Sūtra* 1.2.7.
38. See "The Doctrine of Pratibhā in Indian Philosophy", in Gopinath Kaviraj, *Aspects of Indian Philosophy*, the University of Burdwan, 1966.
39. Note: Actually, if we are looking for the word *pratibhā*, there is, as Dr. Kaviraj himself points out, only one major instance to be adduced in the Vedānta literature: in the ninth *anuvāka* of Sureśvara's *Vārtika on the Taittiriya Upaniṣad.*
40. Śaṇkara in his comment on the *Chāndogya Upaniṣad* 1.1. says exactly this.
41. Note: Sir John Woodroffe (Arthur Avalon) and Dr. Gopinath Kaviraj are the foremost among those who have done signal service to the world of learning by making available to us the products of their profoundly sympathetic and often belief-ful studies of Tantra, thus enriching our knowledge of it.
42. G. Sastri, *The Philosophy of Word and Meaning*, p. 102.
43. M. Heidegger, *Being and Time* (*Sein und Zeit*), trans. J. Macquarrie, and E. Robinson, New York and Evanston, Harper and Row, 1962, p. 206.
44. Ibid.
45. Ibid. p. 209.
46. Ibid. p. 204.
47. Ibid. p. 209.
48. Ibid. p. 204.
49. Ibid. p. 205.
50. F. Max Müller, "Comparative Mythology", in *Chips from a German Workshop*, Vol. 2, p. 7.
51. F. Max Müller, *Lectures on the Science of Language*, Reprint, Delhi, Munshiram Manoharlal, 1965, p. 387.
52. F. Max Müller, *Chips from a German Workshop*, Vol. 2, p. 53.
53. Note: This derivation, however, is different from *Nirukta* 3.7, according

to which *asura* comes from *a-su-raḥ*, meaning, delighting in evil places, or from the root *as* (to throw), meaning, having been expelled from places. The difference is only formal and not really substantial in the last resort.

54. Quoted from Sir Ganganath Jha's translation of *Chāndogya Upaniṣad with Śaṇkara's commentary*, Poona, Oriental Book Agency, p. 15.

55. Ibid. p. 26.

56. *The First Epistle to the Corinthians* 14.19.

The Word as a Category of Revelation

K. Sivaraman

I

The semantic issue that dominates a philosophy of language on the Indian scene arises, in its foundational sense, as part of the 'by what and whence' question. The origin question, characteristic of the approach of the Upaniṣads, concerns the source of the nature of things—in connection with which the question asked simply is: by what is something as it is?[1] Asked in connection with the 'ground' of things, the origin question concerns the form, Whence and by what do things arise? Asked likewise in connection with one's knowledge of things it is of the form, Whence and by what do things become known? What is the light by which things are rendered intelligible?

The stranger announcing himself by his name is, in a trivial sense of the term, the cause of the words spoken to that effect. The word originates from the speaker, as action issues from an agent. But in another sense, of special significance for the semantic problem, speech, i.e. the word spoken, is the means whereby the speaker becomes known.[2] The 'illucutionery' utterance of one's name on one's advent is that by which or *in* which,[3] knowledge about the being of that person arises on the part of the hearer. In a logically odd but semantically significant sense we may say that one's speaking is the cause, and the referent, in this case oneself, is the consequence.

One of the major Upaniṣads derives its name by the very form of such a question with which it begins its discourse.[4] The questions phrased in the instrumental case refer to the cognitive sphere of knowing, thinking, etc., and to what, in a peculiarly Indian manner, is conceived as the correlate coefficient of the cognitional phenomenon namely, the vital function (*prāṇa*). Of special significance are the question and the answers relating to speech. The question is: "By whose intention or will (so to speak is 'this speech' spoken?"[5] The answer *inter alia* that is given is suggestive as setting the stage for the Hindu philosophies of language analyzing the cognitive and revelatory aspects of the word. The answer is to the following effect: That by what and whence speech speaks, that presumably cannot itself also be speech—there speech goes not (*na vāg gaccati*). If anything it is 'speech of the speech' (*vāco ha vācam*)—something itself not spoken but which grounds speaking itself (*yad vācā nabhyuditam yena vāg abhyudyate*).

The issue that is portended for a theology of the word by this discourse about the limits of discoursing is a simple, and an infinitely difficult issue: is the transcendent ground of speech speakable? The solution or the resolution that is implied in the issue is typical of philosophical Hinduism: the validity of verbal knowledge. This resolution, bequeathed almost in a mandatory way to subsequent thought by the Mīmāṃsā, and acceptance of it *vis-a-vis* consciousness and its self-grounded certainty by Vedānta are the chief landmarks in the early history of Indian philosophy of language.

II

The field of application of hermeneutics which sets the context for these philosophies consists of the efforts to interpret the claim of sacredness of the sacred texts. The 'sacred text' is scripture in the eminently Hindu sense; that is, it is not a written composition.[6] Writing is a secondary function and has no standing reference in the religious tradition whose hermeneutical task lies rather in reconstructing the relationship between text and speaking.[7] In a transformed sense this task is interpreted in higher hermeneutics (*uttara mīmāṃsā*) to entail reconstruction of the isomorphism between the structures of revelation and experience so that it is permissible to disclaim ultimacy even to the revealed word. In the words of its most illustrious commentator, the word finds its consummation in one's intuitive experience of one's identity as Pure Consciousness.[8] Be that as it may, it should be borne in mind that the word in a foundational sense is sacred language. Only in its objectivised periphery is language human and 'profane'. It is essentially *revealed*, part and parcel of what is authoritative in its own right.

The sacredness of language is reflected in the doctrines of the eternity of the Word, of the eternal, non-contingent nature of word-object relation and the non-objective and non-objectifiable character of language. These are the broad philosophical presuppositions implied in the recognition accorded to scriptural revelation, and it is within their framework that the Indian philosopher of language perceives his task to lie. There is no attempt or motivation to deduce the nature of language or meaning from some principle of intrinsic rationality. Strictly, there is here no counterpart to the concept of essence or form or reason which is so pivotal to western philosophy (thanks to the legacy of Plato.)[9] The criterion of intelligibility, that the generality of the Hindu philosopher of language (the Grammarian not excepted) strives after, is one which is conditioned by the understanding of language primarily as revealed.

One of the clear indications of such motivation may be seen in the circumstance of the close association between linguistic speculations and the phenomenon distinctive not only of Hinduism but of Indian religion as a whole, viz., *mantra*. The quasi-esoteric doctrine called *mantra-vidyā* is concerned less about its own philosophical premises and presuppositions and is more a practical application in the form of prayer, worship, meditation and yogic integration. But, significantly, *mantra* is not looked upon as the name of the activity of praying or worshipping or the activity of muttering vocables or syllables. *Mantra* is, definitionally, revelatory.[10] In theological language, only that *mantra* in which the deity has revealed its particular aspects can convey or manifest that aspect and is therefore the *mantra* of the particular deity, the "words rising from the depths" as it were (as the *mantra* is described by the Veda itself).[11] The *mantra* has, necessarily, a mental and verbal form (being neither nonsensical nor only a paraphrase of silence).[12] What really is constitutive of it, investing it with its mandatory power, is its transcendent reference.[13] The creative word is the transcendent principle to see or hear 'whom' is not for all. The Mīmāṃsā philosophy of the word, the Vedānta thesis of 'two Brahmans' the *Śabda-Brahmavāda*, and Agamic Saivism—these among other religious systems—can be viewed as representing, in their speculations about language as a whole, complementary approaches to the idea of revelation implicit in *mantra.*[14]

III

The conception of *mantra* implicit in the 'hymn to the deities' in the Veda must be discerned in relation to its context. The context is the circumstance that the *mantras* are chanted in the different stages of the performance of the sacrificial ritual and especially the circumstance that they are chanted invoking the presence of deities. This, among other things, reflects an understanding of language which has proved decisive for later speculations. Language is invested with a function which over-extends the function of expressing ordinary meaning. The very sound aspect of the words and their characteristic combinations are assigned a causal efficiency in invoking the unseen presence and ensuring happiness on earth and enjoyment in the life to come.

A rationalised basis for the belief in the efficacy of the *mantras* was provided by the Mīmāṃsakās in their theory of the word. The sound produced in pronouncing a word is not an accidental phenomenon. Every '*śabda*' is eternal *qua*, the sound representative of an eternal principle.[15] The Vedic *mantra* is not a case of word-combinations composed by an agency; they are eternally there representing the eternal principles which co-exist with the cosmos and its pulsations. 'There never was the world conceivably different from what it is now' (*na kadācid anīdṛśam jagat*). The Vedic sages are the 'seers' of the mantra (*draṣṭāraḥ*) not their makers (*kartāraḥ*); they are aided in their sight or vision both by the transparence of their being and by the power of *vāc* to render articulate their visions. What is significant is that the ṛṣi-vision entailed the Mīmāṃsā claim that aspects of the eternal truth revealed themselves to the seers in the form of sound representations. Such then are the *mantras*.

The *śabda* of the Mīmāṃsakās, while thus laying claim to be the unconditional, does not assume the creative role of God or Absolute being. Gods are admitted in a manner of speaking but they are not accorded existence independent of the *mantra*. The *mantras*, indeed, represent the divine essence; a god's power or potency is but the power or efficacy that is intrinsic to the *mantra*.[16] Otherwise, asks the Mīmāṃsakā, how can the deity, alledgedly different from *śabda*, be present simultaneously at more places than one when invoked in the performance of rituals at different places.[17] The conclusion that is begged here, significant for language, is that *śabda* even when it is envisioned as sound-representation is different from its corporeal material embodiment and that, therefore, it is universal and identical; were it not so, the difficulty raised in connection with gods would apply also in the case of the *mantra*. Words uttered in different contexts being different words, how, conceivably, could they exert their capacity of invoking (as in that case of the Vedic ritual), the deities—pleasing them, so that happiness for the performer would result.

IV

With this emphasis on the eternal nature of *śabda*, originating as speculation about *mantra* of the Veda, stands another strand of thinking which approaches the question dialectically. The issue of equating language (*śabda*) *qua* revelation with reality itself (Brahman) is answered, as it were, with systematic ambiguity. Speech indeed is Brahman[18] and yet thither speech goes not.[19] The paradox of speaking about it as "other than the known and other than the unknown"[20] is less a reflection on the predicament of speech than on the nature of Brahman itself. The uniquely authoritative character of verbal testimony is duly acknowledged and the claim of its self-validity is conceded, but the implication of the eternity of *śabda* is resisted. The only valid implication is that legitimate trust in language and its sacredness can be found in its groundedness in self-validating consciousness. Veda in the sense of an assemblage of words is not exactly the 'higher knowledge' by which alone is realised the immutable consciousness.[21] "There are indeed two Brahmans, verily to be meditated upon—*śabda* and *a-śabda*", runs a significant text. "By *śabda* is the *a-śabda* revealed (*śabdenaivāśabdam āviṣkrīyate*)."[22]

There are other significant lines of development marking a fusion of the idea of Mīmāṃsā and Vedānta over the issue of word in relation to reality. One such is the Grammarian perspective of word as *Śabda-Brahman* meaning by the hyphenation the ultimate reality itself.[23] It represents, one may say, a sustained re-conception of the twin notions of consciousness and power, of ideation and creative vibration which in a sense are already foreshadowed in the Vedānta. The idea of verbal authority implicit in the concept of word as revelation is interpreted in a refreshing manner.[24] The Veda is acknowledgedly the means of attaining *Śabda-Brahman*. The Veda, indeed, is its 'image' (*anukāra*). The *ṛṣi* sees the ultimate and eternal word-principle in the form of *mantras. Śabda tattva* is one and without inner sequence. In order that it be imparted to others, only an 'image' of it, a copy of it like an icon can suffice. Such is Veda. Just as the forms that one perceives in dream are representations of the forms that one has perceived in his wakeful state, the Veda too is an image-adaptation of the *mantra*, i.e., *śabda tattva* perceived by the Vedic *ṛṣi*.

Śabda tattva, then, is the transcendent reality which reveals itself as many and manifold because of its 'powers'. Without a disruption of its unity, it 'reveals' itself[25] at once as the two poles of language, word and its meaning, and the two poles of experience, viz., subject and object. A 'philosophy' of grammar resting on this premise accounts for linguistic apprehension accordingly, through espousing a fusion of levels or layers of speaking—that of the empirical speech which represents discursive and diversified speech at the audio-visual level, and a layer of speech which involves an intuitional apprehension of meaning as a whole (*sphoṭa*). The former is the sphere of a grammatical analysis of language, of its sentences, words and their constituents in terms of strict logical or semantic rationality. The latter, however, is discovered by means of transcendental reflection on the actual dynamics of speaking. 'Purification' of speech is the goal aimed at through this process of awakening of the word to its original pristineness. To know the essence of its function is the means to the attainment of Brahman.

V

The Śaiva thinking about the revelatory nature of the word and of language in relation to reality represents the effort to integrate many of the key notions in the spectrum of theories outlined so far. The Śaivaite's own thesis of language as sound-essence (*nāda tattva*) may be postponed to the final section, but here one broad characteristic of the approach may be mentioned.

The validity of verbal testimony is a crucial issue for the Śaiva thinker whose involvement in the decisiveness of the issue may best be described as as much existential as it is theoretical. The *āgama* is the generic name for the highest revelation of knowledge, and it is, eminently, verbal. The 'self-validity' of the revealed word is not only zestfully endorsed in the style of Mīmāṃsā-Vedānta, but it is understood to typify all knowledge and all discourse but in the precise sense in which 'self-validity' is interpreted.[26] After all, what is it that leads one to discover 'invalidity' in relation to speech save the circumstance of conflicting with experience. The originating source of invalidity pertaining to speech is not the speech itself nor any of the manifesting media that facilitates the operation of speech at its different levels. Once doubt is entertained regarding them, there is no option open other than to grope in the open ended trail of epistemological scepticism. Invalidity of speech, therefore, is traceable to one and only factor, viz., the inadequacy of the source, that is, the speaker's knowledge. In the case of the *āgama*, the speaker, or more properly the revealer, is God who represents for Śaiva theology the transpersonal dimension of consciousness as such, personifying both omniscience and freedom. Applying this model to the case of the alleged unspoken speech, viz., the Veda, the Śaiva thinker argues (*contra* Mīmāṃsā and Vedānta traditions) that the 'self-sufficiency' of the Veda is acceptable in all but one respect, that is, its 'origin' (*utpattau nāprāmāṇyam svataḥ*). What uniquely determines the validity of verbal testimony is the validity that is intrinsic to its 'whence' and 'whither', such source in the case of the word being the intelligent revelatory power (*citśakti*) that the word mediates. There is an isomorphic relation between the transcendent power and the word which also is conceived as an ensemble of power. They may be held together (as in the concept of *parāvāk* of Kashmir Śaivism) or held apart (as implied in the concept of *nāda* of Śaiva Siddhānta)[27] but their parity of functions is the common presupposition underlying the Śaiva theory of language.

VI

The Śaiva thesis about word understood as the category of revelation may now be explained (*vis-a-vis* Rāmakaṇṭha's *Nādakārikā*, the text and translation of which are given in the sequel to this paper). The 'word' is primarily transcendental in relation to the two orders of experience–experience in the causative sense (*bhogajayitri*) and experience in the sense of the accusative (*bhogya* or *bhoktavya*). Language in its original sense of arouser of meaning pervades these two structures but transcends them (*atiriktam*) in the order of being. It grounds the two alike (*preraka*) in so far as experience–both with reference to itself and with reference to things which are experienced–partakes of 'word'. The 'word', then, is what alone accounts for intelligibility independent of the conditions relating to the structures of experience–both those pertaining to its subjective pole, the complex called the psyche and its components, and those pertaining to the objective pole like the sound-complex and other physical accessories to speech.[28]

The common basis which the Nāda doctrine shares with the Mīmāṃsaka and the Grammarian is that the sounds uttered by the speaker and heard by the hearer are momentary like any audible sound. The only distinction about the 'spoken' sound is its function of *conveying* the 'word' which *manifests* meaning. The physical sound is the effect of vibration and arises from its matrix of the plenum (*vyoma*). From this must be distinguished letter or phonemic sound which transcends the plenum (*vyomātīta*).[29] The latter is 'sound', as it were, without vibration, and over-extends in significance the mere fact of its audibility to the biological ear. Hearing is an integrative process in which the phonemes are perceived as meaningful. This apperception entails the operation of the 'word', (*nāda*).

What is the precise nature of the word or, to put it differently, who is the best candidate for this role of the 'word' in respect of arousing meaning? Over this question the Śaiva disagrees with the classical answers, finding them not gratuitous but insufficient.[30] The *nāda* concept includes and over-reaches these solutions.

Let us see how: Uttered words in their determinate pattern, whether the pattern be that of the primary form of a phoneme or of the consequential one of words and sentences standing together, alike face the same predicament. They do not themselves constitute the 'word' except in the trivial sense that they are heard. What is implied in the assumption that these units cause the rise of consciousness of meaning is as follows: These units and primarily the phonemes which are, after all, the linguistic molecules, manifest a determinate 'formal' power (*jñāpaka śakti*). This power is the constitutive ingredient of all linguistic units, potential *qua* the power, but actualised in the manifestation of meaning. It is the counterpart of its material mode, viz., the power which is logically implied in the concept of a thing understanding it as agent, instrument etc., in respect of some action. The Grammarian for example, estimates the concomitant instrumentalities incidental to such a concept (*kāraka*) by an intuitive analysis of syntactical usage. The *kāraka śaktis* are internally differentiated but they allow themselves to be sorted out in a sequential order, notwithstanding the fact that they are all of them potentially present at the same time.

What serves as the catalyst facilitating the sorting out and thus introducing order and meaning in cognitive experience is the intention of the speaker. The potentiality yields to an actualised state of affairs structured commensurately with the intentional structure of experience. Likewise, the 'formal' power of a word embodies or translates the intention of the speaker which in turn calls forth utterances in a specific order of patterning of the phonemes. The 'formal' power or function, as it were, exists potentially 'one' with what it illumines, investing the latter with a fitness to be the accusative of speaking. *Nāda* is the name for a complex of such functions which are intrinsic to a comprehension of thinghood. The functions or powers in their substantive mode (*śaktimān*) is *nāda* which is therefore, ontically, no more different from them than a class exists differently from its members. The understanding of a thing as an integer of multiple powers, materially productive (*kāraka*) and formally illuminative (*jñāpaka*) underlies this formulation of the thesis of Nāda.

A very plausible objection that is raised and answered in the textual exposition of the Nāda doctrine deserves attention before we close.

The 'word' that arouses meaning may in the final resort require it to be understood as continuous with the thing as what is indeed presupposed in one's apprehension of a thing. But the thing that is denoted is after all objective, and the 'formal' power unveiling it—that is what word is—is non-objective, pertaining to mind (*buddhyārūḍha*). Are the two not incommensurable? No word as such, by virtue of its own nature, denotes a thing. Its 'power' makes itself felt only when it represents in thought the thing that is to be denoted. This representation of the nature of thought-form (*parāmarśa jñāna*), therefore, is a better candidate than *nāda* for exercising denotative power.

The Nāda theorist admits the claim, as amounting in effect to the truism, that what arouses the consciousness of meaning is really a significant form of consciousness. But the point that is crucial is: thought (in the discursive sense) despite its logical independence to what is external is still a contingent phenomenon. The 'thing' to which it relates itself is not its own product. The reflection of the external thing which is subject to discursive thinking is something already indeterminately comprehended or prehended by a function more ulterior and less polarised from the object than the thought-form. The thinking act does not improvise its own datum and has no scope without the data that the senses provide. What makes possible the 'origin' of the act of thinking, what causes the inner speech (*antaḥ sanjalpa*) in terms of which discursiveness in consciousness is formed is, therefore, the true arouser of meaning.[31]

This also explains how similarly meaning is received by the hearer of the word. *Nāda* provides to the thought of the speaker the unified word and meaning in the form of inner speech (posterior to the stimulation of the sense). The thought-form 'judges' it and communicates it through audible speech to the hearer. The audible speech manifests the *nāda* in the hearer and the entire process is then repeated. The underlying idea is that all expressions and their meanings pre-exist in an undifferentiated unity and representation of it in one mind gives rise to similar representations in other minds through the medium of spoken speech.

The Word, thus understood in the light of the doctrine that *nāda* imports, is 'revelatory' in a linguistically primordial sense, as underlying the form of any particular language. The expressive-expressed structure, present initially in its undifferentiated unity, becomes subsequently differentiated and diversified conforming to the infinite modalities of language. *Nāda* spans the entire spectrum of sentient life—ranging from the lowest forms of life where language seems inapplicable, to new-born babies which have not begun learning the language of the speech-community, to the unlettered shepherd and the house-wife whose language-habits have not been cultivated, to the primitive and the savage with their dialects deviating from the norms standardized by grammar. At the other side of the spectrum are the cultivated languages with their infinite sophistications. All exemplify the phenomenon associated with the concept of word as sound-essence: the word eternally linked to meaning becomes 'exteriorized' in multiple levels and manifests its power of communicating meaning, of transferring the sense immanent in word from one sentient center to another.

The revelatory significance of the Word, indeed, is more than linguistical. The religious motive that undergirds the attempt to provide a transcendent vindication of language may not be overlooked. If the aim is to counter scepticism and combat solipsism, it is because the latter imply a refusal of religious meaning. All scepticism, one may generalize, is scepticism of the word. The word is after all the means whereby the unknown becomes known, the hidden is brought to light. If this is not perceived, reflectively and in faith, language remains opaque with regard to its dimension of depth. Nāda is a theory of transparence of language whereby its potential as the medium of sacred knowledge, its inherent fitness or power to communicate transcendent intention, stands disclosed. In this sense knowledge of the Word may be said to be the portal toward Fulfillment. The 'End of *Nāda*' (*nādānta*) consists of the insight that speech in its primordial translucence is 'revelatory' of its ontological Depth. The promise of transcendence of the word is implied in the very concept of the Word: (nādātītam śivam natavānāda jñāna prasiddhaye).[32]

VII

The text of *Nāda Kārikā*[33] is as under:

buddhyasmitāmanobhyo vidyāto rāgataḥ kalāyāś ca /
māyā-puṃ-śaktibhyo nādo'nyo dṛśyate dhvanibhyo'pi ⟨1⟩

śrotra-grāhyā varṇā uccaritadhvaṃsinaḥ krama-sthitayaḥ /
aparasparopakārādaviśiṣṭānārtha-vācakā yuktāḥ ⟨2⟩

na ca varṇavyatriktaṃ padam anyac chrūyate'tha vākyam vā /
yac cākṣam iti niṣiddhaṃ tat sad iti niṣidhyate'nyato jñātum ⟨3⟩

gauriti nāmādi-padaṃ śrotragrāhyam sadasti cennaivam /
nagakāraukāra-visarjanīyabāhyaṃ yadato'nyadatrāsti ⟨4⟩

teṣām yugapad bhāvātparopalambhena pūrvayor bhāvaḥ /
prāptād visarjanīyātkhurakambalalakṣaṇā na cidvyaktiḥ ⟨5⟩

atha ced visarjanīyātpurvākṣarajātasaṃskṛtisahāyāt /
iṣṭaiva vācyabuddhiraviśiṣṭādyā na saṃbhavati ⟨6⟩

naitat saṃskāra api yair buddhau purvamāhitāsteṣu /
vijñānahetavaḥ syurna tato'rthe dhīḥ prakalpyate yena ⟨7⟩

tad-buddhyadhirohapadaṃ karmavṛttasya krameṇa vijñānam /
vācakamiṣṭamaduṣṭaṃ hetuś cet sthūla-śabda-jātasya ⟨8⟩

astvitthaṃ vācakatā vācyebhyo naiva bhidyate yena /
tad vastu niravaśeṣamaviśeṣeṇaiva buddhyupārohi ⟨9⟩

vācakataiva viśeṣo vācyāccet tad-vimarśa-rūpatvāt /
asya vimṛśyā vācyā bhedābhedair idaṃ ca sat kintu ⟨10⟩

rūparasagandhaśabdādyarthā yenāvamṛśyataṃ nītāḥ /
so'ntaḥ saṃjalpātmā nādaḥ siddho na viṣayabhāvena ⟨11⟩

viṣayīkurvan sarvānśabdārthāneṣa vācako nānyaḥ /
dṛṣṭaṃ sad-apyasattadyasmādete sadā parāmṛṣṭam ⟨12⟩

buddhyākāro nāsmānna mano'haṅkārayoḥ kṛtiryena /
tatkāryaśarīrendriyavikṛteḥ pṛthagevamavyaktam ⟨13⟩

avyaktatvānnādassūkṣmaśśabdastu vācakatvena /
vākyapade pravibhinnaḥ padārthabuddherasaṇkaro yasmāt ⟨14⟩

smvedyate na tadvaccāgopālāṇganādipaśubṛndaih /
bālairbhinnā nādā utpatyapavargayoginastena ⟨15⟩

seyamavasthā kaiścit padavidbhirvarṇyate kriyāśakteḥ /
iha punaranyaivoktā puruṣāsamavāyinī vāg yasmāt ⟨16⟩

avikāryatrātmoktas tacchaktiś capyato na yogyau tau /
bahudhā sthātuṃ yadvā caitanyavinākṛtau vikāritvāt ⟨17⟩

tatpuṃśakter bhinno nādopādānakāraṇatvena /
acidapi śuddhatvānmāyāto' pyanyā tad ūrdhvagā kathitā ⟨18⟩

śuddhaṃ vidyātattvaṃ vidyeśānāṃ ca bhogadaṃ bhuvanam /
adhvanyuktaṃ cānyaissadāgamaiś śreyase ca taddhetuḥ ⟨19⟩

vāgbrahmaṇi niṣṇātaḥ cid-brahmāpnoti yena kathayanti /
siddhir muktiś ca parā nādajñānakriyā ca saphaleti ⟨20⟩

mantrādi kāraṇatvāt vidyārāgādi-kañcukādibhinnam /
tatkāryam abhiṣvangād dṛk-kriyayor mīlanācca bhinnaṃ yat ⟨21⟩

sa mahāmāyājanyo nādaḥ paramārthavācako yuktaḥ /
yena sthūlaṃ śabdaṃ mantraṃ tantrātmakaṃ pravartate* vāpi ⟨22⟩

sā pratipuruṣam bhinnā vākśaktirvācikāsthiteti tataḥ /
vācakajātaṃ nirmāyāntaratastadvyanakti bāhye' pi ⟨23⟩

sthūlaiś śabdair vyaktāssūkṣmānādātmakāstatodhvanayaḥ /
vācyavibhinnaṃ buddhiṃ kurvanto vardhayanti janayātrām ⟨24⟩

iti nādasiddhim enāmakaroc chrībhaṭṭarāmakaṇṭho' tra /
nārāyaṇakaṇṭhasutaḥ kāśmīre vṛttapañcaviṃśatyā ⟨25⟩

* bhavedvāpi iti pāṭhabhedaḥ.

VIII

The following is a free, annotated rendering of the text of *Nāda Kārikā.*

Intellect, I-am-ness (=egoity) mind, *cognoscens*, appetition, particle (unveiling sentience), *māyā*, the power of the experient (-agent)–from these *nāda* may be seen to be different. From the physical sound (of vibration) also. ⟨1⟩

Apprehensible by the ear the phonemes are (fluxional being of the nature of) rising and perishing. Existing but serially they are devoid of co-operation *inter se* (to constitute a verbal unit.) Incapable of grouping (by mutual coherence) they are unfit to be revealer of meaning. ⟨2⟩

Nor does one hear differently from the phonemes (in succession) the 'word' or 'sentence'. What thus stands refuted on (audio-) perceptual grounds, to claim existence on grounds (of speculation) stands *afortiori* refuted. ⟨3⟩

Nominatives etc., like the ensemble '*gauh*', indeed are apprehended by hearing, if it be, No, because (on analysis) outside (the phonemes) of *ga*, *au* and the aspirate there is (perceived) differently no such thing as '*gauh*'. ⟨4⟩

'(It only means) they (i.e., the phonemes) being simultaneously existing (though manifest in sequence) by due apprehension of what is later in terms of what occurs earlier, is meaning determined. By (apprehension of) the mere aspirate (which comes later), the meaning of words (which terminate in aspirates) like *khurah* or *kambalah* surely do not loom into (the horizon of) intelligibility'.⟨5⟩

True, by means (only) of the assistance of the residual impressions generated by the preceding phonemes, indeed, is (possible) a determination of meaning. Without the composite (resulting from uniting with the impressions generated by the precedent) meaning cannot, conceivably, arise. ⟨6⟩

Not so; even the residual impressions become the *causa cognoscendi* only of such things as have become impressed on the intellect through previous experience of them; they cannot give rise to a different kind of experience. ⟨7⟩

'Let the *cognoscens* in due association with the word impressed on the intellect (through previous experience), and the cause of the sequential occurrence of the collocation of overt sound be the serial revealer of meaning, (jointly and) unerringly'. ⟨9⟩

Be the revealer of meaning so; (i.e., the thought-form of the *cognoscens*.) (The predicament will then be:) the revealer of meaning will be non-distinguishable from the being of what is revealed. Because all things without exception are indiscriminately associated with the determining thought-form (of the cognoscible mind). ⟨9⟩

'(No;) while still being of the form of discursive thought the being of what is revealed, conceivably, can be distinguished from what serves to reveal it. By (differences of) revealing discursive modes differences in what is being revealed, have, (become plausible)'. True, but ⟨10⟩

Whereof things (differentiated in terms of sense-modalities) like visual form, taste, smell, and audible hearing become fitted for discursive apprehension thereof is established *nāda* of the essence of inner speech. Not because of the differences in the things themselves. ⟨11⟩

(This *nāda*) makes possible apprehending of all, the word (that reveals meaning) as well as the meaning (that is revealed by the word), wherefore it is the one and only revealer of meaning. By *nāda* is it perceived that all things both of the order of being and of non-being alike become thinkable. ⟨12⟩

For this reason it is not (identifiable as) of the form of *buddhi* nor (identifiable) with the operations of *manas* and *ahamkāra*; nor with their consequent modification of body and sense. Different also from the unmanifest. ⟨13⟩

Unmanifestly present *nāda* is subtle, but functioning as the revealer of meaning it is differentiated (overtly) as (the semantic units of) word and sentence of a language (uniquely in the case of each knowing mind) in answer to the (commonplace of a) non-promiscuous nature of the comprehension of things (in respect of their reciprocal difference) by a knowing mind.⟨14⟩

Known thus as not present homogenously is *nāda* (but as operating multiformly) by the shepherd, (the unlettered) women as well as other sub-human forms of life, babies, etc. Wherefore also (one may see) *nāda* as having the fitness to emerge into being and also terminate. ⟨15⟩

Some knowers of (the nature of) the word say that it is (but) a state of the power of (sentient) action. Here it is reiterated (by us) as other than (sentient action) because of non-inherence of the word with the (sentient) experient-agent. ⟨16⟩

(The experient-agent) is of the essence of changelessness. So is his power. Wherefore neither is fit to be united with the feature of being or becoming manifold. Otherwise being subject to change it will forfeit its (character as) consciousness. ⟨17⟩

Different from that power of sentient agent (is) present in him the non-sentient (knowable) as the material cause of *nāda*. Despite non-sentience because of its purity it is other than even the *māyā* and is said to be higher (in the order of being) than it. ⟨18⟩

As the pure way, the *vidyā tattva* and the universe (of experience comprehended under *tattva*) meant for the experience of the *vidyeśa* beings are held differently by the good *Āgamās*. The cause of the good (reachable by treading that way,) is (the above-mentioned pure *māyā*). ⟨19⟩

He that comprehends the word-reality realises the reality of consciousness, thus has it been said. (Besides,) spiritual accomplishments, liberation that is (of the) highest (kind) and spiritual acts (of initiation) also accrue as fruits (thus has it been said). ⟨20⟩

Because it is the causal source of *mantra* etc., (it follows that the aforementioned *nāda* is consequential to *mahāmāyā*;) it is different from the (super-psychic) vesture composed of *vidyā*, *rāga* etc., being different from their function of appetition, cognition and action. ⟨21⟩

(It thus follows that) *nāda* that is generated by the *mahāmāyā* is (alone) fit to be the unconditional word (revelatory of meaning). By it comes into operation the manifest forms of sound of the nature of *mantra, tantra*, etc. (which are therefore revelatory *qua* manifesters of *nāda*). ⟨22⟩

Functioning differentially as the revealer of meaning by being present differently in each experient-agent, the power of the word causes to manifest a collocation of (meaning-bearing) words within as well as without. ⟨23⟩

Manifest by means of gross (overt) sound, the subtle sound-complex of the essence of *nāda* makes possible cognition of diversified meaning and contributes to a proliferation of the humal weal. ⟨24⟩

Thus for realising *nāda*, Sri Bhattarāmakaṇṭa, son of Nārāyaṇakaṇṭha in (the terrain of) Kashmir composed this text named thereafter in twenty-five verses. ⟨25⟩

Notes

1. Martin Heidegger, *Poetry, Language, Thought* (New York: Harper & Row, 1972), p. 17.

2. Cf. the two ways of interpreting *śāstra yonitvāt*, as *śāstra* being the *yoni* (*causa cognoscendi*) of Brahman and Brahman (omniscient that he is) being the *yoni* (*causa essendi*) of *śāstra*. Śaṃkara's Commentary, *Brahma Sūtra* 1.1.3.

3. J. L. Austin, *How to do Things with Words*, Oxford, 1965, p. 109.

4. *Kena Upaniṣad* thus named after the way it begins: *keneṣitam patati preṣitam* etc.

5. *keneṣitam vācam imām vadanti*. Ibid.

6. Cf. the remarks of Śabara to the effect that the relation between *śabada* and *artha* being *autpattika* does not preclude the hermeneutical demand that Scripture be construed like any written composition in terms of *laukika* usage of words. *Sabara Bhāṣyam*, (Poona: Anandasrama Edition, 1934), p. 754.

7. The historical relation of writing to the Judaic-Christian tradition of the West was the theme of the seminar given by H. G. Gadamar on *Religious Speaking* at McMaster University in 1974. The writer's participation in it helped to clarify his thinking about the Hindu understanding of the relation of text and speaking. See also Apte. V. M., "The Spoken Word in Sanskrit Literature," Poona, *Bulletin of the Deccan College Research Institute*. pp. 227f.

8. *anubhava avasāntvāt bhūta vastu viṣayatvācca brahmajñānasya*. Śaṃkara's Commentary, *Brahma Sūtra* 1.1.2.

9. Plato's theory of Forms as developed for example in the *Phaedo* is an ontology of Forms, in which a Form or Idea is, among other things, intellectually apprehensible and capable of definition by means of pure ratiocination. Arithmetic and Geometry which embody unrestrictedly general truths representing ideal limit concepts are among the considerations that influenced Plato's doctrine.

See Plato's *Phaedo*, Introduction by R. Hackforth, Cambridge, 1955. From this point of view one has to be specially cautious in understanding the following remark of Professor T. R. V. Murti: "The eternality of words as propounded by the schools of Mīmāṃsā and Grammar is the Indian counterpart of the doctrine of Ideas." *Some Thoughts on Indian Philosophy of Language* Chandigarh, 1963. p. xiii. Of there being some kind of aesthetic resemblance between some of the arguments employed by Plato including his semantic considerations, i.e. meaning of subject-predicate structure of truths and falsehoods, and the well-known arguments of the Mīmāṃsaka and the Grammarian, there can be no gainsaying. Neither can one rule out the element of thinking that is part of the elucidation of the doctrine. A wise man, says Bhartṛhari, should see through logic's eye even the thing that he perceives with his mere eye. (*Vākyapadīya* 1.141). On the other hand his fling at the *kuśalair anumātr* (ibid. 1.34) recalling to the reader Śaṃkara's classical critique of *tarka* (*Brahma Sūtra* 2.1.11) and his use of the jeweller illustration in the next verse with the express disclaim that the intelligibility that is the issue is rationality (*nānumāṇikam*) makes one pause. Perhaps he is a thinker who advocates less of reasoning based on human intelligence alone. See for more of this, and especially the place of *pratibhā* in the matter: Iyer, *Bhartṛhari*, Poona, 1969, pp. 83ff.

10. *Nirukta* 7.12.

11. *niṇyā vacāṃsi Ṛgveda* 4.3.16.

12. See Yāska's reply to the criticism of Kautsa, *Nirukta* 1.16. Frits Staal's remarks about *bīja mantra* in a recent article ("The Concept of Metalanguage," *Journal of Indian Philosophy* 3:333) to the effect that they do not *have* meaning but are *given* them meaning and that in accordance with the principle of Humpty Dumpty, are not convincing. It does not reflect the understanding of *Mantra Vidyā* of the Hindu Tantra not even that of Mantrayāya Buddhism. Vasubandhu says that absolute meaninglessness is the meaning of *mantras* and that therein indeed lies its power which helps the *sādhaka* in realising the nature of the universe as absolute void. (*Bodhisattva Bhūmi*, ed. Unari Wogihara, Tokyo, p. 273) What seems implied is not that mantras are nonsensical but that they have lost their etymological meaning, or had never an etymological meaning. See S. B. Dasgupta, *An Introduction to Tantric Buddhism* (Berkeley: Shambala, 1974), p. 54.

13. See *Nirukta* 1.20 Yāska's comment on *Ṛgveda* 10.71.5 about the flower and the fruit of the Word and its alternate meanings either as referring to rituals and gods or referring to gods and self. The three levels of interpretation of special significance for Tantra in terms of ontology, are the well-known triad: *ādhyātmika, ādhibautika* and *ādhidaivika. sarva tattvanām mantra vindanti* of *Sarvajñānottara Āgama, mantrātma prakaraṇa* 2.3 sums up the metaphysics underlying applied *mantra vidyā* as for example in the case of *garuḍa bhāvanā*.

14. It is profitable to read S. B. Dasgupta's insightful section on the role of

mantra in Indian Religion for comprehension in terms of historical interconnectedness. *Aspects of Indian Religious Thought*, Calcutta, 1957, p. 22.

15. For the classical arguments in defence of the Mīmāṃsā point of view at their best see Parthasarathi Misra's *Śāstra Dīpikā*, Poona: Nirnaya Sagara pp. 116ff.

16. *śabda mātram hi devatā, Mrgendra Āgama, Vidyāpāda* 1.7; Nārāyanakaṇṭha cites the following text of *Śloka Vārttika* in his *vṛtti: stutivāda krtascaiṣa jananām mativibhramāh, paurvāparya parāmrstah śabdo 'nyam kurutem itim.* The Kashmir series of Texts and Studies, No. 50, 1930, p. 26. That the ontological significance of the God-language of the Veda is but in terms of the Vedic *mantra* is the thesis put eloquently in the mouth of Indra as *purva paksa* before the latter begins his discourse on the Śaiva doctrine.

17. *śabda itaratve uygapat bhinna deśeṣu yaṣṭṛṣu na sā prayāti sānnidhyaṃ, mūrtatvāt asmadādhivat.* Ibid. 1.8.

18. *Bṛahadāraṇyaka Upaniṣad* 4.1.2.

19. *Taittīriya Upaniṣad* 2.4.

20. *Kena Upaniṣad* 1.3.

21. Śaṃkara's Commentary, *Mundaka Upaniṣad* 1.1.5.

22. *Maitri Upanisad* 6.22. Also the lines *śabda-brahmaṇi niṣnātaḥ param brahmādhigacchati* are significant for bequeathing the language of discoursing about the ontological reality to the philosophies of grammar. The commentator of *Nāda Kārikā* cites it under *Kārikā* 19 as if wresting it from the mouth of the author of the *Kārikā.*

23. *anadi nidhanam brahma śabda tattvam yadakṣaram*
vivartate 'rthabhāvena prakriyā jagato yataḥ. Vākyapadiya 1.1.

24. Ibid. 1.145; Also Iyer, op. cit. p. 95.

25. *śabda tattva brahmaṇi ekatva avirodhinyaḥ samucitaḥ atmabhutah śaktayaḥ santi etc. Vṛtti, Vakyapadiya* 1.2.

26. For a fullfledged reconstruction of *svataḥprāmaṇya* thesis along lines of Umapati's *Bhāṣya* on *Pauṣkara Āgama* and other texts see K. Sirvaraman, *Śaivism in Philosophical Perspective*, Delhi: Motilal, 1972, Chapter 13.

27. A detailed analysis of the issue between the two families of what, perhaps, is a single tradition is not possible, but the following may be said: Abhinavagupta employs the notion of *śabdanam* to explain the Word as 'inner word' (*samjalpa*)—an inner recognition (*pratyabhijñā*) of the identity of *śabda* and *artha*, as proximal (*abhisambhandha*) as only it can be in the case of a tautology like 'this is this' (*so'yam*). The *samjalpa*, consequently, does not overlap ontologically speaking on the side of the object (*viṣaya pakṣe na vartate*), but is intrinsically one with the light of consciousness (*prakāśa*). *Iśvara Pratyabhijñā Vimarśini* 1.2.1,2.

The Nāda theory, in contrast, rests on the metaphysical distinction between consciousness and language which, however, is creatively interpreted to bear both in respect of Being and in respect, as it were, of Becoming. The order of *māyā* is metaphysically distinguished from that of *citśakti*, but the former admits of levels or grades in terms of increasing transparence and greater disclosure of its depth. The Word (*nāda*) represents, micro-cosmically speaking, the very limit of this tractability. *Nāda* is like the mellowed light of the moon (with its increasing digits) which serves as the condition of intelligibility in a night of phenomenal life, itself a species of what is not conscious (*acit/aśiva*) like the world which it renders intelligible and yet, standing aside from it, contra-distinguished as the condition without which 'the world' will be dark. It is the condition which makes possible world as well as world-transcendence (*bhoga* and *mokṣa*). The Word, then, is the foil of consciousness with which consciousness is 'one'. The oneness is intentional (*parigraheṇa*), not substantial (*tādātmya*), so that one is not precluded from viewing it as the 'power' (*śakti*) of consciousness. It is not power in the sense of *vimarśa*, that constitutive aspect of consciousness entailing a fusion of two poles of self and the object, (of the simultaneous knowing of oneself as knowing something and a knowing of that something) which permits one to view consciousness as a field of force as well as pure stasis. The Word which grounds language acts as a foil (*upādhi*) to the *vimarśa śakti*, and, likewise, in relation to finite consciousness (*puruṣa*) and its 'power', (which locus, micro-cosmically, it makes its dwelling) it acts as its primordial embodiment (*para sarīra*) without infringing into the 'embodied' structure. Consciousness, infinite or finite, is of one homogeneous nature and its integrity cannot be compromised by a literal assimilation of the 'being diversified' (*bahudhā sthātum*) character that is structural to word denoting meaning. (see verses 17 and 18 of *Nāda Kārikā*)

28. The opening *kārikā* defines the transcendent scope of *nāda* in relation to the following: (i) the three-fold functions of psyche explained in terms of *ahaṃkāra*, *manas* and *buddhi*, (ii) the non-varying super-psychic complex acting as the 'vesture' (*kaṇcuka*) that swathes a person preparing him, as it were, to enter his scene of action; these involve *vidyā, rāga kalā* and *māyā*. (iii) the 'person' (*puruṣa*) and his intelligence partially unveiled by the help of the configuration of (ii) and (iv) the audible sound (*dhvani*). Extending the list (from the hint in '*dhvanipyo'pi*' of the *kārikā*) the commentator adds (v) the phonemic *śabda*. Indeed the text proceeds, in the next five *kārikās*, to examine the claims principally of the unmentioned (v) and, by implication, (again according to the commentator without much textual warrant) of the claims of *Sphoṭa* as an extended version of the phoneme-thesis.

29. The plenum as the matrix of physical sound is the *conveyor* and the phonemes which are also 'sound' are the *conveyed*: *abhivyanjakam vyoma vyangya varṇa vyasvasthitah, Pauṣkara Āgama* 6.305. There is also, as it were, an 'overarching' plenum standing in similar relation to the *vyangya* 'sound' itself but with a significant difference; it is the ground wherein the conveyed Word, even the one transcending *pasyanti* exists as only a possibility. It is 'plenum without collision' (*anāhata vyoma*). Incidentally, the language of *vyangya-vyanjaka* must not be confused with that of the semantically significant *vachya-vacaka*. This distinction indeed is utilised by the *Pauṣkara Āgama* text to bring home the point in favour of

nāda as against *varṇa: artha vācakah varṇah vyanjaka na kadācana; nādastu vyanjyate varṇaih.* (6.318) The *vācakatā* of *varṇa* pertains to *varṇa*, not unconditionally, but because of *nāda*. In relation to *nāda* the *varṇa* considered by itself has only the role of *vyanjaka*.

30. Rāmakanṭha rejects the following theses in order in *Kārikās* 2 to 7, employing a method of immanent criticism: (i) the audible sound-cluster which is immediately heard has the first claim to be the word which manifests meaning. (ii) the phonemes, and not the merely audible sounds particular and perishing and incapable of mutual assistance to group themselves into meaningful units, constitute the word. They are eternal and ubiquitous, and they co-exist in cognition in such wise that they can function as one unit to denote meaning. (iii) the entity standing over against the phonemes, articulated in a progressive manner and becoming unveiled, this entity is primarily of the form of a whole as sentence or word—all-pervasive and eternal within as well as without—and qualifies better for the role of meaning-bearing word. There is not the *tour de force* of crediting residual traces causing remembrance with the power also of conveying meaning which is the rationalisation of (ii). In the present case the whole pre-exists as sentence or word units, which becomes revealed by and by through the utterances of the speaker until toward the end, thanks to the impressions bequeathed serially by the preceding utterances, it becomes fully unveiled coinciding with grasping of meaning. The option of Sphoṭa as a clear alternative to the Varṇa thesis, and the lines of clear demarcation if any between Nāda and Sphoṭa—these and other associated issues are not clarified by Rāmakanṭha or even his commentator. The implied and express criticism of (ii) in the formulation of the position (iii) is utilised in support of the thesis of Nāda, but the table is turned against (iii) with the help of the arguments drawn from the standpoint of (ii): "the individual words and sentences are only a grouping of phonemes." The *Pārākhya Āgama* text that the Commentator cites under *Kārikā* 12, *purva varṇaja saṃskara yukto 'ntyor no 'bhidhayakah* is interpreted by him very much in keeping with the spirit and letter of Sphoṭa thesis: the last letter of the word with the revived residual impressions of the preceding letters, *through manifesting nāda* becomes expressive of meaning. The language of '*spoṭa*' is also used as inter-changeable with *nāda* in the text of *Pauṣkara Āgama* at many places. Distinguishing the Sphoṭa and the Nāda theories as answers to the semantic problem (without considering their respective ontological horizons) remains a serious exegetical task.

31. It is useful to note that the text typifies an understanding of the problem that serves to define a non-idealistic point of view original to the generality of the Āgama but which becomes blurred in the Spanda sāstra and a target of criticism in the Pratyabhijña literature. While it is through language that the world arises for us and in this sense, surely, our experience is linguistic, experience is not a case of projection of personal or reflective consciousness, but is, the medium by which the being of a thing as it is is disclosed. Language is equiprimordial and co-eval in relation to experience. The distinction of *savikalpa/nirvikalpa* which is structural to perception is occasioned through mediation, not of mind, but of language. See

Srikanṭha's *Ratna Traya Parīkṣā*, 59,C (Devakottai, 1926). For a refutation of this position by arguments reminiscential of Buddhist Vijñānavāda, see Abhinava's *Īśvara Pratyabhijña Vimarśinī*, Jñānādhikāra, āhnika V, verses 8 and 9.

32. The commentator's *mangalācaranam* to the commentary of *Nāda Kārikā*.

33. The Text of *Nāda Kārikā*, reproduced here in Roman transliteration and translated for the first time in a European language, was printed along with Aghora Siva's Commentary in 1925 in Devakottai along with other similar manuals. Always describing himself as the son of Bhatta Nārāyaṇa Kanṭha in his works and thus, luckily for the modern historians, identified in contra-distinction from other Rāmakanṭhas, in the present work the author refers, in addition, to his Kashmir ancestry. Dr. K. C. Pandey assigns him to the first quarter of the 12th century A.D. on the very plausible ground that he was the teacher of Aghora Siva who in his *Paddhati* gives out his date as 1158 A.D. The Text is remarkably lucid and represents the only book of its kind focusing on language. The author draws freely from the *Pauṣkara Āgama* both in language and in substance as one may see on reading the two texts.

Bhartṛhari's Dhvani: A Central Notion in Indian Aesthetics

Harold G. Coward

STANDARD HISTORIES OF INDIAN AESTHETICS described *dhvani* (suggestion) as a central notion.[1] The agreed authoritative definition of *dhvani* is given within the context of poetics by Anandavardhana as follows: "That kind of poetry wherein either the (conventional) meaning or the (conventional) word renders itself or its meaning secondary (respectively) and suggests the implied meaning, is designated by the learned as DHVANI or 'suggestive poetry'."[2] The earliest example of *dhvani* is usually taken from Vālmīki's *Rāmāyaṇa*; the particular incident runs as follows. Once Vālmīki went to the river for his mid-day bath. While walking in the beautiful forest, he came upon a pair of birds (called *Krauñca*) engaged in the act of mating. As Vālmīki stood gazing at this sight an arrow came from behind, killing the male bird. The shock of this terrible turn of events changed the female's joyous twitter into a terrified shriek. Vālmīki was deeply moved by her plight. He completely forgot himself and for a moment fully identified with the helpless female bird. From his lips burst forth a poetic expression of grief: "Hunter, may you never get any peace. You have killed one of the pair of krauñcas in the state of being carried away with love."[3] This spontaneous outpouring is said to be the first poetic expression in classical Sanskrit, as well as the first example of *dhvani*. K. C. Pandey analyzes the poetic expression as follows:

> [Vālmīki] speaks not as Vālmīki, but as the female Krauñca universalized. He views the situation as the latter. He, therefore, experiences the loss of what was the dearest and most precious. This has meant to him the irrecoverable loss of peace of mind. He looks upon the hunter as the author of his perpetual grief. He feels his helplessness against the enemy. And, therefore, in the characteristic manner of a widowed woman [whose husband has been senselessly murdered], he curses the hunter with a lot very much worse than his own.[4]

In Indian aesthetics this is considered inspired poetry because of the deep feeling of grief which the words in their rhyme, meter, juxtaposition, etc., arouse. It is *dhvani* because the expression of grief is accomplished without the use of the word 'grief' or any of its synonyms. The feeling is too deep, intense and universal to be directly expressed in conventional words–it can only be evoked or suggested indirectly, and this is the notion of *dhvani* in aesthetics. However, prior to this usage in aesthetics, the notion of *dvani* had been carefully formulated by the great Indian philosopher of language, Bhartṛhari, in his *Vākyapadīya*.

In this paper we will briefly examine the way in which Bhartṛhari's notion of *dvani*, along with his whole language model, is taken over and further developed by the Indian literary critics. We will analyze this development first in terms of its philosophic aspects and second in terms of its psychology. The latter is judged to be as important as the former in that a complete analysis of the aesthetic experience should bring out not only its philosophical plausibility, but its psychological possibility as well.

Bhartṛhari's Dhvani as Developed by the Literary Critics

In Indian literature, Bhartṛhari is held to have been a great poet and philosopher of language. His date has been variously given from 450–650 A.D.[5] It is in the *Vākyapadīya*, his great work on the philosophy of language, that the term *dhvani* appears. The commentary on *Kānda* 1, *Kārikā* 5 states that the Veda though ONE has been put into a diversity of poems or hymns (*dhvanis*) by the *Ṛṣis*. Although the various manifestations of the one Veda may vary in *dhvani* (form and style of expression) from poet to poet and from region to region, it is same *dharma* or truth that is being voiced throughout.[6] This is the basic model upon which Bhartṛhari constructs his theory of language. The central or essential idea of the poem is a given which is inherently present in the poet's consciousness (as well as in the consciouness of everyone else). At the first moment of its revelation the poet is completely caught up in this unitary idea, or *sphoṭa*, as Bhartṛhari calls it. However, as he starts to examine the idea with an eye to its communication, he withdraws himself from the first intimate unity with the idea, symbol, or inspiration itself, and experiences it in a twofold fashion. On the one hand there is the objective meaning which he is seeking to communicate; on the other hand there are the words and phrases he will utter. Further on in the *Vākyapadīya*[7] Bhartṛhari provides a technical analysis which could be diagrammed as follows:

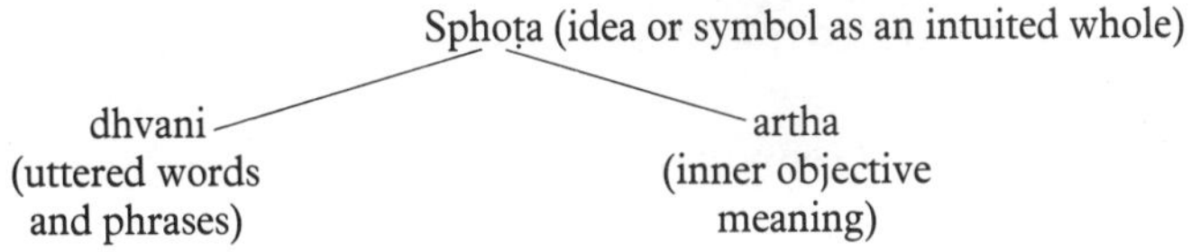

For Bhartṛhari the sentence, play, poem, essay or book taken as a meaning-whole is the *sphoṭa*. The technical term *sphoṭa* is difficult to translate into English. Sometimes the word 'symbol' is used for *sphoṭa*, while at other times the Greek conception of *logos* and the Platonic notion of the innate idea have been suggested as approximating *sphoṭa*. In his *Sphoṭavāda*, Nāgeśa Bhaṭṭa describes *sphoṭa* in two ways: as that from which the meaning bursts or shines forth; and as an entity which is manifested by the spoken letters or sounds.[8] The *sphoṭa* may thus be thought of as a kind of two-sided coin. On the one side it is manifested by the uttered sounds, and on the other side it simultaneously reveals the inner meaning. In a more philosophic sense, *sphoṭa* may be described as the transcendent ground in which the spoken syllables and conveyed meaning find themselves united.

The process of speaking is described as follows: At first the whole idea exists in the mind of the speaker as a unity or *sphoṭa*. It is, as it were, an immediate intuition with, as yet, no subject-object distinction. However, when the speaker utters it, he produces a sequence of different sounds so that what is really one—the *sphoṭa* or whole idea—appears to be many: namely, all the words of the sentence, poem or drama. From the listener's point of view, the process is reversed. The listener, although at first hearing a series of uttered words, ultimately perceives the uttered sentence as a unity—the same unity or *sphoṭa* from which the speaker began—and it is then that the moment of communication between speaker and listener occurs.[9]

Before proceeding, let us briefly note the presuppositions involved in this philosophy of language. In opposition to our usual modern way of thinking in which language is seen as essentially conventional or man-made, Bhartṛhari assumes that language is a given (a divine given) which is coextensive with human consciousness. Therefore the *sphoṭas* (ideas or symbols) are always present, although not always known, in every individual's consciousness. Further, there can be no cognition without words.[10] This seems to agree with the contention of at least one modern linguist. Edward Sapir maintains that there is no thought without language.[11] As T. R. V. Murti puts it, it is not that we have a thought and then look for a word to express it; or that we have a lonely word we seek to connect with a thought. "Word and thought develop together or rather they are expressions of one deep spiritual impulse to know and to communicate."[12]

Development by the Literary Critics

Among the literary critics of India, Anandavardhana seems to have been the first to make use of Bhartṛhari's notion of *dhvani*. It is *Kārikā* 47 of *Kānda* I that directly provides the basis for interpreting *dhvani*. It is *dhvani* in terms of 'suggestion.' There Bhartṛhari says it is the spoken words which suggest that inner meaning (*artha*) and eventually evoke the unified *sphoṭa*.[13] Anandavardhana picks up the notion of *dhvani* as the suggestive power of the spoken words, but also uses *dhvani* to refer to the thing suggested, namely, the principle poetic mood or meaning.[14] Let us examine each of these usages in turn.

Dhvani refers to the suggestive function (*vyañjanā*) of the words and phrases of the poem or drama. But whereas for Bhartṛhari it is the conventional inner meaning or *artha* which is called forth, Anandavardhana specializes the notion of *dhvani* so that it refers to the specific poetic sense evoked rather than to the ordinary meaning. The traditional example offered is the phrase, "a hamlet on the Ganges." What is meant here is more than just the conventional meanings of the individual words since that would result in a house in the middle of the river Ganges. Therefore the secondary (lakṣanā) sense of a house on the bank of the Ganges is understood. But if the phrase were part of a poem, yet another level of meaning would be involved. The words "a hamlet on the Ganges" would suggest not just a house on the river bank, but a house which, due to its proximity to the Ganges, is cool, pure, and holy. Of course all this could be spelled out word for word, but then it would lose its special poetic sense. Sankaran clearly analyzes this distinction:

> This idea of the coolness and sanctity of the hamlet is delightful when suggested from 'a hamlet on the Ganges', but it is not so when understood expressly from 'a hamlet on the bank of the Ganges is very cool and holy'; for in getting at the idea there is in the former a peculiar exercise to the mind which only an intellectual man can take, and it delights him, while in the latter this is totally absent. The Dhvani school holds that the presence of the suggested idea above the express sense distinguishes poetry from ordinary language.[15]

The presence of a larger suggested sense (inclusive of idea, mood and mystic intuition) over and above the primary (*abhidhā*) and secondary (*lakṣanā*) meanings makes the passage poetry rather than ordinary language.

Sankaran provides an example from the great Indian poet Daṇḍin to further clarify this distinction:

> Depart my dear! If thou dost, then may thy paths be safe! Let me also be born again in that place whither thou wouldst be gone. (Daṇḍin, *Kāvyādarśa* 2:141).

The verse is spoken by a lady to her beloved on the eve of his departure on a long journey. In its conventional or primary meanings the verse simply wishes the lover a happy journey and says that she wishes to be reborn in the place where her lover is going. This is the exact meaning of the words. But the poetic sense suggests much more. By desiring rebirth in the land to which her beloved is going, she is suggesting that he should not leave for if he does she will die due to the pain of their separation. To put it very plainly she could have said, "My dear, I love you intensely; so do not go. If you do, I will certainly commit suicide."[16] But in this form no poetic feeling and none of the subtle aesthetic sense of the poetic passage is evoked. Here the term *dhvani* refers to the special suggestive function (*vyañjanā*) of the poetic phrases.

But Anandavardhana also uses *dhvani* to refer to the total mood and/or idea that is suggested. In the example of the lady and her beloved, both an idea (*artha*) and a dominant mood (*rasa*) are evoked by the suggestive power of the poetry. The idea that the beloved should not depart and the mood of intense love in the face of impending separation are both termed *dhvani*. With reference to Bhartṛhari's language model, this usage would seem to parallel the notion of *sphoṭa* as the meaning-whole manifested by the spoken words (*dhvanis*). Thus we see that Anandavardhana expanded Bhartrhari's usage of *dhvani*, which referred to the manifested sounds, to include the *artha* and *sphoṭa* as well. But whereas Bhartṛhari's *sphoṭa* connoted more the abstract unitary idea,

Anandavardhana's *dhvani*, as the end poetic experience, includes an emphasis on the aesthetic feeling or mood as well as the unitary idea. These added aspects that distinguish Anandavardhana's *dhvani* from Bhartṛhari's *sphoṭa* occur as a direct result of the poetic rather than the ordinary way of speaking.[17] This use of *dhvani* to refer to the aesthetic mood or feeling itself also allowed Anandavardhana to subsume the older notion of *rasa* under *dhvani.* Some centuries earlier, possibly around the Sixth Century A.D., Bharata in his *Nātyaśāstra* had established *rasa* as the 'soul' of poetry and drama.[18] The term *rasa* primarily means 'taste', 'flavor' or 'relish', but metaphorically it refers to the emotional experience of beauty in poetry and drama.[19] Bharata emphasized the inner aspect of the aesthetic experience—*rasa* as the 'soul' of poetry or drama. After Bharata the pendulum swung in the opposite direction and the essence of poetry was identified with its external aspects—its figures of speech (*alaṃkāras*) and poetic style (*rīti*).[20] However, in his *Dhvanyāloka*, Anandavardhana was able to subsume all of the pendulum swings of previous aesthetic theorizing. This he accomplished by basing himself on the *sphoṭa* model of Bhartṛhari and developing the notion of *dhvani* so that it referred not only to the evocative function of the uttered sounds (*alaṃkāra* and *rīti*) but also to the inner mood/idea (*rasa*). In this way Anandavardhana established *dhvani* as the central notion of Indian aesthetics, and provided a definition for poetics that would include all rhythmic expression. Thus his *dhvani* theory presents itself as a development of the definition given by the first Indian poet Vālmīki—that rhythmic expression, which is the spontaneous outlet of the mind overpowered by the grief caused by the death of one of the pair of *krauñca* birds, would alone constitute poetry.[21] Anandavardhana not only included all rhythmic expression in his definition but also showed *dhvani* to be a key characteristic of such aesthetic experience.

After Anandavardhana, the next important *dhvani* literary critic is the great philosopher and poet of Kashmir, Abhinavagupta. Abhinavagupta lived c. 1000 A.D. His two works on aesthetics are the *Locana*, a commentary on the *Dhvanyāloka*, and the *Abhinavabhāratī*, a commentary on the *Nātya-śāstra*. Of these two it is the *Locana*, based upon Anandavardhana's *dhvani* theory, that Abhinavagupta himself judges to be most important. Of the two aspects of *dhvani* developed in the *Dhvanyāloka*—outer *dhvani* as the suggestive function of the uttered words, and inner *dhvani* as the suggested aesthetic mood itself—Abhinavagupta pays more attention to the latter. His interest here is both philosophical and religious. Whereas Anandavardhana seems to have paid equal attention to the inner and outer aspects of *dhvani* (although with an evident preference toward the inner), Abhinavagupta shifts the emphasis almost completely to the inner *dhvani*, which he calls the *kāvya* or soul of the aesthetic experience.[22]

This development takes to its logical conclusion the direction that was already evident in the *Dhvanyāloka* and allows Abhinavagupta to make several theoretical moves in rapid order. In one stroke he overcomes rivalries between the Rasa school and the Dhvani school since they both now champion the same goal–i.e. the inner essence of the aesthetic experience, which Abhinavagupta calls *rasadhvani*. In terms of philosophical analysis, the essence of poetry and drama is no longer located at the level of phenomenal experience (i.e. the external *dhvanis* of spoken words and heard sounds). Through aesthetics one is now seen to rise above the level of the individual enjoyment to the universal experience.[23] The uttered words and the meanings (*arthas*) they manifest are the mere particularities, like the outer adornments of the body. The true inner soul (which in Eastern thought is often conceived of as common to all men) of the aesthetic experience is the *rasadhvani* that the words and ideas evoke. Being beyond individual words and cognitions, *rasadhvani* is, according to Abhinavagupta, transcendental. There is intuitive union with ultimate reality. One is completely caught up in the aesthetic experience. Subject-object duality is overcome and there is a oneness with the universal *rasadhvani* itself. Pandey summarizes Abhinavagupta's final position as follows: "He holds that aesthetic experience at its highest level is the experience of the Self [Divine] itself, as pure and unmixed bliss."[24] It is the pure bliss of this highest universal *rasadhvani* that phenomenalizes itself into the various *rasas* and *dhvanis* of our aesthetic experience. Although this is not the place to enter into a long discussion of the various categorizations in terms of numbers of *rasas*, it is perhaps interesting to note that Anandavardhana added the unorthodox *śānta* (spiritual serenity) to the orthodox list of eight *rasas*. In line with his universalizing and spiritualizing tendency, Abhinavagupta not only includes *śānta* but makes it the storehouse *rasa* for all others. In his view, all *rasas* proceed from *śānta* and subside into *śānta*. *Śānta* is therefore not merely one of the *rasas*, but the vitalizing energy of all the other *rasas*.[25] *Śānta* therefore is the nature of the absolute *rasadhvani*, and gives *mokṣa* (spiritual self-realization) when one identifies with it fully.

Before turning to the psychological analysis, let us briefly note one of the criticisms entered against the *dhvani* philosophy of aesthetic experience.[26] Mahimabhaṭṭa, a younger contemporary of Abhinavagupta, is a representative of the *anumāna* or inference school of philosophy. In his *Vyaktiviveka* he attempts to show that *dhvani* is simply a variety of inference and therefore not different from *lakṣaṇā*. It is the unexpressed conclusion which the learned person reaches on hearing the poem that gives rise to aesthetic pleasure. The learned person is simply filling in the inferential steps that the poet has left out, and often this 'filling-in' inferential activity will go on subconsciously so that the reader or spectator is not aware of it—suddenly the conclusion appears as if from nowhere, and one experiences *dhvani* or elation. Thus, in Mahimabhaṭṭa's eyes, *dhvani* is not a special poetic function in itself but is reduced to simply unconscious inference.[27] In this Mahimabhaṭṭa strongly attacks the Sphoṭa theory of Bhartṛhari and the Dhvani theory of Abhinavagupta, because they claim to transcend dualistic (subject-object) cognition in the inner realization—*sphoṭa pratibha* for Bhartṛhari, and the transcendental *rasadhvani* for Abhinavagupta. Of course if, as Mahimabhaṭṭa contends, these are really only cases of unconscious reasoning (which is necessarily dualistic), then *sphoṭa pratibha* and *rasadhvani* are merely fictitious. Since Mahimabhaṭṭa's criticism rests on assumptions as to what happens within the unconscious during the aesthetic experience, let us now turn to a psychological analysis to see if he or Sphoṭa/Dhvani theory is supported.

The Psychological Processes of Dhvani

Having philosophically analyzed the notion of *dhvani*, let us now examine the psychological processes involved in having the actual aesthetic experience. We must attempt this, to begin with at least, not in the terms of modern psychology, but rather from the viewpoint of the traditional psychology adopted by all medieval Indian thinkers[28]—the Yoga Psychology of Patañjali.[29] Once the psychological processes have been described in the terms which Bhartṛhari, Anandavardhana and Abhinavagupta would have used, we can perhaps also apply modern psychological theory to the notion of *dhvani*.

The Yoga Psychology Underlying Bhartṛhari's Sphoṭa Theory

Recent discussion of both Sphoṭa and Dhvani theory has dwelt almost exclusively on the philosophical analysis and ignored Yoga psychology which, in the medieval debates, was evidently assumed and valued for both theoretical and practical purposes. The ancient Yoga scholars arrived at their psychological description by subjectively analyzing thought processes. In our experience of a thought, a particular idea (*artha*) seems to arise, momentarily appear as self-illuminated before our mind's eye, and then pass away. Movement (*rajas*) therefore was conceived as a principal element of thought. Apart from *rajas,* thought, when its sensuous contents are removed, seems to exhibit a sort of universal form or mold. This *a priori* form appears to assume the structure of all contents presented to it. This is the universal knowing aspect of consciousness (*sattva*) which provides the substratum upon which the idea particulars impose themselves for understanding. In the Yoga view the contents of thought are simply limitations of this universal aspect of *sattva.*[30] *Tamas* is the material aspect of consciousness (i.e. the neural tissue of the brain) that becomes infused with energy and at the same time conserves energy, preventing its dissipation and providing for potentiality. In Yoga theory, *sattva, rajas* and *tamas,* like three strands of a single rope, compose *all* the 'stuff' of consciousness (*citta*).[31] Consequently, if it were possible to suddenly stop one's mental processes and take a cross-section through one's psyche, it would reveal a quantitative relationship between *sattva, rajas* and *tamas* that would be in keeping with the qualitative nature of the experience of that particular moment. For example, if it were a moment of clear intelligence, *sattva* would be predominant and the other two aspects (*rajas* and *tamas*) would be proportionately reduced. A moment of pure passion would see *rajas* as predominant. An experience characterized as dullness or inertia would mean that one's *citta* was dominated by *tamas.* The infinite variety of relative weightings between the three aspects of citta correspond to the seemingly infinite variety of our mental states. Such states (*citta-vṛttis*) include all the possible modifications of citta that may be experienced in ones phenomenal existence. Dasgupta points out that we cannot distinguish these states of consciousness from consciousness itself, for consciousness is not something separate from its states. Consciousness exists in its states.[32] Thus, as was stated earlier, thought or language and consciousness are one and the same.

Another basic finding of the Yoga analysis is that this unity of language and consciousness is identified with the Divine (*Īśvara*—consciousness as the universal forms of pure *sattva*) and is constantly seeking to burst forth into expression at the phenomenal level of thoughts and words.[33] In Bhartṛhari's language theory these seed or *a priori* forms of word/consciousness are the universal *sphoṭas* which manifest themselves through *rajas* and *tamas* as inner meanings (*arthas*) and uttered words and phrases (*dhvanis*). Such a primordial, noumenal *sphoṭa* is psychologically analyzed as a pure concentrated intuition (*prajña*) which is unitary in nature. Only as it becomes bifurcated into thought, as the first step towards uttered speech, does the subject-object duality of our ordinary cognition appear.[34]

Perhaps it would be helpful to illustrate the above Yoga description with an introspective examination of our own experience in the act of speaking.

At its earliest genesis the speaking act would seem to involve: some kind of mental effort to tune-out distracting sensations and thoughts, an inwardly focused concentration of mind, and an effort of the mind to bring into self-awareness some idea (glimpse of reality) that is only vaguely within our ken. Although we may feel very sure of its presence just beyond the fringes of our conscious awareness, and although we may find ourselves impelled by a great desire to reveal that idea to ourselves in discursive thought, a great effort at concentrated thinking is often required before any clear conceptualization of it is achieved. Even then we may well feel dissatisfied in that the laboriously conceived conceptualization proves to be inadequate and incomplete in comparison with our direct intuition of the noumenal 'thing-in-itself' which remains stubbornly transcendent in the face of all our attempts to capture it in discrete thought.

To return to Bhartṛhari's terminology, the noumenal idea or intuition would be the *sphoṭa*, the conceptualized inner meaning would be *artha*, and the spoken expression of that conceptualization would be *dhvani*. Let us now see if this psychological description,[35] which clearly supports the language theory of Bhartṛhari, can be extended to also include the development of the *dhvani* notion by the literary critics as outlined in Section I.

Application of Yoga Psychology to Rasadhvani

The above introspection into the speaking act is a helpful beginning point for illustrating the special claim made by the aesthetic theories of *dhvani*. The difficulty in conceptualizing the noumenal idea into the words and phrases of ordinary language was very evident. Although Bhartṛhari maintained that each uttered word or *dhvani* manifested the whole of the *sphoṭa*, it did so only vaguely, so that the full or *prajña* intuition was not accomplished on the first try. Subsequent words and phrases of the sentence would each again attempt to reveal the whole *sphoṭa*, and each would remove a little more of the vagueness until finally with the cognition of the last word, (taken together in consciousness with the memory traces or *saṃskāras* of all the preceding words), the last obstructing vagueness would be removed and the *pratibha* or unitary intuition of the *sphoṭa* would spontaneously occur.[36] The language critics seem to be suggesting that ordinary speaking, as analyzed by Bhartṛhari, does not have the power to reveal fully or make possible intuitive union with the *sphoṭa*. The ordinary *dhvanis* may well, by the psychological mechanism of *saṃskāras*, evoke inner meanings (*arthas*), but this will still be at the discursive level of subject-object cognition—the point at which philosophic enquiry inevitably seems to have to terminate. This is unsatisfactory, however, because it leaves one in the impotent situation of having vaguely glimpsed the truth 'academically', as we say, yet having been unable 'to make it one's own'. It is precisely at this juncture that the aestheticians see themselves as offering a helping hand to the philosopher or theologian who has become entrapped in the limitations inherent in his own rational processes. This helping hand comes in the aesthetic evocation of the underlying emotion (*rasadhvani*) in which the *artha* in its *a priori* form is embedded. Emotion is needed for the overcoming of dualistic cognition so that the unitary intuition of the *sphoṭa* can occur. Since the dualistic nature of ordinary language or rationality and inference can only vaguely suggest the *sphoṭa* it is only by the *vyañjanā* or suggestive power of poetic and dramatic words and its resultant emotion (*rasadhvani*) that one can identify with the non-dualistic intuition of the poet and so escape from the duality inherent in ones own ordinary cognition. This is the special power and function which the aestheticians claim for their use of language. Perhaps the contempoary poet A. E. Housman put it well when he said,

> And I think that to transfuse emotion—not to transmit thought but to set up in the reader's sense a vibration corresponding to what was felt by the writer—is the peculiar function of poetry.[37]

The 'vibration' or *rasadhvani* is potentially present in all consciousness. The poet or dramatist does not create it as a new thing; he simply discovers what is already present through the excellence of his own intuition. His contribution is the skillful creation of a set of words and phrases that will awaken the spectator's sensitivity to that same intuition—but this time in the spectator's consciousness. The beginning point for the poet and the ending point for the listener are the same universal intuition or *rasadhvani* which is inherent in all consciousness.

Abhinavagupta's description of the mental processes involved in the aesthetic experience is consistent with the above analysis. In his view, each psyche has implanted within, certain basic *sthāyibhāvas* or 'instincts'[38] The *sthāyibhāvas* are the divinely given *saṃskāra* series of pure *sattva*, which, for Patañjali, compose Īśvara's pure forms. These pure *sattva* forms are the unmanifested *sthāyibhavas*, and are but limitations within *sattva* of pure universal consciousness. This would be the Yoga description of the *rasa śānta*—the ground *rasadhvani* out of which the others arise. At this level of collective consciousness (*buddhitattva*), there is no subject-object distinction, and, as Vyāsa puts it "all we can say is that it exists."[39] The poet or playwright first comes to know this universal *rasadhvani* as a unitary supersensuous perception (*pratibha*). Since *sattva* is by definition pure bliss, and this is a 'knowing by becoming one with *sattva*', the author's experience at this point is also bliss—but with a *rajas* impulse towards outer expression or manifestation. From this moment of highest inspiration flows forth his aesthetic creation, the rhythmic phrases and dramatic situations which evoke in the consciouness of the listener that same supersenuous perception which the author experienced. The better the poet, the more effectively will his words (outer *dhvanis*) raise us away from the dullness (*tamas*) of our ordinary experience to an aesthetic climax (inner *dhvani*) which is pure and blissful (*sattvic*) in nature.[40]

One thing that the above psychological analysis makes clear is that, in terms of Yoga psychology at least, the *rasadhvani* is a case of suggested or evoked intuition, and not a rational conclusion from unconscious inference as Mahimbhaṭṭa maintained.[41] The *rasadhvani* aesthetic philsosophy is thus supported by traditional Yoga psychology.

Application of Modern Western Psychology to Rasadhvani

It is of considerable interest to note that an increasing number of contemporary psychologists are coming to support the ancient Indian contention that the mind contains its own structuring mechanism (*sphoṭas* or *rasadhvani*) without which aesthetic knowing would be impossible. For example, Karl Pribram, a neurophysiological psychologist, while studying memory, found evidence suggesting that the brain contains structuring patterns within individual nerve cells which seem to resemble laser-produced holograms. When the appropriate sensory input patterns are presented, the latent hologram is aroused resulting in the words and symbols that function as our means for knowing.[42] In Abhinavagupta's aesthetic theory, *rasadhvani* would be the functional equivalent of the nerve cells' hologram, and the outer *dhvanis* would correspond to the sensory input patterns. Another point of contact between Pribram and Dhvani Theory is the former's emphasis upon inner feelings or dispositions as the motive power by which the external sensory patterns and the inner holograms are, as he puts it, grafted onto one another.[43] Following a similar line of theorizing, Wilder Penfield, a neurologist, likens the cerebral cortex to a carpet of nerve cells in which consciousness is recorded in a kind of permanent fashion.[44] Such 'permanent' recordings (of past experiences) provide a *sphoṭa*-like model against which present experience is interpreted as meaningful. But, while there are many formal and functional similarities between the above modern scientists and Dhvani theory, it must be clearly understood that for modern Western thinkers inner mechanisms of consciousness (e.g. *sphoṭa* or *rasadhvani*) are usually taken as a learned expression of the external world, and not a beginningless inner entity which is related to both the individual's previous lives and the universal or collective consciousness of all beings.

Perhaps the only modern Western psychologist to maintain that all consciousness is collective and contains within itself in seed form the knowledge of reality is Carl Jung. In this regard Jung provides the closest modern Western approximation to the Yoga conception of consciousness. The psyche is defined by Jung as the totality of all conscious as well as unconscious mental processes.[45] For Jung, as is the case for Yoga, the stuff of consciousness is no less real than the physical matter of the external world.[46] The core constituents of consciousness are the archetypes which Jung defines as mankind's universal reactions to typical human situations of fear, hate, love, birth, death, the divine, etc.[47] The Jungian archetypes bear some formal resemblance to the *sphoṭa* or *rasadhvani* in that it is described as a universal and eternal presence which represents the sum of the latent potentialities of the individual psyche.[48] In agreement with Yoga psychology, Jung conceives of the archetype's external expression as occurring by a process of individuation. Jung calls the external expression a symbol and it may take the form of a word, gesture or, more often for Jung, a pictorial image. This expressed symbol would parallel the outer *dhvani*. Such external expressions (i.e. the poem, play or painting) are never devised consciously but are gradually clarified as the pictorial or word motif moves from the level of the personal consciousness to the deeper level of the collective unconscious. There, says Jung, "the symbol becomes increasingly dominant, for it encloses an archetype, a nucleus of meaning that is not representable in itself but is charged with energy."[49] Jung's conception of the archtype as "not representable in itself" seems to correspond to the *rasadvanis* as pure potentialities (*sattvic saṃskāra* series) in the universal consciousness (*buddhitattva*). The 'nucleus of meaning' aspect of the archetype would relate to the *artha*, and the pictorial or word form to the outer *dhvani*. The energy charge of the archetype would be Jung's version of the emotion (*rasa*) required for the aesthetic unification of juxtaposition of all these aspects so that the unitary *rasadhvani* could be realized. It is interesting to note that in describing this process of symbol formation Jung gives the 'feeling' and 'intuiting' functions of the psyche priority over 'thinking' (logical inference) and 'sensing'. Emotion and intuition are the basic processes through which man must first make contact with his archetypes. Thinking and sensing, (pure abstract philosophizing) on their own, cannot firmly engage or evoke the archetype —although they are the necessary copartners of feeling and intuition once the latter have made contact with the archetype. Before meaningful external expression can take place, (in the speaking act, for example), there must first be an inner intuition which reveals the meaning to be expressed. Both Yoga and Jung maintain that this is only achieved when the psyche, through emotion and intuition, gives priority to the eternal archetypes, *sphoṭas* or *rasadhvanis* which are universally present in consciousness. Herein Jung notes, lies part of the difficulty for modern technological man. Because of the emphasis on 'surface discursive thinking' and 'empiric sensing' that our technology requires, there is a limited possibility for intuitive symbolization of the archetypes within consciousness[50]—for the deeper aesthetic experiences (*rasadhvanis*).

Although the above analysis suggests close parallels between Jung and Yoga in terms of aesthetic psychology, there are at least two basic differences. An idea entirely contrary to the Yoga notion of *sphoṭa* or *rasadhvani* as a pure *sattvic* form (experienced as divine bliss) occurs when Jung describes archetypal experience as the latent ancestral experience of the human race. Thus, for Jung, consciousness, at its core (or archetypal level), is colored by the darker hues of human passion and cultural history. As Jacobi puts it, "every collective, representing at the same time the sum of its single members, is stamped by the psychic constitution of those members."[51] In the Yoga view, *rasadhvani* as pure *sattva* is identified not with the darker hues of human history but with the eternal bliss of the divine. This difference would seem to be a direct result of Jung's Western individualistic or egocentric criterion for the highest level of consciousness. For Yoga, Bhartṛhari, and Abhinavagupta, the nature of consciousness is primarily identified with the divine—the personal ego being consigned to a relatively low location in the hierarchy of the evolution of consciousness. The difference is clearly seen in the direction of movement required for achieving the height of aesthetic experience. Whereas Jung seeks to appropriate the universal archetypes to the self-conscious ego via the process of individuation, Yoga (and Dhvani theory) seeks to appropriate the self-conscious ego to the universal (the divine *śānta rasadhvani*).

Concluding Comments

This paper, through philosophical and psychological analysis, has shown some basis for the thesis that Bhartṛhari's *dhvani* is a central notion in Indian aesthetics. But the analysis itself points out several problems requiring further study.

The most important of these would be a careful examination of the Dhvani theorists' claim that only via *vyañjanā* or aesthetic suggestion, consciousness be realized. This unity, it is held, could not be achieved via the ordinary manifesting power of words which is described by Bhartṛhari's *dhvani-artha-spoṭa* analysis. In short, it suggests that Bhartṛhari's *sphoṭa pratibhā* would be somehow incomplete when compared with Abhinavagupta's *rasadhvani*. Yet an impartial look at Bhartṛhari's *dhvani* indicates that it includes all aspects of the aesthetic expression—all gesture, accent, style, metaphor, etc.—so, would it not also include this notion of aesthetic suggestion (*vyañjanā*)? What then is really the difference between these two theories?[52]

Something which is not a technical problem, in the sense of the point just discussed, but which does need clarifying, is the relation of Dhvani theory to the modern Western discussion of aesthetics. K. C. Pandey, in Volume Two of his *Comparative Aesthetics*, has made a start in this direction, but his comparison ends with Hegel and his immediate followers. The relating of *dhvani* to recent Western aesthetics has not been thoroughly undertaken, although V. K. Chari is making helpful contributions in this regard.[53] Several recent Western thinkers offer concepts that bear at least a facial relation to various aspects of Dhvani theory and therefore invite serious study. For example, Ernst Cassirer's notion of symbolic language as the universal *a priori* form,[54] based, as it is, on the Kantian notion of a regulative form or idea needs to be carefully compared against the theory of *rasadhvani* as an *a priori* form of pure *sattva*. Then there is the psycholinguist, Noam Chomsky, who proposes some kind of universal grammatical structures as innate within the mind.[55] Chomsky's innate structures also need to be examined in relation to the *a priori* pure *sattva* forms of both Sphoṭa and Dhvani Theory. Such comparative studies, while useful in themselves, may also serve the purpose of making Western students of aesthetics aware of the serious study that has been undertaken in this field within Indian thought.

Notes

1. See for example: K. C. Pandey, *Comparative Aesthetics*, vols. 7., 2. Banares: Chowkhamba Sanskrit Series, 1956; S. K. De, *History of Sanskrit Poetics*, vols. 1., 2. (Calcutta: K. L. Mukhopadhyay, 2nd ed., 1960), and P. V. Kane, *History of Sanskrit Poetics* (Delhi: Motilal Banarsidass, 4th ed., 1971). *Rasa* The dominant emotional mood) is another central notion which appears to be initmately related to *dhvani*. Other common notions include: *doṣas* (flaws), *alamkāras* (figures of speech), *rīti* (style), *guṇas* (special qualities).

2. Anandavardhana, *Dhvanyāloka*, trans. K. Krishnamoorthy (Poona: Oriental Book Agency, 1955), 1.13, 9. This important work on Indian Aesthetics is dated C850 AD in Kashmir.

3. *Vālmīki Rāmāyaṇa* as quoted in trans. by K. C. Pandey, op. cit. 1:260–61.

4. Ibid., p. 263.

5. K. A. Subramania Iyer, *Bhartṛhari* (Poona: Deccan College, 1969), pp. 1–2. For an example of the poetry attributed to him see the *Vairāgya-Śatakam* of Bhartṛhari. Calcutta: Advaita Ashrama, 1963.

6. *Vākyapadīya of Bhartṛhari* trans. K. A. Subramania Iyer (Poona: Deccan College, 1965, 1:5, 7–8.

7. *Vākyapadīya*, op. cit. 1:44–48, 53–56.
Nāgeśa Bhatta, *Sphoṭavāda* (Madras: The Adyar Library, 1946), p. 5.

8. Nāgeśa Bhatta, *Sphoṭavāda* (Madras: The Adyar Library, 1946), p. 5.

9. *Vākyapadīya*, op. cit., 1:44–46, p. 52ff.

10. *Vākyapadīya*, 1:123. Related to this point is Bhartṛhari's rejection of gestures as vehicles for communicating meaning. As Punyarāja puts it, the shaking of the head indicating negation does not communicate independent of words. The gesture serves to make one think of the word 'no' before it can communicate the meaning of negation or refusal. P. K. Chakravarti, *The Linguistic Speculations of the Hindus* (Calcutta: University of Calcutta, 1933), p. 72.

11. Edward Sapir, *Language* (New York: Harcourt, Brace and World, Inc., 1949), p. 15.

12. T. R. V. Murti, "Some Thoughts on the Indian Philosophy of Language" (Presidential Address to the 37th Indian Philosophical Congress, 1963), p. 3.

13. *Vākyapadīya*, op. cit., 1:47, 55.

14. *Dhvanyāloka*, op. cit., 1:13, *vṛtti*, p. 14.

15. A. Sankaran, *Some Aspects of Literary Criticism In Sanskrit* (Madras: University of Madras, 1929), p. 66.

16. Ibid.

17. *Dhvanyāloka*, op. cit., 1:13, 9.

18. S. K. De, *History of Sanskrit Poetics*, op. cit., 1:16.

19. P. V. Kane, *History of Sanskrit Poetics*, op. cit., p. 356.

20. P. C. Lahiri, *Concepts of Rīti and Guna in Sanskrit Poetics* (Ramna: University of Dacca, 1937), pp. 85–90.

21. A. Sankaran, *Some Aspects of Literary Criticism in Sanskrit*, op. cit., p. 79. For a detailed analysis of how Ananda's *dhvani* encompasses and supersedes all previous aesthetic theories see pp. 79–84.

22. For a detailed presentation of Abhinavagupta's aesthetic theory see K. C. Pandey, *Comparative Aesthetics*, op. cit., vol. 1.

23. Although a Western reader can follow this move in terms of its logic, i.e. from the level of the phenomenal or conditioned to the universal or unconditioned, he will not perceive the total implication for the Eastern mind, until some grasp of the underlying psychology is also attained. This is attempted in the next section of the paper.

24. K. C. Pandey, *Comparative Aesthetics*, op. cit., p. 140.

25. A. Sankaran, *Some Aspects of Literary Criticism in Sanskrit*, op. cit., p. 116.

26. Readers wishing a comprehensive review of the criticism against *dhvani* and *rasa* are referred to A. Sankaran, *Some Aspects of Literary Criticism in Sanskrit*, op. cit. Mahimbhaṭṭa's view is reported here in that it could perhaps be the most potent criticism against both *rasa* and *dhvani*.

27. A. Sankaran, *Some Aspects of Literary Criticism in Sanskrit*, op. cit., pp. 132–36.

28. In support of this statement it is noted that M. Eliade states that Yoga is a basic motif of all Indian thought (See *Yoga: Immortality and Freedom* [Princeton: Princeton University Press, 1958], p. 3), and the Russian scholar Stcherbatsky observes that yogic trance (*samādhi*) and yogic courses for psychological training of the mind in the achievement of *mokṣa* appear in virtually all Indian schools of thought–be they Hindu, Buddhist, or Jaina. (*The Conception of Buddhist Nirvāṇa* [London: Mouton & Co., 1965], pp. 16–19.)

29. *Patañjala-Yogadarśanam*, Sanskrit Edition. Varansi: Bhāratīya Vidhyā Prakāśana, 1963. Best English translation is by Rāma Prasāda, *Patañjali's Yoga Sūtras* with the 'Commentary' of Vyāsa and the 'Gloss' of Vācaspati Miśra. Allahabad: Bhuvaneswari Asrama, 1924. *The Sacred Books of the Hindus*, vol. 4.

30. S. N. Dasgupta, *The Study of Patañjali* (Calcutta: University of Calcutta, 1920), p. 49.

31. Yoga psychology adopts a kind of common sense identification or ontological unity between the whole (the universal) and the parts (the particular manifestations). The three *guṇas* of *sattva, rajas* and *tamas* are the one universal genus, and it is the *guṇas* in various collocations that show themselves as the particular manifestations. Thus Patañjali (in *Mahābhāsya* 5.1.129) identifies

substance (*dravya*) with both the particular object (in all its qualities) and the substratum which remains constant amidst change. (S. N. Dasgupta, *Yoga Philosophy*, [Calcutta: University of Calcutta, 1930], pp. 120–26.)

32. *The Study of Patañjali*, op. cit., p. 94.

33. *Yoga Sūtras*, 1:24–26. The underlying metaphysical assumption here is that Braham freely phenomenalizes himself as Īśvara (as an act of grace) so as to provide the means (i.e. Īśvara's pure *sattva* as the pure form of the Vedic revelation) by which beings can attain *mokṣa* or spiritual self-realization. On the psychological level, if this revelation is to be capable of human understanding, it must function through human cognition, thus there is a kind of continuum between Īśvara's *sattva* and that of the lowest being (*jiva*).

34. *Yoga Sūtras*, 3:17.

35. Limitations of the context of this paper have prevented a full and detailed elucidation of Sphoṭa Theory in terms of Yoga Psychology. This I have done in my book entited, *Bhartṛhari* (Boston: G. K. Hall, 1976).

36. *Vākyapadīya* 2:143–145.

37. From A. E. Housman as quoted by Oscar Williams in the "Introduction" to his *A Little Treasury of Modern Poetry* (New York: Scribners, 1952, p. xxxvi).

38. A. Sankaran, *Some Aspects of Literary Criticism In Sanskrit*, op. cit., p. 194.

39. *Yoga Sūtras* 2:19, Bhāsya.

40. Due to the limitations arising from the nature of this paper, a full technical description cannot be given of the evolution of the author's initial intuition through his *buddhi* (intellect), *ahaṃkara* (ego), *manas* (mind), sense organs, etc. into verbal utterances which travel through air waves, impinge upon the spectator and ravel through his sense organs, *manas*, *ahaṃkara*, etc., and induces into manifestation the same *sattva* intuition.

41. It should be noted here that a number of modern Western psychologists are following a similar line of thinking to that of Mahimbhaṭṭa. C. R. Peterson and L. R. Beach, for example, attempt to argue that unconscious reasoning is at the base of all man's so called intuitive processes. (See C. R. Peterson & L. R. Beach, "Man as an Intuitive Statistician," *Psychological Bulletin*, 1967, 68:42–43.) While this approach may be able to quantify the technical problem solving intuition of a scientist, logician, or mathematician, in terms of unconscious inference, the aesthetic intuition seems to be a qualitative 'something other than' the sum total of all quantitative inferences. In the experience of art, music, and literature, it is the 'being caught up in' that seems to be the essence–as Dhvani theory maintains.

42. See K. H. Pribram, "The Neurophysiology of Remembering," *Scientific American*, Jan., 1969, pp. 73-86, and K. H. Pribram, "Neurological Notes on Knowing," (Proceedings of Second Banff Conference on Theoretical Psychology), Banff, 1969.

43. K. H. Pribram, *Neurological Notes on Knowing*, op. cit., p. 16.

44. "The Recording of Consciousness and the Function of the Interpretive Cortex," in *Speech and Brain-Mechanisms* by W. Penfield and L. Roberts (Princeton: Princeton University Press, 1959), pp. 38–55.

45. Jolande Jacobi, *The Psychology of C. G. Jung* (New Haven: Yale University Press, 1958), p. 5.

46. Ibid., p. 2.

47. Ruth Monroe, *Schools of Psychoanalytic Thought* (New York: Dryden Press, 1955), p. 541.

48. *The Psychology of C. G. Jung*, op. cit., pp. 43–48.

49. Ibid., p. 92.

50. *Schools of Psychoanalytic Thought*, op. cit., p. 550.

51. *The Psychology of C. G. Jung* op. cit., p. 204.

52. Dr. V. K. Chari, in a recent personal communication, has suggested that the special notion of *dhvani* is not really needed—all one needs is Bhartṛhari plus *rasa*. But this then raises the question, why 'plus *rasa*'? Perhaps Bhartṛhari's *dhvani–artha–spoṭa* is all that is needed to fully account for the aesthetic experience. It is claimed that he was a poet as well as a philosopher, therefore it would not seem surprising if his philosophy of language could also include the poetic experience. Further study is indicated.

53. See V. K. Chari, "Poetic Emotions and Poetic Semantics: A Critique of the Indian Theory of *Rasa*." (Unpublished paper read at the English Studies Society, Carleton University), Dec., 1974. Also, " 'Rasa' as an Aesthetic Concept: Some Comments from the Point of View of Western Criticism." (Unpublished paper presented at the International Sanskrit Conference), March 1972, New Delhi. Dr. Chari appears to be more drawn to *rasa* than *dhvani*.

54. E. Cassirer, *An Essay On Man*. Toronto: Bantam Books, 1970, and *Philosophy of Symbolic Forms*, vols. 1, 2, 3. New Haven: Yale Univ. Press, 1957.

55. Noam Chomsky, *Language and Mind* (New York: Harcourt, Brace and World, 1968), p. 76.

Bibliography

1. Indian Philosophy and Aesthetics

Aesthetic Rapture: The Rasādhyāya Of The Nātyasāstra, vols. 1, 2. Trans. J. L. Masson and M. V. Patwardhan. Poona: Deccan College, 1970.

Sir Ashutosh Mookerjee Silver Jubilee Volumes, vol. 3. Article by S. D. De on *History of Rasa*.

Brough, J. "Audumbarāyana's Theory of Language." *Bulletin Of The School Of Oriental And African Studies* (1952), 14:73–77.

Chakravarti, P. K. *The Linguistic Speculations of the Hindus*. Calcutta: University of Calcutta, 1933.

Chari, V. K. *'Rasa' As An Aesthetic Concept: Some Comments From The Point Of*

View Of Western Criticism (Unpublished paper presented at the International Sanskrit Conference), March 31, 1972, New Delhi.
______. "Poetic Emotions and Poetic Semantics: A Critique of the Indian Theory of *Rasa*." (Unpublished paper read at the English Studies Society), Carleton University, Ottawa, December 1974.
Chatterjee, Satischandra. *The Nyāya Theory of Knowledge*. Calcutta: University of Calcutta, 1965.
Chabrabarti, Tarapada. *Indian Aesthetics And Science Of Language*. Calcutta: Sanskrit Pustak Bhandar, 1971.
De, S. K. *Studies in the History of Sanskrit Poetics*, vols. 1, 2. London 1923, 1925.
Dhvanyāloka of Anandavardhana, trans. K. Krishnamoorthy. Poona: Oriental Book Agency, 1955.
Iyer, Subramania K. A. *Bhartṛhari*. Poona: Deccan College, 1969.
______. "The Conception of Guna Amount The Varyyakaranas." *New Indian Antiquary*, 5, 6:121-130.
______. "The Doctrine of Sphoṭa." *Journal Of The Ganganath Jha Research Institute*, 5:121-147.
Kane, P. V. *History of Sanskrit Poetics*. Delhi: Motilal Banarsidass, 4th ed., 1971.
Lahiri, P. C. *Concepts of Riti and Guna in Sanskrit Poetics*. Ramna: University of Dacca, 1937.
Murti, T. R. V. "Some Thoughts on the Indian Philosophy of Language." (Presidential Address to the 37th Indian Philosophical Congress), 1963.
Nāgeśa Bhaṭṭa, *Sphoṭavāda*. Madras: The Adyar Library, 1946.
Pandey, K. C. *Abhinavagupta*. Varanasi: Chowkhamba Sanskrit Series Office, 1963.
______. *Comparative Aesthetics*, vols. 1, 2. Varanasi: Chowkhamba Sanskrit Series Office, 1959.
Raja, K. Kunjunni. *Indian Theories Of Meaning*. Adyar: Adyar Library and Research Center, 1963.
Sankaran, A. *Some Aspects of Literary Criticism*. University of Madras, 1929.
Sarva-Darśana-Samgraha by Madhava Acharya, trans. E. B. Cowell and R. E. Gough. London: Kegan Paul, Trench, Trubner & Co. Ltd., Chowkhamba Sanskrit Series Reprint, 1961.
Sastri, Gaurinath. *The Philosophy Of Word And Meaning*, Calcutta: Sanskrit College, 1959.
The Vākyapadīya, Cantos 1 and 2, edited with English Translation by K. Raghavan Pillai. Varanasi: Motilal Banarsidass, 1971.
Vākyapadīya of Bhartṛhari, Cantos 1 and 2, trans. K. Raghavan Pillai. Delhi: Motilal Banarsidass, 1971.

2. *Traditional Indian Psychology*

Eliade, M. *Yoga: Immortality and Freedom*. Princeton: Princeton Univ. Press, 1958.

Dasgupta, S. N. *The Study of Patañjali*. Calcutta: Calcutta Univ. Press, 1920.

———. *Yoga Philosophy*. Calcutta: University of Calcutta, 1930.

Patañjala-Yogadarśanam, Sanskrit Edition. Varanasi: Bhāratīya Vidhyā Prakāśana, 1963.

Patañjali's Yoga Sūtras with the Commentary of Vyāsa and the Gloss of Vācaspati Miśra, trans. Rāma Prasāda. Allahabad: Bhuvaneswari Asrama, 1924, *The Sacred Books of the Hindus*, vol. 4, 3rd edition.

Stcherbatsky, T. H. *The Conception of Buddhist Nirvana*. London: Mouton & Co., 1965.

The Yoga-Sāra-Saṅgraha of Vijñāna Bhiksu, trans. Ganganatha Jha. Madras: Theosophical Pub. House, 1932, rev. ed.

The Yoga System of Patañjali with the *Bhāsya of Vyasa* and the *Tīkā of Vāchaspati Miśra*, trans. J. H. Woods. Delhi: Motilal Banarsidass, 1966, a reprint of "Harvard Oriental Series," vol. 17.

3. Western Psychology and Aesthetics

Cassirer, E. *An Essay On Man*. Toronto: Bantam Books, 1970.

———. *Language and Myth*, trans. S. K. Langer. New York: Dover Pub., 1953.

———. *Philosophy of Symbolic Forms*, vols. 1, 2, 3. New Haven: Yale Univ. Press, 1957.

Chomsky, N. *Language and Mind*. New York: Harcourt, Brace and World, 1968.

Jacobi, J. *Complex/Archetype/Symbol in the Psychology of C. G. Jung*, trans. R. Manheim. New York: Pantheon Books, 1959.

———. *The Psychology of C. G. Jung*. New Haven: Yale Univ. Press, 1955.

Jung, C. G. "Approaching the Unconscious," in *Man and His Symbols*, ed. C. G. Jung. London: Aldus Books, 1964.

———. *Psyche and Symbol*. New York: Anchor Books, 1958.

———. *Psychology and Religion*. New Haven: Yale University Press, 1938.

Munroe, R. L. *Schools of Psychoanalytic Thought*. New York: The Dryden Press, 1955.

Penfield, W. and Roberts L. *Speech and Brain-Mechanism*. Princeton: Princeton University Press, 1959.

Peterson, C. R. and Beach, L. R., "Man as an Intuitive Statistician," *Psychological Bulletin*, 68, 1967, pp. 29–46.

Pribram, K. H. "The Neurophysiology of Remembering," *Scientific American*, Jan. 1969.

———. "Neurological Notes on Knowing," (Proceedings of Second Banff Conference on Theoretical Psychology, Center for Advanced Study of Theoretical Psychology), University of Alberta, May, 1969.

Sapir, E. *Language*. New York: Harcourt, Brace and World, Inc., 1949.

Westcott, M. *Towards A Psychology Of Intuition*. New York: Holt, Rinehart and Winston, Inc., 1968.

Man Carries the Power of All Things in His Mouth

Jacob Boehme's Ideas on Word and Language

Klaus K. Klostermaier

ALTHOUGH HE WAS NOT FORMALLY EDUCATED in philosophy or theology, Jacob Boehme (1575–1624), a contemporary of Tulasīdāsa (1532–1623), has attracted the attention of some of the most learned minds for more than three centuries. Philosophers such as Leibniz, F. V. Baader, Schopenhauer, and Hegel acknowledged the profundity of Boehme's original ideas—ideas that earned him the name 'Philosophus Teutonicus'.[1] Poets and writers such as Goethe, Tieck, and Novalis admired the power of his imagination and the forcefulness of his language.[2] In our own time, C. G. Jung helped to rekindle interest in the 'alchemystical' system developed by Boehme.[3]

Although none of Boehme's voluminous writings deal specifically with word and language, in almost every one of his works he mentions or presupposes ideas that allow the reader to reconstruct his philosophy of language. Boehme's philosophy of language develops a dimension of thinking about language which seems to have been left out in contemporary philosophy; it also bears striking resemblance to various Indian schools of philosophy that concerned themselves with language—schools of which Boehme could not possibly have had any knowledge.

Jacob Boehme's biographers tell us that he had a special sense for words. Without having studied either Latin or Hebrew, he was able to identify plants and flowers by the mere sound of their Latin or Hebrew names. When his learned friend, Dr. Balthasar Walther, visited him and mentioned the Greek word for 'idea', Boehme immediately had a vision of a heavenly virgin: wisdom 'Sophia', in the form of a female companion.[4] It is no wonder that he was able to create new idioms to express his insights and to interpret Scriptures.

The contemporary school of linguistic philosophy operates largely under the tacit supposition that 'word' refers to the printed word. This school concentrates only on the 'carrier of information' and basically studies those aspects of language that a computer can store and retrieve. When Boehme speaks of language, however, he means the spoken word. The spoken word contains many dimensions that are inaccessible to the computer: dimensions we perceive when we labor to produce the right words for a thought; when we find ourselves struck by the appropriateness of a great poet's language; or when we rejoice in coining a word that seems to express uniquely what we feel.

Language and Languages

Throughout his writings, Boehme makes use of a classification of languages which distinguishes between five *Hauptsprachen* (principal languages) and seventy-two *Volkssprachen* (peoples' languages). A further subdivision is found within the *Hauptsprachen*.[5] They are: *Natursprache* (nature language); Hebrew; Greek; Latin; and *Mentalische Sprache* ('mental' or spiritual language).

The five *Hauptsprachen* are 'holy' languages, though to differing degrees. The seventy-two *Volkssprachen* are the result of the Babylonian confusion of tongues,[6] but they are rooted ultimately in the *Natursprache*, and are capable of carrying the *Mentalische Sprache*; they partake of the same power and dignity of the *Hauptsprachen*, the sacred languages of the scholarly European Christian tradition (Hebrew, Greek and Latin).[7] The division into numerous languages had its divine purpose over and above the punitive aspect: it made manifest to the angelic world the wonderful works of God.[8] Boehme takes great pain to point out that the *Volkssprache* which he uses is as capable of revealing deep meaning as the sacred languages used by the scholars. He rebukes the conceited scholars who dabble in Hebrew, Greek, and Latin without even really understanding their native German:

> Our scholars want to be called 'doctors' and 'masters'; but not one of them understands his mother tongue. They have no more understanding of the spirit than a farmer has of the tools with which he does his work. They simply use the ready-made form of the gross composite words and do not understand what the Word in *in sensu*; Therefore we see quarrel and quibble about God and His Will: they wish to teach about God and have not the least understanding of God.[9]

Natursprache *and* Volkssprache

The list of five *Hauptsprachen* does not by itself emphasize sufficiently well the prominent role Boehme gives to the *Natursprache*, which seems to have fascinated him.[10] As far as its origin is concerned, the *Natursprache* is the language of Adam, the first of mankind, and consists of the names by which, according to Scripture, he called everything. It also is the *Sensualische Sprache*[11] through which he was able to find each creature's proper name, a name identical with the *Signatura Rerum*[12] and thus inherent in things themselves.

According to Boehme, this was the language of mankind lost by the children of Noah before the Great Flood.[13] Until the time of the founding of Babylon it was still widely understood;[14] the confusion of tongues consists essentially in the inability to understand the common language of the *Natursprache*. The *Natursprache*, however, is somehow present in all *Volkssprachen*, and although not identical with any one of them, it hovers over our tongues in some imperceptible way.[15] Boehme claims to have received an understanding of the *Natursprache* as a special gift from God. On account of this gift, he claims to be better equipped to interpret Scriptures than the scholars of the classical languages who are incapable of deciphering the signature of things.[16] "*Natursprache*," he says, "is the root or mother of all languages in this world; in it resides the whole and perfect knowledge of all things."[17]

Boehme maintains that the events at the first Pentecost[18] made the *Natursprache* again available to mankind and that in spiritual rebirth every man can understand it. Nobody can be a theologican who does not know the *Sensualische Sprache.*[19] The reference to the Pentecost reveals a cross-link between the first and the last of the *Hauptsprachen: Natursprache* carries in itself the language of the Holy Spirit. "But," says Boehme, "nobody will understand the spiritual tongue in the sensual."[20] In a crucial passage in *Mysterium Magnum*, an exposition of Scriptural texts, he writes about the 'sensual' language, *Natursprache*:

> This is the foundation of the *Hauptsprachen*. When all people spoke in one language, all understood each other. When they no longer wanted to use the 'sensual' language, true understanding vanished, because they led the spirits of the sensual languages into a gross form and encapsuled the subtle spirit of understanding in a crude form and learned to speak with this form. Today all people speak only from this same form of their encapsuled sensual languages.
>
> No nation understands the sensual language any longer. The birds in the air and the animals in the woods understand it according to their own natures.
>
> Man may reflect upon what he has lacked and what is to be gained in rebirth, though not here on earth but in the spiritual world; for all spirits converse with each other in the sensual language. They do not need any other language because this is *Natursprache*.[21]

Alphabets and Letters

Paralleling the classification of *Hauptsprachen*, Boehme has five principal alphabets: that of *Natursprache*, Hebrew, Greek, Latin, and ending with the 'alphabet of the Spirit'.[22] The alphabets, he says, have their origin in the *colors* of the Great Mystery.[23]

Boehme's interest in language *per se* leads him into very interesting speculations about the nature of the letters, the 'atoms' of language. He maintains that each one of the twenty-four letters of the alphabet is a spirit and a form of the 'center'.[24] The 'center' of all things is God and each thing's center is its spirit. The center, however, is three-fold, according to three principles:[25] The first center is God's own speech; the second center is the utterance of God's Wisdom; the third center is the *verbum Fiat*.[26] Man's center is the innermost essence of his soul which he must search for through constant meditation.[27] Boehme tells the reader that he himself has received as gift from God the knowledge of this inner center.[28]

The five vowels of the alphabet constitute the *Mentalische Sprache* whereas the nineteen consonants form the *Sensualische* or *Natursprache*.[29] Since all letters have their ultimate root in the Spirit of God, they have great power in themselves.[30] Boehme maintains that we have lost the five vowels and that an understanding of letters, especially in the Scriptures, does not lead to a true and spiritual understanding of the text.[31]

The following is one of the more interesting examples of Boehme's applications of his own principles to spiritual exegesis:[32]

> The spirits of the letters in the alphabet are the form of the One Spirit in *Natursprache*; the five vowels lead the holy tongue of the five holy languages from the name JEhOVAh, from which the Holy Spirit speaks, because the

five vowels are the Name of God according to His Holiness. The name 'Jehovah' contains only the five vowels A, E, I, O, U.[33] The other letters suggest and express the nature of God's name in the formed Word in nature, in love and in anger, in darkness and in light. However, the five vowels denote *only* what He is in the light of His Holiness; for by the five vowels nature is colored so that she may become the realm of joy.

It was with great insight that the wise men of old, who know these tongues, added the H to the name Jeova and called Him JEhOVAh, because the H makes the Holy Name, with the five vowels, manifest in external nature. It indicates how the Holy Name of God breathes Itself into the creature and manifests Itself. The five vowels are the hidden name of God, Who dwells alone in Himself, but the H signifies the divine pleasure of Wisdom, indicating how the divine pleasure breathes Itself out from Itself.

The inner meaning of the five vowels is as follows:

I is the name JESVS;
E is the name Engel (Angel);
O is the formed Wisdom of Joy of the I and is the Heart of GOD or Center;
V is the spirit as the SVS in JESVS;
A is beginning and end, and is the Father.

Further, these five combine with the form into the word, △/. That is: A, O, V, Father, Son, and Holy Spirit; the triangle signifies the threefold nature of the attributes of the Persons, and the V in the triangle points towards the Spirit in the H, as in expiration, since the whole Godhead manifests Itself in a spiritual manner by going forth from Itself.

The other letters, besides the five vowels, proceed from the name *Tetragrammaton*, as from the center of eternal nature; they spell out the differences of the formed Wisdom as the formed Word in the three principles, wherein the whole creation is contained: they are the *sensus* of creation, as the qualities of the faculties and the truly revealed God in the Word of nature.

Sound and Word

For Jacob Boehme, language is spoken language; and spoken language is associated with sounds that are produced by human organs of sound. Spoken language always carries the intentionality of communication: the spoken word is always spoken *by* someone *to* someone. For Boehme, then, it is of utmost importance to observe exactly the production of the word-sounds and to correlate them to the meanings of words. His textual interpretations of Scripture make the fullest possible use of this method. On several occasions he deals with the question of how words are formed and uttered quite apart from textual references. Thus he writes:

When man's joy transforms itself into desire, as in the free will of man, man takes up the whole alphabet. The desire is the *fiat*, and the joy in desire

> is the contemplative faculty of free will, the formed Word of Wisdom wherein free will looks at itself. Into this, he wishes to introduce the joy of wisdom concerning evil or good. When free will has contemplated itself, it operates with joy in the letters and forms this joy into words; it then exists in an inner form, as a thought conceived.
>
> Then free will takes the H as the spirit of expiration, and leads the formed thought before the council of the five senses, which looks at the formed word and determines whether it is good or not. If the senses approve it, the 'H' as the exhaling spirit, takes the word and leads it to the tongue in the mouth. There the workmaster is the *fiat*, the divine instrument, which forms the *sensus* of the qualities of the letters as free will has composed them, into a substance of sound for the purpose of utterance.
>
> Now take note: See how every word assumes substance in the mouth for the purpose of being uttered, how the work-master who is in the senses forms it as the *fiat*. Note also how the tongue cooperates when she takes hold of the word, and also how she tosses it out: through the teeth or above the tongue itself, or with mouth open. Also note how the tongue bends when forming the word, taking back the *sensus* which she does not want to completely send out. Some *sensus* is rarely half-uttered, some completely, some is drawn back again toward the heart. Also mark how the word has been formed in such a manner: the thing in its form and quality which the word describes insofar as free will might give it a right name and does not take on a wrong name because of malice or a defect in understanding.[34]

Boehme uses this method in countless examples of Scriptural exegesis: much of it may be spurious, especially if one considers that he uses only one particular German version of Scripture from which to draw most profound theological verities. Admittedly, however, he succeeds quite often in making the reader aware of the correlation between the sounds and the meanings of words and the importance of the stages by which spoken language is formed. Along the same lines, he quite convincingly argues the basis of interpersonal communication:

> With sound or speech the *Gestalt* (form) imprints itself in another's *Gestaltnisse* (figure): a like sound catches and moves the other and in sound the mind draws its own *Gestaltnisse* (figure) which it has created in the essence and brought into form *in principio*. In this way, the word can be understood as the mind has created it, whether in good or bad. With the same connotation it enters into another's *Gestaltnisse* and arouses in the other a form which is the signature, too. Both *Gestaltnisse* flow into each other in one form; thus it is *one* concept, *one* will, *one* mind, and also *one* understanding.[35]

Word of Man and Word of God

The process through which words orginate is a truly creative one: in a very profound sense man is the creator of his words.[36] This is the basis for man's responsibility for his words: not only for the effects his words may have, but for the words themselves and for himself as well. In man's capacity for words, ever-deeper strata can be uncovered; man is able to speak because he carries within himself God's own Word.[37] The word is not merely a fictitious and wholly subjective creation of man, but it possesses its own reality, because each word evokes its own *ens*. Thus Boehme says:

> From whatever quality of sound each word is formed when it is uttered—either in God's love, as in the sacred *ens*, or in God's anger-*ens*—it will assume that very same quality when uttered. Each man's word issues forth from something eternal, be it the *ens* of God's love, or God's anger, and as it goes forth from such an *ens*, as from its mother, it wants to return to it again as a place of rest, wherein it may work . . .
>
> Every man is a creator of his words, his faculties, and his being: what he does with his free will is what will enter as a work of the revealed Word into each quality of the revealed Word . . .
>
> Whatever a people is, such a god it will have. God's Word is manifest in everything, and in everyone according to its *ens*, wherefrom issues free will: free will is the creator.
>
> There is neither a blade of grass nor any other thing one could mention wherein one would not find an *ens* from revealed Word, both an *ens* of God's love and of God's anger; of the world of light and the world of darkness, for this visible world has been expirated by the same Word. Each *ens* of the expirated Word has from its own *ens* a free will to breathe out what is similar to itself.
>
> The worst of all evils, however, is that the *ens* in its centro has gone out from the equilibrium, and has become many *entia* from one *ens*.[38]

God's Word is the instrument of creation: the fruitful principle allowing the created things to speak their own word and become thus creators in their own way.[39] However, as Boehme sees it, creation has been vitiated and fouled at its second source: in the word. This, according to Boehme, is the reason salvation came into the world through the Word of God.

The term *lógos*, usually translated as 'Word', has been used as a term for Christ since early times; but seldom have others interpreted, so meaningfully as in Boehme's writings, why it is through the Word that mankind is saved and not through some other divine intervention. God, who utters the Word, is at once the utterance and the uttered. The Word of God is, for Boehme, identical with the 'Heart of God' as the essence of all things:[40] it is the 'Great Mystery' enshrined in all things. God always utters his Word: if for an instant he ceased to do so, everything would be annihilated. God in His own nature is the living and speaking Word, and the whole creation is His formed, natural Word.

In this context, Boehme attributes special significance to the Biblical account of man's fall—as due to a lie: the misuse of the word, the poisoning of man's creation at its roots. Adam's fall results in the loss of the essential word. Interestingly, Boehme located the word of the promise of salvation in Eve's *matrix*: woman's body is the instrument of the transmission of this word to future mankind.[41] In Christ, the word that had been lost by Adam has been recovered.[42] Not only does he reveal God's Word to mankind, but he also leads man's word back into the eternal Word of God:

> God works from eternity to eternity, but only through His Word, and the Word *is* God as a revelation of the ground of existence. If the soul no longer speaks its own will, the unfathomable Will shall speak: where creatures stand still, God works. If creatures should work with God, they must enter into God, for God works with and through creatures. This is because the whole creation, heavenly, hellish, and earthly, is nothing but the working Word; the Word itself is everything.
>
> A creature is a compact, cohesive breath of the Word and, as the Word exhales itself from the free will, free will leads it from no-ground to ground. Thus the free will of angels and souls leads the Word into a ground of existence; and this same ground is a creature, a fire-fountain for its re-utterance.[43]

Word of Scripture and Prayer

Boehme's attitude toward Scripture as a whole, related to what he considers to be the essence of religion, is surprisingly detached in view of his closeness to a Christian tradition for which Scripture is the one-and-all of religion. Scripture, he declares, is not really Christ's voice, but only its 'case'; it is not identical with the essential Word, but is only a way leading towards it.[44] Boehme certainly did not endear himself to the Biblical scholars of his time when he declared that Babel, the confusion of minds and tongues, took its beginning in the letters of the Bible.[45] He openly accuses pastors of misusing Scripture because of their lack of the 'sensual' understanding of the words.[46] Thus he writes:

> Christ alone is the Word of God, teaching the way of Truth through its children and members: the literal word is only a guide and a revelation of Christ . . . so that we may enter into the living Word, Christ, and be born in him unto life.[47]

Boehme calls those who lack the 'sensual', that is, the Spirit-inspired understanding, "workmen of the great Babylon, letter-changers without divine insight." He writes:

> They say the written word is Christ's voice. True, it is the sound-box, as the form of the word, but the voice, which moves like a clockwork within

> the case, must be alive. The letter is an instrument, like a tuba, but one must have sound in it, which is one with the sound of the letter.
>
> The Word of the letter is a composite product: whenever a trumpeter blows into it, that will be its sound. Great Babylon has been built up entirely with such work. Everyone blew into this trumpet of the letter according to his own sound: and thus the sound from each trumpeter has been formed into a substance, and this substance is Great Babylon, since good and bad have been worked into one edifice.[48]

For Boehme, it is finally in true prayer that he sees the fulfillment of the word: prayer forms the true and essential word into a substance.[49] Ultimately, Christ himself is the prayer in us:[50] in true prayer all the words used become essential,[51] entering into the Heart of God.[52]

We could not choose a more appropriate example to illustrate both Boehme's exegetical technique and his profound personal involvement in the 'word' than his interpretation of the Lord's Prayer.[53] Suffice it here to give just the beginning:

> When we say *Unser Vater im Himmel* (Our Father in Heaven) the soul arises in all the three principles and makes its own, that from which it has been created. In *Natursprache* we understand this clearly and properly:
>
> *Un* is the eternal will of God to nature;
>
> *Ser* means the first *principium* in which the four principal forms (*Gestalten*) of nature stand;
>
> *Vater* provides two distinctions of two principals:
>
>> *Va* is the *matrix* on the cross;
>>
>> *Ter* is Mercurius *in centro naturae*, and there are two mothers in the eternal will out of which everything has come—one being on the side of fire, and the other in the light of softness and water. For
>>
>> *Va* is the mother from light, giving essence;
>>
>> *Ter* is the mother of fire-tincture, giving great, strong life; and
>>
>> *Vater* is both.
>
> *Im* means the interior, as the heart from which the spirit goes forth, because the syllable comes from the heart and sounds through the lips, and the lips keep the heart at its innermost unawakened;
>
> *Him* designates the creation of the souls; and
>
> *Mel* is the Angelic soul itself, which has apprehended the Heart on the Cross *in centro* between both mothers and make into a creature by the word *Him*. As to *Mel*: Because *Him* is the habitat of *Mel*, therefore the soul has been created in heaven, i.e. in the love-*matrix*.

Conclusion

Jacob Boehme certainly shared predilections and preoccupations with his baroque contemporaries, connections we no longer consider relevant. Much work has been done in linguistics to provide a more complete and historically accurate picture of the world's languages. We have also advanced in research on the physiological basis of word formation. The large amount of solid work in linguistic analysis represents a very valuable basis for further work; we also should not underrate the labor of philologists, who over several hundred years patiently assembled the tools that now allow us to understand from a much better historical and philological point of view the texts that Boehme dealt with. There is, nevertheless, an aspect of Boehme's treatment of word and language which still is attractive: his insistence that "there are three that form the word: the soul, the mind and the body,"[54] and the resulting integrated view of word and language as both creative and self-revealing in all their aspects. It is here, it seems, that Boehme parallels some ideas that have been expressed in Indian schools of thought. (Another paper will develop these themes more fully.) The importance of this type of concern for language lies in its emphasis on the specifically human aspects: language as the foundation of man's identity;[55] as depth-level communication of personality; and as the proper world of man, which he has created and is called upon to maintain.[56]

Notes

All references to the text follow the complete (11 vols.) edition *Theosophia Revelata oder Alle Göttliche Schriften Jacob Boehmens, von Altseidenberg* (1730) arranged as Facsimile Reprint by Will-Erich Peukert Fr. Frommanns Verlag (Stuttgart: 1955). All translations in the text are mine.

Note: The opening quotation is from *Quaestiones Theosophicae* 5.24: "Er führet die Macht aller Dinge in seinem Munde schwebend."

1. According to Boehme's contemporary and biographer A. von Franckenberg, it was his learned friend Dr. Balthasar Walther who gave him the title 'Philosophus Teutonicus'. See '*Abraham von Franckenberg: Lebensbeschreibung Jacob Böhmes*' in Hans Kayser *Schriften Jakob Böhmes mit der Biographie Böhmes von A. V. Franckenberg und dem kurzen Auszug F. C. Oetingers* (Leipzig: Insel Verlag, 1923), p. 31.

2. For details see Charles Waldemar, *Jakob Böhme: Der schlesische Mystiker* (München: Goldmann Verlag, 1959), pp. 29ff.

3. Boehme was strongly influenced by Paracelsus and Weigel. He presupposes a rather intimate knowledge of alchemistical terminology; in the present essay these references have been kept to the minimum but a full understanding of Boehme is not possible without it.

4. A. v. Franckenberg (see n. 1 above), p. 32.

5. *Von dem Irdischen und Himmlischen Mysterio*, 7, 6–10.

6. *Vom dreyfachen Leben des Menschen*, 9:68.

7. *Aurora: Morgenröthe im Aufgang*, 8:73.
8. *Mysterium Magnum*, 35:10.
9. Ibid., 35.
10. W. E. Peukert, op. cit. 10:146.2, points out that one should not consider Boehme's concern with *Natursprache* as idle folly but as an expression of his search for the essential nature of things which was expressed in every thing's language: language is the self-revelation of every thing.
11. *Mysterium Magnum*, 35:57.
12. *De Signatura Rerum*, 1:17.
13. *Mysterium Magnum*, 35:63
14. Ibid., 35:48.
15. Ibid., 29:65.
16. *Epistolee Theosophicae*, 4:27.
17. *Aurora*, 20.
18. *Mysterium Magnum*, 36:6ff.
19. Ibid., 35:63.
20. Ibid.
21. Ibid., 35:17ff.
22. *Von dem Irdischen und Himmlischen Mysterio*, 7:6.
23. Ibid.
24. *Vom dreyfachen Leben des Menschen*, 5:88.
25. *De Signatura Rerum*, 2:11.
26. *Epistolae Theosophicae*, 47:8–11.
27. *Vom dreyfachen Leben des Menschen*, 14:94; *Trostschrift von 4 Complexionen*, 94.
28. *Vom dreyfachen Leben des Menschen*, 2:18.
29. *Mysterium Magnum*, 35:49; 36:75; 37:15.
30. *Von der neuen Wiedergeburt*, 7:1; *Quaestiones Theosophicae*, 5:19.
31. *Mysterium Magnum*, 36:38.
32. Ibid., 35:49.
33. In Latin the letter V is used both for U and V.
34. *Mysterium Magnum*, 35:45; *Vom dreyfachen Leben des Menschen*, 6:3.
35. *De Signatura Rerum*, 1:4.
36. *Mysterium Magnum*, 22.
37. *Quaestiones Theosophicae*, 1:23f.
38. *Mysterium Magnum*, 22:7ff.
39. *De Signatura Rerum*, 16:3.
40. *Von der Gnaden-Wahl*, 8:23; 9:4; *Vom dreyfachen Leben des Menschen*, 1:41.
41. *Mysterium Magnum*, 22:68.
42. Ibid., 73:28.
43. Ibid., 61:43ff.
44. Ibid., 28:56f.
45. Ibid.

46. 'Sensualisch', translated here as 'sensual' means 'what is according to the *sensus*' or the inner meaning of things or words.

47. *Mysterium Magnum*, 28:53.

48. Ibid.

49. Ibid., 22:50.

50. *Von der Gnaden-Wahl*, 12:39.

51. *Mysterium Magnum*, 27:36.

52. Ibid., 31:21.

53. *Vom dreyfachen Leben des Menschen*, 16:30.

54. Ibid., 5:85.

55. *Von der Gnaden-Wahl*, 11:2. Man's identity consists in the oneness of the 'word of the mouth' and the 'word in the heart'.

56. There is a striking parallel between Boehme's care for the right word and Confucius' concern for the 'rectification of Language' as described in *Analects*, 13:3.

The Problem of Self in Buddhist Philosophy

Hajime Nakamura

The Problem of Self in Indian Tradition

When we attempt an overall discussion on the problem of the self or the individual, one stumbling block in the way of synoptical understanding is the general assumption that Buddhism did not admit the existence of an ego or a self, whereas Hindu philosophy in general admitted the self (*ātman*). They seem to contradict each other. When we examine the tradition of India, we notice that at the core of Hindu thought is found the concept of the self (*ātman*) as an independent, everlasting entity regulating both the physiological and the psychological functioning of an individual.

The Sanskrit original for self is *ātman*, which etymologically derives from the same origin as German *atmen, Odem* or Greek *atmos* (meaning air). As can be seen from this etymological investigation, *ātman* originally meant 'breath', then it came to mean 'soul', and finally 'self'. This development of the meaning of the word '*ātman*' is parallel to that of the Greek word 'psyche'. However, in India the 'Self' was identified with *Brahman*, the absolute, in the philosophy of the Upaniṣads and the Vedānta school. (Such an identification did not occur in the West.)

Moreover, in the scriptures of early Buddhism we come across a variety of notions of the self. In a scripture (the Brahmajāla-sutta, ND), sixty-two different heretical postulations regarding the doctrine of the self were thoroughly analyzed and then refuted. Among these, eighteen were seen to arise due to ignorance of the past, and forty-two due to that of the future. For example, the 'Eternalists' characterize the soul and the world as eternal; to others, who are in some respects 'eternalists' and in other respects 'Non-Eternalists', the soul and the world are partly eternal and partly non-eternal; the 'Semi-Eternalists' consider the soul and the world as semi-eternal; the 'Extentionists' believe in the finity and infinity of the world; the 'Eelwrigglers' present misleading statements and do not stick to any specific point (they seem to have been sceptics); the 'Fortuitous-Originists' hold the view that the soul and world originate without a cause; 'Believers in Future Life' think that the soul after death is conscious. Some maintain that the soul after death is unconscious; others hold the uncommitted view that the soul is neither conscious nor unconscious; the 'Annihilists' believe in the annihilation of the soul on the dissolution of the body; and finally, the believers in the 'Theory of Happiness in This Life', think of the complete liberation of the soul in this world.[1]

Moreover, according to a scripture, three forms of personality are commonly acknowledged in the world:

> . . . material, immaterial, and formless. The first has form, is made up of the four elements, and is nourished by solid food. The second has no form, is made up of mind, has all its greater and lesser limbs complete, and all the organs perfect. The third is without form, and is made up of consiousness only.[2]

The Theory of Non-self (Anātman) *in Early Buddhism*

The teaching of non-ego (*anātman*, non-self *anattā*), has been regarded as characteristic of Buddhist thought. The Buddha did not assume any metaphysical substance; this attitude was logically derived from his fundamental standpoint.

The transient character of this present world is emphasized in Buddhism to such an extent that it has come to include not only what man observes around him, but man himself; the whole of man, not excepting what he may call his 'self'.[3] The Buddha reduces things, substances, souls, to forces, movements, functions, and processes, and adopts a dynamic conception of reality. Admitting the transitoriness of everything, Buddhists do not assume any metaphysical substances.

The self, according to the orthodox Indian interpretations, is permanent, substantial, and impervious to change. It remains firm, unshaken, immutable, and identical amidst all kinds of change. On the other hand, nothing that is experienced has a self,[4] because impermanence and unsubstantiality are the very nature of things. "Impermanent are compounded things."[5]

Early Buddhists at first set forth the teaching that, since everything is transient, one should not cling to anything in the objective world. Nothing should be regarded as 'mine' (*mama*) or 'belonging to me'. One should not consider anything as 'one's own' or 'one's property'; one should have no attachment to anything. Everything which is considered to be 'one's own' changes constantly and, therefore, does not belong to any particular person permanently. Possessiveness of selfishness (*mamatta* 'mine-ness') was thus rejected. This teaching was set forth in the oldest poems[6] of the scriptures, and was shared by Early Jains.[7] There was no theoretical ratiocination.

A little later, however, the theory of Non-ego was developed more systematically, as can be seen in the prose sections of Pāli scriptures, which contend that life is nothing but a series of manifestations of becomings and extinctions, a stream of becoming and change. Buddhists repudiated the popular delusion of the individual ego, and of the individual ego as a substance. The objects with which we identify ourselves are not the true self; our fortune, our social position, our family, our body, and even our mind are not our true self. In this sense, the Buddhist theory can be called 'the theory of Non-self', i.e., *anything perceived is not the self.* All the theories about 'souls' (introduced in Section I) are discussed and rejected in the scriptures.[8] In their place, Buddhists advocated 'the theory of Non-ego or Non-soul'.

The 'ego' or 'soul' is the English translation of Pāli '*attan*', Sanskrit '*ātman*', which is more literally rendered 'self'.[9] Occasionally, however, we should use the word 'ego' in order to distinguish 'ego' from the 'true self' stressed in Early Buddhism. There is nothing permanent, and if the permanent deserves to be called the self or *ātman*, then nothing on earth is self. Everything is non-self (*anattā*).[10] This is the theory of *nairātmya*.

The relation of reasoning among propositions in canonical literatures is as follows:

(1) Everything is impermanent (*anicca*); (2) Anything that is impermanent is suffering (dissatisfactory) (*dukkha*); and (3) Anything that is suffering (dissatisfactory) is not myself *i.e.*, 'non-self' (*anattā*).

The above-mentioned relationship is often repeated in canonical literature. Later the theory of 'non-self' came to mean 'non-substantiality'.

To make clear the teaching of non-ego, Buddhists, as is seen in the scriptures, set forth the theory of the Five Aggregates or Constituents (*skandhas*)[11] of our human individual existence—the total of our mind and body. The five aggregates, then, make up the individual. These Five Aggregates or Constituents are:

REALITY	FICTION
1. Form (= matter) (*rūpa*)[12]	Self
2. Feeling (pleasant, unpleasant, neutral) (*vedanā*)[13]	
3. Perceptions (sight, etc.) (*saṁjña*)[14]	
4. Impulses (greed, hate, faith, wisdom, etc.) (*saṁskāra*)[15]	
5. Consciousness (*vijñāna*)[16]	

In order to make this teaching slightly more tangible, we may cite the example of toothache. Normally, one simply says "I have a toothache." But to the Buddhist thinkers this is a very inconsistent way of speaking, for neither 'I', nor 'have', nor 'toothache' are counted among the ultimate facts of existence (*dharmas*). In Buddhist literature personal expressions are replaced by impersonal ones. Impersonally, in terms of ultimate events, this experience is divided up into:

1. There is the physical *form*, i.e., the tooth as matter;
2. There is a painful *feeling*;
3. There is a sight-, touch-, and pain-perception (ideation) of the tooth; perception can exist only as ideation;
4. There are by way of *volitional* reactions, resentment at pain, desire for physical well-being, etc;
5. There is consciousness—an awareness of all the above-mentioned four.[17]

The 'I' of ordinary talk has thus disappeared: it is not the ultimate reality. Not even its components are reality. One might reply, of course: an imagined 'I' is a part of the actual experience. In that case, it would be placed in the category of consciousness, the last one of the five mentioned above. But this consciousness is not ultimate reality, for our human experience is only a composite of the five aggregates (*skandhas*). None of the Five Aggregates is the self or soul, nor can we locate the self or soul in any of them. A person is in process of continuous change, with no fixed underlying entity. In this way Buddhism swept away the traditional conception of a substance called 'soul' or 'ego' which had hithertofore dominated the minds of the superstitious and the intellectuals alike. Instead, the teaching of *anattā*, non-self, has been held throughout Buddhism. The constituents of a person are not elements or entities as exist in the outer world; they are of provisional reality. Once one attains enlightenment by true wisdom, the constituents of a person are brought to the state where they do not operate. Thus, they might be called 'realms', (or 'functions', from another viewpoint). Buddhism believes that our existence is maintained and formed in the area of the five 'components' of a person. Our existence is formed in the areas of these five different classes of provisional functions. The combination of everything that exists in such realms is provisionally called 'self', or 'I' (*ātman*) from the worldly, conventional point of view, but the subject of human existence cannot be included in any of the above-mentioned realms. With regard to material things (the first of the five) Buddhism propounds: material things are impermanent; what is impermanent is suffering; what is suffering is not one's self; it is something other than oneself. What is not oneself does not belong to oneself; in it one's self does not exist; it is not one's *ātman*. The same argument is set forth regarding the other four constituents: feelings, ideations, impulses, and consciouness. Everything that worldly people consider to be *ātman* is not *ātman* at all.

Thus, the Buddha explained[18] the nonperceptibility of the soul:

> The physical form is not the eternal soul, for it is subject to destruction. Neither feeling, nor ideation, nor impulses, nor consciousness, together constitute the eternal soul, for if it were so, feeling, etc., would not likewise tend towards destruction.[19]

In another passage it is taught:

> Our physical form, feeling, perception, impulses and consciousness are all transitory, and therefore not permanent [and not good]. That which is transitory, suffering, and liable to change, is not the eternal soul. So, it must be said of all physical forms whatever past, present, or to be; subjective or objective; far or near; high or low: "This is not mine, this I am not, this is not my eternal soul."[20]

Body, feeling, perception, impulses, and consciousness—all these are impermanent and suffering (dissatisfactory). They are all 'non-self'. Nothing of them is substantial; they are all appearances empty of substantiality or reality. There can be no individuality without a putting together of components, for this is always a process of 'becoming': this is becoming different; and there can be no becoming different without a dissolution, a passing away, or decay.

Besides the theory of the Five Constituent Aggregates, early Buddhists set forth a theory of systems of 'realms' in which our cognitions and actions are formed. They are the sense of visual function, the sense of hearing, the sense of smell, the sense of taste, the sense of touch, and mind. They are called the Six Realms (or Situations). At the same time, corresponding to these six, another system of 'Realms' was established. This is the system of the Realms of the Six Objects, which include: visual forms, sounds, odors, tastes, things touched, and things thought. In living human existence there is a continually succeeding series of mental and physical phenomena, and it is the union of these phenomena that makes the individual. Every person, or thing, is therefore put together, a compound of components which change. In each individual, without exception, the relation of its components is always that no sooner has individuality begun, than its dissolution, disintegration, also begins.

Many Buddhist terms are very difficult to translate into English. For certain technical terms there are no exact equivalents, and so terms used in Western languages can only give a rough understanding of Buddhist teaching on this subject. However, the purport of this theory is rather simple. In daily life, we assume that something is ours, or that we are something, or that something is ourselves; but this is wrong. Buddhism denies the assumption of the existence of *ātman* as a metaphysical principle; hence this Buddhist theory is called the theory of 'non-self'. However, it never denies *ātman* itself. It merely insists that any object which can be seen in the objective world is not *ātman*. Regarding the question whether *ātman* exists or not, Buddhism gives no answer, neither affirming nor denying the existence of *ātman*. The Buddha exhorts us to be philosophical enough to recognize the limits of philosophy. As *body* (corporeality) is a name for a system of functions, even so *soul* is a name for the sum of the states which constitute our mental existence. Without functions no soul can be admitted. Therefore, it is not correct to understand Buddhism as the theory of the nonexistence of soul.

The Practical Implication of the Non-self Theory

If we apply this method of analytical reflection properly, it has a tremendous power to disintegrate unwholesome, selfish tendencies. Early and later conservative (*Hīnayāna*) Buddhists strongly felt that the meditation on the component elements alone could not uproot all the evil in our hearts. They did, however, believe that it was bound to contribute to our spiritual development to the extent that, when repeated often enough, it would set up the habit of viewing all things impersonally, free from our selfish tendencies. This way of thinking may be applied with efficiency by modern psychiatrists.

In early Buddhism, those who got rid of the notion of 'ego' were highly praised. This kind of denial, however, did not mean nihilism or materialism. The Buddha clearly told us what the self is not, but he did not give any clear account of what it is. It is quite wrong to think that there is no self at all according to Buddhism.

> He among men, O Brahmin, who eschews
> All claims of me and mine; he in whom thought
> Rises in lonely calm, in piety rapt,
> Loathing all foul things, dwelling in chastity–
> Herein proficient, in such matters trained,
> Mortal can reach th' immortal heav'n of Brahma.[21]

The Buddha did not, as a rule, dwell on illusion (*māyā*) in general as is done by most Hindu scholars, but dwelt on the concept or illusion of the ego. In the situation of *Nirvāṇa*, the ego cannot be noticed:

> As a flame blown about by the violence of the wind goes out, and cannot be reckoned [as existing], even so a *Muni*, delivered from name and matter, [the 'self'] disappears, and cannot be reckoned [as existing].[22]

The Buddha was not a mere materialist. Both in the West and in all Indian systems except Buddhism, souls and the gods are considered as exceptions to transiency. To these spirits is attributed a substantiality, a permanent individuality without change. But the Buddha did not want to assume all these exceptional substances. In early Buddhism, traditional ideas were torn away from their ancestral stem and planted in a purely rational justification. Phenomenalistic doctrines were developed with great skill and brilliance.[23]

> The wandering monk Vacchagotta asked whether there is an ego or not. The Buddha was silent. Then that monk rose from his seat and went away. Then Ānanda asked the Buddha: "Wherefore, Sire, has the Exalted One not given an answer to the questions put by that monk?" The Buddha replied: "If I had answered, "The Ego is," then that would have confirmed the doctrine of those who believe in permanence. If I had answered: "The Ego is not," then that would have confirmed the doctrine of those who believe in annihilation."[24]

The Buddha neither affirmed nor denied the existence of *ātman*. He urged people to be philosophical enough to recognize the limits of ratiocination. The scope of philosophy was made clear. As 'body' is a name for a system of some functions, even so 'soul' is a name for the sum of the mental states which constitute our mind. Without such functions no soul can be admitted. Here again, it may be concluded, the Buddha was more concerned with the practical, ethical implications of the *an-attā* doctrine than with any metaphysical discussion of the subject–ethical implications which have been emphasized throughout Buddhist history. As we have observed, he was concerned to eschew, in this respect, "all claims of me and mine."[25]

The True Self–The Basis of Moral and Early Buddhism

If the reality of the self were doubted, the pursuit of moral ideas and of liberation would become meaningless and morality would be deprived of its basis. Self-realization is not possible if the self itself is denied.

The Buddha seems to have acknowledged the true self in our existence as it appears in our moral conduct conforming to universal norms. The Buddha did not want to assume the existence of souls as metaphysical substances, but he admitted the existence of the self as the subject of action in a practical and moral sense; thus the Non-self theory does not mean that the Buddha completely denied the significance of the self. He always admitted the significance of the self as the subject of actions in the moral and practical sense. According to the Buddha, the self cannot be identified with anything existing on the outside; we cannot grasp the self as something concrete or existing in the outer world. He cuts off identification with all objects in turn by the thought, "I am not this, this is not mine, this is not myself."

The self is not experienced at all. The true self in one's existence can be realized only when we act in conformance to universal norms of human existence; when we act morally, the true self becomes manifest. In this connection the self of Buddhism is not a metaphysical entity, but a practical postulate: *ātman* as the basis of human acts.

In early Buddhism 'one who knows the self'[26] was highly esteemed, and the virtue of relying upon oneself also was highly stressed. The Buddha taught his disciples in his last sermon:

> Be a lamp to yourself. Be a refuge to yourself. Betake yourself to no external refuge. Hold fast to the Truth as a lamp. Hold fast as a refuge to the Truth. Do not look for refuge to anyone (anything else) besides yourself.[27]

One's self should be ennobled. A man who is devoted to religious practice is extolled as follows: "He thus abstaining, lives his life void of cravings, perfected, cool, in blissful enjoyment, his whole self ennobled."[28] It means: "Depend on the self (*ātman*). Depend on the law (*dharma*). Make the self a candlelight. Make the law a candlelight." He thought that the true self should be expressed whenever human law is practiced. The Buddha asked a group of young men who were searching for a missing woman: "Which is better for you, to go seeking the woman, or to go seeking the self?;" he did not say 'your selves'. This means he did not think that each individual had its own self as an entity.[29] The above-cited statements imply that there are two selves. One is the empirical self in daily life, and the other is the Self in the higher sense. The former should be subdued: "If a man were to conquer in battle a thousand times a thousand men, and another conquer one, himself, he indeed is the greatest of conquerers."[30] "If a man holds himself dear, let him diligently watch himself."[31]

The empirical self has to be guided, tamed, and liberated from bondage.

> The self is the lord of self; who else could be the lord?
> With self well subdued a man finds a lord who is difficult to obtain.[32]
>
> The evil done by oneself, born of oneself, produced by oneself, crushes the fool even as a diamond breaks a precious stone.[33]

The self, i.e., the empirical self, should be trained ethically with a view to achieving a wholesome development and perfection:

> Rouse your self by your self, examine your self by your self.
> Thus guarded by your self and attentive, you, mendicant, will live happy.[34]
>
> For self is the lord of self; self is their refuge of self; therefore curb your self even as a merchant curbs a fine horse.[35]
>
> The whole wide world we traverse with our thought,
> Finding, to man naught dearer than the self,
> Since aye so dear the self to others is
> Let the self-lover harm no other men.[36]

One should know himself that he is not wise enough. "The fool who knows his foolishness, is wise at least so far. But a fool who thinks himself wise, he is called a fool indeed."[37] So we may be able to conclude that the realization of *Nirvāṇa* can be explained as taking refuge in one's true self. On this point the Buddha's assertion comes to be very similar to that of the Upaniṣads and the Vedānta philosophy (*paramātman*, Supreme Self). But the latter's self (*ātman*) is rather metaphysical, while the Buddha's self is genuinely practical. Based upon this thought, Mahāyāna Buddhism developed the theory of the 'Great Self'.[38] The attitude of eliminating one's own selfishness means lifting up the barriers between oneself and others. In this state of mind all living beings in the universe are identified with oneself. This ideal was expressed with the term 'the Self of All' (*sabbattatā*).[39]

In a canon of the scripture of early Buddhism the practice of the meditation of the Four Sublime States (*brahma-vihāras*) is encouraged. The sentences read:

> He lets his mind pervade one quarter of the world with thoughts of Love (*mettā-sahagatena cetasā*), and so the second, and so the third, and so the fourth. And thus the whole world, above, below, around, and everywhere, with the feeling that all the world is his self (*sabbattatāya*), does he continue to pervade with heart of Love, far-reaching, grown great, and beyond measure . . . and he lets his mind pervade one quarter of the world with thought of pity (*karunā*), . . . sympathy (*muditā*), . . . equanimity (*upekhā*), and so the second, and so the third, and so the fourth. And thus the whole wide world, above, below, around, and everywhere, with the feeling that all the world is his self (*sabbattatāya*), does he continue to pervade with heart of pity . . . sympathy . . . equanimity, far-reaching, grown great, and beyond measure.[40]

The mental attitude to regard all the world (including other human beings) as one's self is closely related to the ethical virtues of love, pity, sympathy, and equanimity. This mental attitude, however, does not imply the thought that one's self is identical with the Universal Self as the metaphysical substance as was held by Upaniṣadic and Vedāntic thinkers. It is of ethical and practical implication. From this attitude emerges the thought: "I am a friend of all. I am a companion of all."[41] This thought harbingers the formation of the idea of the 'Great Self'.

To summarize: The Non-self theory in early Buddhism does not mean that the Buddha completely denied the significance of the self. According to the Buddha, the self cannot be identified with anything existing on the outside; we cannot grasp the self as something concrete. The self can be realized only when we act according to universal norms of human existence; when we act morally, the true self becomes manifest. The Buddha did not want to assume the existence of souls as metaphysical substances, but he admitted the existence of the self as the subject of action in the practical and moral sense. 'One who knows the self' is highly esteemed.[42]

We would say that in early Buddhism two kinds of self are virtually admitted. The first is the empirical self of ordinary daily life, and the other is the latent self in the practical sense. The empirical self should be subdued, tamed, and disciplined. This means that a change in the structure of ego occurs by means of disciplinary practice in various traditions. The second, the latent self, which might be called the fundamental self, is the nonperceivable subject, which can be observed in terms of human behavior. It is not an entity in the objective world, but it can be manifested through human subjective actions.

The latent self was called 'the lord of self'. "The Self is the lord of self; who else could be the lord? With self well subdued, a man finds a lord such as few can find." One should be earnest in carrying out own's duty, in compliance with the demand of the true self. Further, to be true to oneself comes to be the same as to be true to others. In early Buddhism to control oneself was regarded as the starting point for altruistic activities.

The Modification of the Non-self Theory

This theory of Non-self was modified in later days. Hīnayāna teachers explained the theory as follows: Things are nothing but names. 'Chariot' is a name as much as 'Nāgasena' (the name of a Buddhist elder). There exists nothing real beneath the properties or events. The immediate data of consciousness do not argue the existence of any unity which we can imagine. In like argumentation, Nāgasena drew a negative inference that there was no soul[43] from the silent attitude of the Buddha on the problem of the soul. This opinion became the orthodox teaching of Hīnayāna Buddhism. The teaching of the Buddha himself, however, seems to have been slightly different, as has been shown above. From the investigation we have done so far, it is clear that the assertion of the denial of the ego appeared in a later period.[44] The Buddha did not necessarily deny the soul, but was silent concerning it. Moreover, he seems to have acknowledged what might be called a 'true self' which appears in our moral conduct conforming to universal norms.

According to early Buddhism an individual existence is nothing but an uninterrupted and unbroken series of psychical states which are called *dharmas*.[45] In this case *dharmas* mean constituent elements of the direct experience of one individual at one moment. In the philosophy of the Sarvāstivādins these *dharmas* were regarded as a discrete and existent entities. In ancient India, belief in rebirth or transmigration was generally current, and this conception was associated with the doctrine of *karma* (literally 'act', 'deed'), according to which good conduct brings a pleasant and happy result, while bad conduct brings an evil result. The *karma* committed previously will come to fruition, either in this life or in future lives. These concepts were adopted by Buddhists. However, this acceptance gave rise to a difficult problem: how can rebirth take place without a permanent subject which is reborn?

The relation between existences in rebirth has been explained by the analogy of fire which maintains itself unchanged in appearance, yet is different in every moment. In order to solve this vulnerable problem, some Buddhists of later days assumed a sort of soul, calling it by different names (e.g. *pudgala*, which means 'person').[46] In the discussions between the Theravādins and the Pudgalavādins, the latter held to the permanent and abiding character of the self, considering the self as real. They denied the Theravādins' assertion that 'the person' is known in the sense of a provisional fact.[47]

Following this controversy, Nāgārjuna declared his theory based upon his standpoint of the Middle Path: "The self is neither different from the constituent functions nor identical to them; the *ātman* without constituent functions does not exist nor does it not not exist' "[48] This Middle Path means the negation of both extremes. This is ascertained firmly, while the theory of existence of the individual (*satkāyadṛṣti*) is refuted.[49] This tendency finally gave rise to the conception of the fundamental consciousness (*ālaya-vijñāna*) of the Yogācāra (or Vijñānavāda) School in Mahāyāna. As early Buddhism did not deny the self in the ethical sense, Mahāyāna developed the concept of *Buddha-nature* latent in everyone. Based upon this thought, Mahāyāna Buddhism developed the concept of the 'Great Self'.[50] Some teachers overtly and defiantly criticized the theory of Non-self in early Buddhism. The concept of the 'Great Self' was especially emphasized in the *Mahā-parinirvāṇā-sūtra* of Mahāyāna, extant only in Chinese, and then generally admitted in Vajrayāna texts. This is not found in Conservative Buddhism, and is criticized by some as being very close to Vedānta philosophy. However, this idea is generally held by Chinese, Korean, and Japanese Buddhists.[51]

The Standpoint of the Philosophy of Voidness to Transcend the Extremes of self and Non-self

In Mahāyāna, especially in the Mādhyamika school founded by Nāgārjuna, the theory of Non-self became interpreted in a slightly different way. In this school non-self (*nairātmya*) meant 'without self-nature' or 'without self-existence', 'without essence', and this was explained as 'the true nature of being'. Teachers of this school set forth two kinds of non-self. First is the 'non-self' of 'an individual existence' (or of soul), which is tantamount to 'the nonexistence of the individual existence as a substance' (*pudgalanairātmya*), which theory was maintained by the Hīnayāna schools.

The other kind of 'non-self' is 'the non-self of the constituent elements of the individual existence' (*dharma-nairātmya*), a theory which was newly set forth by Mahāyāna teachers. Things being so, 'non-self' in this school is almost the same as 'non-substance', 'substancelessness'; this is equal to 'voidness' (*śūnyatā*). The concept of self (*ātman*) in this sense was severely analysed and criticized by Nāgārjuna in the eighteenth chapter of a work called '*Mādhyamika-śāstra*'. When one tries to make the standpoint of voidness consistent, one is led to the conclusion that one should not adhere to the tenet that 'there is no ego'. Nāgārjuna boldly said: "The Buddhas have provisionally employed the term *ātman*; they have also the term *anātman* (non-self). They have also taught that there is no entity called *ātman* or *anātman*."[52]

The standpoint of the Mādhyamika school transcends all opposites, therefore it cannot be refuted, as they asserted. It transcends both opposites of *ātman* and *anātman*. Here even the theory of Non-self is not of absolute significance, but of provisional value to bring one to enlightenment. Such a dialectical argumentation had already been set forth in Mahāyāna sūtras,[53] but Nāgārjuna makes this point clear.

The Realization of the True Self– The Discipline of Meditation

Then how shall we be able to realize the true self? This search brought about the practice of meditation, especially in the medieval East and also in the West. Meditation was essential to the contemplative life. The central theme of the *Mahāvairocana-sūtra* is 'knowing the true self'. It unfolds the *bodhicitta*, the primal nature of enlightenment. Zen Buddhists practiced Zen meditation, as the practitioners of the Hindu sect practiced Yoga, and Western mystics meditated on God. This point has been discussed by many scholars. The requirements for meditation were more or less the same in the various advanced religions. Practitioners need composure of mind, abstinence from sensual enjoyments, and perseverance in concentration of mind. They should practice in quietude.

Meditation in Zen Buddhism is called '*Zazen*' (i.e., sitting for meditation). It has biological and psychological effects. In the enlightened state of mind dualistic antagonisms, such as good and evil, or right and wrong, disappear. This state of mind may be compared to the fourth or ultimate condition of mind which is the awakened life of supreme consciousness, and which is set forth in the *Māṇḍūkya-Upaniṣad* and *Māṇḍūkya-Karikās* of ancient India.

Zen Buddhism teaches intuitive knowledge of the absolute. A well-known motto of Zen, "Direct pointing to the mind of man," emphasizes that we originally have the Buddha-mind and need the actual experience of it. That is, the master points to the Buddha-nature, or Reality itself. Enlightenment takes place in a 'timeless moment', i.e., outside time, in eternity; it is an act of the Absolute itself, not our own doing.

In medieval Japan, Master Dōgen made meditation the essential practice of Zen. "Why do you encourage others to practice meditation?" His answer: "This is the right gate to the teaching of the Buddha." "Meditation is the gate to comfort and happiness." He taught to "forget oneself." Dōgen said that practice and enlightenment are not two things but one. Enlightenment is not something to seek in the future because people are already at this moment in the world of enlightenment though they are not awakened to this fact. The innate Buddha-nature is the *a priori* basis of the practice which itself embodies enlightenment in the process of one's endeavor. Dōgen says: "In Buddhism practice and enlightenment are one and the same. Since practice has its basis in enlightenment, the practice even of the beginner contains the whole of original enlightenment."[54]

Zen dispelled all kinds of ratiocination on the absolute. The Buddha dwells hidden in all inconspicuous things of daily life. To take them just as they come, is enlightenment. Justification of moral virtues is possible based on the fundamental supposition that we human beings are in our essence good and pure. In Zen Buddhism they say that "living beings are by origin (essentially) Buddhas."[55] After such consideration we are led to the conclusion that daily life is in itself the enlightened self, and the mind of ordinary people is in itself the Buddha's mind. The process of the phenomenal world is activity, mighty self-positing, a procreation not under the compulsion of laws or blind impulse but in the creative power and freedom of sublime wonder.

On the other hand, Asian thinkers who were highly interested in psychological analysis by way of self-reflection made value judgments on mental functions. Scholars of traditional Buddhism of ancient India, i.e., Abhidharmikas, and Buddhist idealists (*Vijñānavādins*) accepted some mental functions of the human mind as evil, some good, and others neither good nor evil. To illustrate: belief, courage, equanimity, modesty, shame, noncovetousness, non-hatred, noninjury, dexterity, endeavor—these ten mental functions are regarded as *always good* in the eyes of Buddhist psychologists. Anger, hypocrisy, envy, jealousy, approving objectionable things, causing harm, breaking friendship, deceit, trickery, complacency—these purely mental functions, which are of limited occurrence, are *always bad*. Feeling, sensation, perception, attention, memory, concentration, etc. are *neither good nor bad*, in themselves. This kind of scholarly classification has been preserved up to the present time in some cathedrals and authoritative monasteries, as well as in prestiged temples of our ancient capital of Nara, such as the Horyūji, Yakushiji, and Kofuku-ji.

To seek one's self has also been a problem of Western thinkers; and it is likely that psychological study of Asia will give some clues to solve the problem of the self, the individual, and its psychological implications in the future. One could suggest that Asian ways of psychological approach will be justified in many respects. Among the various mental functions of the human mind, perception and various functions evolving from it may occur just like natural phenomena. But the movement of feelings and emotions must be quite different from that of natural phenomena. They do not move in the same way as movements of physical objects in the natural world.

Human feelings and emotions are often of utmost ethical and aesthetic significance. They can develop in different ways. The law of functioning of feelings and emotions, which is greatly tinged with ethical, aesthetic, and even religious implications in actual human life, will be effective only in the real sphere of activities of the human mind. Secondly, they can effectuate some results in some cases. The Sanskrit and Pali technical term for 'meditation' is *bhāvanā*, which derived from the word "to cause to be." It implies that, if one continues to meditate on the peaceful state of mind, one's own mind finally becomes quiet and peaceful. Mental process in terms of feelings and emotions is not a process of natural objects, but one which can result in transformation of our own personality. This way of evaluation has been quite conspicuous not only in Buddhism, but also in Asian thought in general.[56]

The effects thereof may not be able to be measured so easily in terms of calculation by way of experiments. But this way of approach is especially needed in the present-day situation of spiritual confusion and chaos in which we are unavoidably placed.

Conclusion

According to the investigation conducted so far, we can say that, although we can locate some common features in various theories of Non-self, there existed a variety of teachings on that problem, teachings that were not always consistent and that occasionally were contradictory to each other. What, then, is the genuinely authentic teaching?

We need not be particular with it. All sorts of teaching of 'non-self' were set forth for the purpose of eliminating the deep-rooted selfishness in our individual existence and of realizing loving-kindness among ourselves. If a teaching was useful for the purpose, it was admitted. Thus the teaching of 'non-self' was not necessarily a tenet, but an expediency.

Notes

1. T. W. Rhys Davids, trans., *Dialogues of the Buddha*, Part 1, *Sacred Books of the Buddhists*, vol. 2 (Reprint, London: 1956), pp. 26–54.

2. *Ibid.*, pp. 259–260.

3. "In part the difficulty in understanding the teaching of annattā is due to the difficulty of translating the original basic terms into Western languages." (H. Nakamura: *Buddhism in Comparative Light*, in press).

4. *Sabbe dhammā anattā* (*Dhammapada*, v. 279).

5. *Sabbe saṃkhārā aniccā.*

6. This thought is especially clear in the poems of the *Suttanipāta.*

7. This is most clear in the first half of the *Āyārāṅga.*

8. *Dīgha-Nikāya* 1.

9. The Indian philosophers spoke of personality in the ethical and psychological sense with the term 'Self' (*ātman* in Sanskrit), whereas Confucius seems to have held that habit makes up a personality. Although both theories are of utmost psychological significance, the Indian way of approach to the individual was rather metaphysical, whereas the Chinese way was rather practical or behavioristic.

10. The term *anattā* is defined as follows: "Non-recognition of the existence of soul regarded as imperishable according to orthodox Hindu philosophy." (S. C. Banerji, *An Introduction to Pāli Literature*, p. 140); "non-ego: absence of a permanent, unchanging self or soul, substanceless." (K. W. Morgan: *The Path of the Buddha*, p. 407).

11. Or it might be translated as 'constituent aggregates'. "*Khandha*: a part of a whole thing, ingredients of the worldly existence; the constituents of the individual; form, feeling, notion, mental dispositions, clear consciousness or discrimination." (S. C. Banerji. *An Introduction to Pāli Literature*, p. 141). *pañcaskandha* in Sanskrit, *go-un* or *go-on* in Japanese.

12. In many cases 'physical form' (*rūpa*) (*shiki* in Japanese) means 'physical form pertaining to the body' or 'the body of a human being'. Occasionally it is rendered as 'matter', a rough translation. According to interpretations by later Abhidharma teachers, it can mean 'matter', including everything both spiritual and material. Spiritual effects also were regarded as a kind of 'latent matter'.

13. *Vedanā* (*ju* in Japanese). There are three kinds of feeling, i.e., pleasant, unpleasant, and neutral. Later teachers of Abhidharma and China interpreted it as 'feeling, signifying the acceptance of impression within one's consciousness'.

14. *Saṁjñā* (*sō*) in Japanese), ideation, meaning: to form an image within one's consciousness, according to the *Abhidharmika* and Chinese dogmaticians. The Pāli word *sañña* is occasionally translated as 'consciousness'. Consciousness is

the concept closest to the concept of 'self' or 'soul'. However, early Buddhists made a distinction. To the question: "Is the consciousness (*sañña*) identical with a man's soul (*atta*), or is consciousness one thing, and the soul another?" The Buddha replied, "Granting a material soul, having form, built up of the four elements, nourished by solid food; still some ideas, some stages of consciousness, would arise to the man, and others would pass away. On this account also, you can see how consciousness must be one thing, and soul another." (T. W. Rhys Davids, trans., *Dialogues of the Buddha*, Part 1, pp. 252-53).

15. *Saṁkāra* (*gyō* in Japanese) is a difficult term to translate. 'The confections' (T. W. Rhys Davids); 'the predispositions' (Warren); 'the constituent elements of character' (T. W. Rhys Davids). When we consider the interpretations by later Abidharma and Chinese teachers, we can translate it as 'latent, formative, phenomena' or 'formative forces, including activeness and latent formative forces'. *Saṁkhāra* is explained by A. K. Warder: *Introduction to Pāli* (Luzac, 1963), p. 277, as follows: "Force, energy, activity, combination, process, instinct, habit (a very difficult word to find an exact equivalent for: 'force', with a restricted technical sense attached to it, is probably the best. *Saṁkhāra* means force or forces manifested in the combination of atoms into all the things in the universe, in the duration of such combination—as in the life-span of a living being—and in the instincts and habits of living beings, which are to be allayed by the practice of meditation (*jhāna*). It is one of the five basic groups (*khandha*) of kinds of things in the universe: matter, sensation, perception and consciousness being the others)."

16. *Vijñāna*, (*shiki* in Japanese). Later Abhidharmika and Chinese teachers interpreted it as 'cognition' denoting the act of distinguishing every object and recognizing it.

17. These illustrations were taken from E. Conze's *Buddhism*. cf. *Samyutta-Nikāya* 3.46 etc.

18. In the Buddha's allegedly first sermon addressed to the five ascetics in Benares, (*Dhammacakkappavattana-sutta*), the nonperceptibility of the soul was set forth.

19. Or it can be translated as: "it is subject to destruction."

20. *Vinaya, Mahāvagga* 1.6.38f; 1:13f; *Vinaya, Mahāvagga* 1.21. cf. *Samyutta-Nikāya* 4.54.

21. *Dīgha-Nikāya* 2:241, *gāthā*.

22. *Suttavipāta* 1073.

23. In Greece, Heraclitus had very similar ideas, and similar ideas are found in post-Buddhistic Indian works also (*Kāthakopaniṣad* 2.10; *Bhagavadgītā* 2.14; 9.33); but in neither case are they worked out in the same uncompromising way. In European and in all Indian systems, except the Buddhist, souls and the gods are considered as exceptions to the rule of transience. To these spirits is attributed a substantiality, an individuality without change. But in Early Buddhism, phenomenalistic doctrines were developed with great skill and brilliance.

24. H. C. Warren. *Buddhism in Translation*, op. cit., p. 134.

25. Much the same may be said of Christ's admonition: "If any man would come after me, let him deny himself and take up his cross, and follow me." (Matthew 16.24) He who hates life in this world will keep it for eternal life, but "whosoever will save his life shall lose it." (Mark 8.35).

"If anyone comes to me and does not hate his own father and mother and wife and children and brothers and sisters, yes, and *even his own life*," (*heauto psykhēn = tasya ātmānam*), "he cannot be my disciple." (Luke 14.26) That soul which "he who hates his life in this world will keep it for eternal life." (John 12.25) but "whoever would save his life will lose it." (Luke 9.24) "If any man would come after me, let him deny himself." (Mark 8.34).

26. *Attannū*. *Anguttara-Nikāya* 4:113; *Dīgha-Nikāya* 3:252.

27. *Mahāpadāna-sutta* 2:101; *Dīgha-Nikāya* 2:101. "And whosoever, Ananda, either now or after I am dead, shall be a lamp unto themselves, and a refuge unto themselves, shall betake themselves to no external refuge, but holding fast to the Truth as their lamp, and holding fast as their refuge to the Truth, shall look not for refuge to any one besides themselves—it is they, Ananda, among my bhikkhus, who shall reach the very topmost Height!—but they must be anxious to learn." (T. W. and C. A. F. Rhys Davids, trans., *Dialogues of the Buddha*. 4th ed. London: Luzac, 1959.)

"I have taken refuge to myself (*kataṁ me saraṇan attano*)." (*Dīgha-Nikāya* 2:120).

28. *Dīgha-Nikāya* 3:232–33.

29. *Vinaya* 1.23, i.e. *Mahāvagga* 1.14, cf. *Visudhimagga* 393.

30. *Dhammapada* 103. "He who is slow to anger is better than the mighty, and he who rules his spirit than he who takes a city." (Proverbs 16.32). "He who overcomes others is strong; he who overcomes himself is mighty." (*Tao Te Ching* 32.1.)

31. *Dhammapada* 157. "And what I say to you I say to all: Watch." (Mark 13.37) "Loathe ourselves for our iniquities (Ezekiel)".

32. *Dhammapada* 160. (Radhakrishnan's translation)

33. *Dhammapada* 161.

34. *Dhammapada* 379.

35. *Dhammapda* 380.

36. *Udāna*, trans. F. L. Woodward, p. 56.

37. *Dhammapada* 63. cf. "Nothing is worse than to think one knows what one does not know." (Apol. 29B.)

38. In the West also we find similar assertions. Aristotle is nearer to the Buddha when he counsels a man to be a true lover of himself. In Judea, Jeremiah, who is said to have appeared nearly at the same time as the Buddha, said, "I will put my law within them, and I will write it upon their hearts." (Jeremiah 31.33).

39. *Sabbattatā* is translated as 'nondiscrimination ('all = self-ness'), unselfishness'. (*Introduction to Pāli*, op. cit., pp. 320–29).

40. *Dīgha-Nikāya* 13.76–69, 1:250–51. T. W. Rhys Davids, *Dialogues of the Buddha*, Part 1, (London: Luzac and Company, 1956), pp. 317–18. Rhys Davids

did not translate the Pāli word '*sabbattaya*'. So, I translated the term and inserted in the translation. Such an important word should not be overlooked when we are going to discuss the problem of 'self'.

41. *Theragātha* 648.

42. Professor Arasteh suggested that already in the thought of Zoroaster there existed the problem of the personal Self and the universal or cosmic Self (cf. his paper included in *Proceedings of the Twentieth International Congress of Psychology*, August 13–19, 1972, University of Tokyo Press, 1974). With regard to the Chinese concept of the self we are not yet so clear as in other traditions. However: "For the Confucianist 'cultivation of self' (*hsiu-shen*) was a basic ideal in life." (See also notes 51 and 56).

43. *Milindapañhā*, op. cit. pp. 25–27.

44. Common elements in the Buddhist and the Christian self was discussed in *Buddhism in Comparative Light*, p. 52.

45. Stcherbatsky: *The Soul Theory of Buddhists*. 'Being the appendix to the *Abhidharmakośa* of Vasubandhu, trans. and notes'. (*Bull.d.l'Academie d.Sc. de Russie*, pp. 823–958. St. Petersbourg, 1919).

46. *puggala*: Individual person as distinguished from a group or class. It also means character or soul. (S. C. Banerji. *An Introduction to Pāli Literature*, p. 143).

47. S. Z. Aung and Mrs. Rhys Davids, trans., *Points of Controversy* (London 1915), pp. 8–9.

48. *Mādhyamika-śāstra* 27:8.

49. Cf. *Madhyamakāvatāra* 6.120, quoted in *Mādhyamaka-vṛtti*, ed. by P. L. Vaidya, p. 145.

50. "The doctrine of a self shines brilliantly like the rising of the world-end fire, wiping away the faults of the philosophers, burning up the forest of egolessness." (*Laṅkāvatāra-sūtra* 5.766.284).

51. Arasteh: op. cit. (note 42).

52. *Mādhyamika-śāstra* 18.6.

53. " 'That everything is permanent' is one extreme; 'that everything is transitory' is another. 'That *ātman* is' (*atmeti*) is one extreme (*anta*); 'that the *ātman* is not' is another. However, the middle between the *ātman* and *nairātmya* view is the Inexpressible. It is the reflexive insight of the truth of things (*dharmāṇām bhūta-pratyavekṣa*)." *Kāśyapa-parivarta* (ed. Baron A. von Stael-Holstein, Shanghai, 1926), pp. 86–87.

"Those who hold the theory of nonego are injurers of the Buddhist doctrines; they are given up to the dualistic views of being and nonbeing . . ." *Laṇkāvatāra-sūtra* 5.765.284 (Str.).

54. On the other hand, the way adopted by Confucius was empirical, i.e., to change the nature of men by learning. Confucius said: "By nature, men are nearly alike, by practice they get to be wide apart." If we substitute the term 'Self', *ātman*, for 'nature' in the above-mentioned sentence, we can get exactly what Indian thinkers assert. This conjecture is not arbitrary, for in Chinese versions of

Buddhist scriptures we very often come across cases in which the Chinese word 'nature' is used as an equivalent for the Indian word *ātman*, self. This assumption will not be preposterous, for some Indian scholars also use the term 'the nature of man'.

55. The theory of human nature as being good was set forth by Mencius also and it is likely that this point was stressed by Sung period Neo-Confucianists in later days under the influence of Zen. The Neo-Confucianists also practiced meditation in a fashion slightly different from Zen. In the West the way of practice advocated by Pelagius and medieval mystics may correspond to the above-mentioned thoughts in some sense.

56. Professor Arasteh said in his paper (cf. note 42): "In a practical sense, Persian psychology, along with other Asian psychologies, can contribute to education, therapeutical, and clinical processes." *Proceedings of the Twentieth International Congress of Psychology, August 13–19, 1972*, Tokyo, Japan (University of Tokyo Press, 1974), pp. 80–82. This is especially true in the case of Zen Buddhism, which is being approached more and more psychologically and scientifically by some scientists, such as Professor Kesamatsu and Professor Akishige.

Trikāya in Buddhist Philosophy Tibetan and Chinese Hua-Yen Interpretation

By Herbert V. Guenther

It is the nature of all speculative thought that it progressively moves away from the problem at hand, loses itself in the maze of its own fictions, and ultimately dies of sheer exhaustion in the wastes of its own barrenness. The accompanying feeling of frustration and the growing sense of diminished being imply a prior awareness of fullness and happiness. That is to say, happiness is the release from a state of frustration and, if happiness is the criterion of fullness of Being, it is, and always must be, the direction our striving is to take. Fullness of Being and the feeling of happiness which is at the same time the awareness of this fullness, are not two contrasting entities, but the two aspects of a single reality. Awareness carries with it the certainty that awareness *is* and Being *is* in so far as there is awareness of it. The one is the other and the distinction is a matter of emphasis rather than of difference.

This single experience has significant ramifications within the life of man. It is these ramifications that are referred to by the technical term *trikāya* (*sku gsum*), commonly, though quite ludicrously, translated as the 'Three Bodies of the Buddha', due to the fact that the early Western translators and their later copyists failed to understand or to note the purely descriptive character of the word *buddha* (*sangs-rgyas*) owing to the primitive anthropomorphism involved in the equally primitive theistic background of Western thought, which, to make matters worse, mistook the purely mythological concept of *mahāpuruṣa* ('Absolute Man') for a literal designation of an historical person.[1] The word *buddha* is a past participle of the verb *budh* 'to wake up', and its exclusively adjectival use describes the experience a person has had, but not the person. Similarly, the Tibetan term sangs-rgyas is not just a mechanical translation, but an interpretation of an experience.[2] These considerations should suffice to show that it is meaningless to speak of 'bodies'. An experience tends to get expressed, but it is neither fact nor bare ideas that get expressed but 'values'; how it feels to be; and the meaning of fullness of being is apprehended as embodied. 'Value' is a two-sided notion, subjective as well as objective; how it feels to be fully alive may be said to be a strictly incommunicable private subjective feeling, but the way in which a person who feels fully alive presents himself (i.e. his feeling) is its objective counterpart, and our experience of such a person derives in part from his delight in his being. What we perceive are the observable qualities of the aesthetic object which we then mistakenly impute to the (postulated) physical object. Similarly, 'embodiment' is a subjective-objective on-going process, involving total situations whose 'meaning' is only to be found within the system of being itself.

In this total situation which is both 'existential' and 'cognitive' it is the existential pattern acting as a 'founding stratum' for the 'founded' cognitive processes,[3] that is indicated by the term *kāya* (Tibetan *sku*). Since as human beings we can only talk about the *human* situation, about *our* life world, centering in *our* body, animals having different life worlds and life world experiences—Vimalamitra aptly declares:

'Founding stratum' (*sku*) is so called by analogy with the different bodies (*lus*) of the six kinds of beings.[4] For the body is an orientational center without which there would be no world with its multiple objects, organized around the body and perceived by it in as much as the body is the bearer of localized sensations. It is from this orientational point of our physical existence (*lus*)[5] that we move towards meaningful existence (*sku*) by enacting the values of being, or as Vimalamitra says:

> Bodily existence moves in the direction of meaningful existence; its way is related to our bodily existence and implies enactment, but the goal is not just physical existence.[6]

In other words, the goal is, as it were, a deliberate creation of something new arising out of the delight in the value of being. Not that 'value' is something vaguely floating about somewhere, waiting to be caught somehow; rather it stands for a total existential pattern felt and experienced as being so highly charged with values or meanings that we are prompted to act upon them. Hence "to make the three *kāyas* the way" is the Buddhist way of speaking of an on-going process of embodiment of value, which can never be equated with a static absorption in a spurious absolute.

Of primary importance is Dharmakāya (Tib. *chos-kyi sku*) which is interpreted by Vimalamitra as follows:

> *chos* refers to universal and particulars; *kyi* to their connection, and *sku* to an existential pattern which is (envisaged and acted upon as) the mystical foundation of values (*rin-chen gsang-ba'i sbubs*).[7]

The word 'mystical' is used here to emphasize the experience of value in the sense that it comprises both vision and enactment. In such an experience we see the world in a different light and consequently all our actions become more significant because they occur in a different framework. We feel at our best and are fully aware only in acting, and in acting we feel at our best and become intrinsically aware. Hence, as Vimalamitra points out,[8] Dharmakāya "is the ground or foundation of all values," and, since values are primarily 'meanings' (*chos*), not dead entities, Dharmakāya is realized (known and felt) as a 'founding stratum of meaning' that becomes manifest through pristine cognitions' (*ye-shes*).

As a peak value, experienced when we feel at our best, Dharmakāya underlies and gives sustenance to our feeling of a relationship, as individuals, with life. In other words, as individuals we participate in a 'life-world' as a horizon of meanings and actions; we do not look at our world in a detached way, but we participate in it through the way we are 'seeing' our world. Man's positive feeling toward life is termed Sambhogakāya (*longs-sku*) and his value as an individual is termed Nirmānakāya (*sprul-sku*). As facets of a peak value Sambhogakāya and Nirmānakāya share in the existential value of Dharmakāya, which is never an arbitrarily assigned value and hence, no value at all. As manifestations of a peak value, Sambhogakāya and Nirmānakāya are summed up in the term Rūpakāya (*gzugs-sku*), and the relationship between these values can be shown as follows–letting D stand for Dharmakāya, R for Rūpakāya, S for Sambhogakāya, and N for Nirmāṇakāya:

D = primary, intrinsic value (is)
R = manifest, extrinsic value as S = participating value and
N = presentative value.

Values are unique patterns which give an underlying unity and distinctiveness to man's actions. This is how sGam-po-pa defines the term *sku* (*kāya*):

> Since the *chos-sku* ('founding stratum of meanings', a peak value pattern) is all-encompassing and is the foundation of the *gzugs-sku* (manifestation patterns), it is a 'pattern' (*sku*),[9]

and

> Why is the *chos-sku*, being an open dimension (*stong-pa*), called a pattern? Because pristine cognitiveness (*ye-shes*) is continuous.[10]

Here sGam-po-pa reiterates the basic idea of Tantrism that Being-as-such and knowledge-as-such are synonymous, that the one cannot be added to or subtracted from the other, and that they are continuous by not being limited in space and time. Lastly he says:

> Why are the two *gzugs-sku* (manifestation patterns) called a pattern? They are called so because, generally speaking, everything that has become a configuration is a manifestation (*gzugs*); the two *gzugs-sku* (manifestation patterns) have become the special patterns of Buddhahood.[11]

Inasmuch as reality is constituted by values which give meaning to man's life, they are of the highest importance for his existence as an embodied being. By committing himself to values he not only retains his dignity as a human being, but also, in recognizing the value of others, he acts with respect towards the value and dignity of others. sGam-po-pa, to quote only one author, speaks of an 'existential value commitment' (*sku'i dam tshig*) and relates it to our body (*lus*):

> As far as our body is concerned, to refrain from killing, stealing, and sexual excesses constitutes an existential value commitment.[12]

Even more so,

> To take a divine pride in our body is an existential value commitment.[13]

'Pride' is here understood as the feeling of worth and dignity, which spurs us on to better our best; it must not be confused with arrogance and conceit which prevent us from seeing ourselves truly and which are an indication of the loss of our sense of value. The way that we feel about our body has important consequences for our health as well as our relationship to our environment, because our body is a unique orientation point. To the extent that we do not despise, but appreciate, our body, we also are able to appreciate the world around us. In feeling ourselves intrinsically valuable, seeing ourselves as gods and goddesses, as the religious language would express it, we take a different view of the world as well. It becomes a 'divine mansion', shining in beauty, and a place in which we can feel happy. If, on the other hand, we despise our body and consider its value only in terms of its fitness to be drafted as a guinea-pig for the war-industry and in inverse proportion to the dividends paid out to the shareholders, our relationship to our fellow-beings and to surrounding nature is badly affected: genocide, defoliaton and other forms of destruction become accepted 'moral' standards, possibly of the 'silent' and pious majority.

kLong-chen rab-'byams-pa interprets the technical term *sku*, which I have rendered as 'founding stratum of meaning, an existential value pattern', in two different ways which are nevertheless intimately related to each other. The one may be called 'epistemological' and the other 'ontological'. The 'epistemological value-pattern' is 'intrinsic awareness with its object-appearance'. It is

> That which appears before our senses (in its immediacy) without being in need of being asserted or denied, and that which can be analyzed into (i) the senses (as controlling powers), (ii) the psycho-physical constituents, and (iii) the (complex of the) objective situation and the owner of the objective situation.[14]

To term this complex a 'value-pattern' is justified by the fact that value does not reside in one aspect alone, but in the totality of what constitutes the pattern.

The 'ontological value-pattern' as a 'form of creativity' is represented as two patterns, the one holding to what it is on the unerring path, the other just being the being-there as pure existence. Of the former, kLong-chen rab-'byams-pa says:

> As it holds to what it is in its triad of facticity, actuality, and cognitive responsiveness, and leads to fullness of being as goal, it is known (by such terms) as 'great playful fascination pattern', 'crown-jewel patterns', 'life-style supporting pattern'.[15]

The pure existence pattern is said to be

> The triad of the ground, path, and goal. The ground is the presence of absolute pristine cognitiveness; the path is the invariablesness of an outward appearance in radiancy and as an (aesthetic) field pattern. The goal is the absoluteness of the three existential patterns in effortless presence.[16]

The existential value-patterns which are both intrinsic and extrinsic, are by no means to be considered as static entities to which man has to submit. Rather they are man's very life, pulsating with wondrous experiences. The manifestation of these value-patterns holds a fascination which is felt as pure playfulness, quite different from the strain and the frustration attendant upon those 'values' that are vainly looked for outside one's Being. kLong-chen rab-'byams-pa discusses these existential value-patterns and the ease with which they manifest themselves in concise terms reflecting his metaphysical awareness:

> The facticity of Being-as-such (*ngo-bo*) as a founding stratum of meanings and value-patterns (*chos-sku*) is an open and vast intrinsic awareness (*rig-pa*); the ease with which it manifests itself (*rol-pa*) is the ocean of pristine cognitiveness (*ye-shes*) in which no dichotomic thought obtains. The actuality of Being-as-such (*rang-bzhin*) as the shared value-pattern (*long-sku*) is the effortlessness of irradiativeness (*gsal-ba'i lhun-grub*); the ease with which it manifests itself is the five 'life-styles' or action-patterns adorned with the major and minor marks (of Buddhahood). The cognitive responsiveness (*thugs-rje*) of Being-as-such as the representative value-pattern (*sprul-sku*) is the basis upon which the all-encompassing pristine cognitiveness operates: and the ease with which it manifests itself is the Teacher appearing to anyone and anywhere.[17]

In the linking of values with Being-as-such, a very important observation has been made. Values are relevant to our concrete existence as we are here and now, and they spur us to action. They operate from within and are not inventions that are supposed to inhabit a special realm of their own. They reach into the limitations of the concrete human individual —and man is good when he really is himself, but evil when he tries to succumb to imaginary, constructed values. The consequence is that good and evil are not fixed properties, but ways of existing. However, to speak of good and evil has its dangers, particularly when we do not remind ourselves of the absoluteness of Being. The absoluteness of Being is its goodness, its valuableness, hence there cannot exist any evil, anything not valuable. In making (ethical) judgments we can only determine in which way and to what degree something is good. Since judgments are relative, the absolutization of judged goodness is evil, so much more so because every judgment is a relativistic qualification and misses the absoluteness of what it attempts to judge.

In the same way that the question, whether true knowledge as against seemingly true opinion is possible, already presupposes knowledge, so also the question, whether life is meaningful and valuable, indirectly reaffirms the fact that true values and meaning are existential, rather than postulational and arbitrarily dogmatized. To live by values, grounded in Being-as-such, is to 'make them the path'. There are several steps in the transition from external, imposed rule to inner values which alone have effectiveness and cogency for man's life, and the stages, in turn, are marked by increasing intensity of awareness. Although we tend to speak of a transition from external standards to inner motives, this must not be understood as implying that now man can give in to any random whim. It is unfortunate that we have come to equate the within with the ego and have absolutized it in grossly anthropomorphic form. Thereby we have lost sight of the real within and turned it into an 'external' postulate. The observable fact is that a person who begins to live by his 'inner', that is, existential values, becomes less ego-centered and more 'open', and to the extent that he becomes 'open', it is meaningless to speak of an 'outer-directed' or 'inner-directed' person. Vimalamitra concisely brings out this point. He distinguishes several aspects. The first belongs to the beginner:

> When first the yogi does away with all positive and negative imputations concerning the without, the within, and the mystical, by means of an appreciative-discriminative awareness (*shes-rab*) that is born from listening, thinking about (that which has been heard), and attending to (what is intended), then, when all propositions have been suspended, there is Nirmāṇakāya. Since he enjoys both the 'word' and the 'thing' when he is at the stage (of distinguishing between the fiction of) individual and real, (he is in a state of) Sambhogakāya. When he has discarded (the idea of) the real, then due to the fact that his original awareness (emerging) from intrinsic awareness (or the basis of his Being) cannot be added to or detracted from (absolute Being) as there is no parting from the absolutely real appearing as such, (he has realized) Dharmakāya.[18]

It should be obvious that all judgments miss the point and therefore are incapable of revealing the existential values by which man lives. To refrain from judgments, be they directed towards ourselves or others, makes us realize the 'representational values' (*sprul-sku, Nirmānakāya*) of whatever there is. To this end the development of the appreciative-discriminative awareness (*shes-rab*) which is said to derive from listening, thinking and attending, is the main task. The first process (i.e., listening) operates in the framework of words which are arbitrary symbols given meaning by their use by human beings. Here we take the words as they are used by our fellow human beings, without questioning their function. The second process introduces a division between the word and the thing symbolized by the word. It sees that words are no more than labels of things, they have no closer relationship to the things than a price-tag on a piece of merchandise does to the piece of merchandise. The third is not concerned with either the 'word' or the 'thing'. In a sense, it has a liberating effect, because it goes beyond the cognitive meaning (of what propositions assert or deny) and their emotive meanings (what feelings they cause). Then, to 'let things be', whether these 'things' be ourselves or other beings, person and natural objects, is the first recognition of the value of things in their own right. It is through this recognition of their value that we can 'enjoy' them, because we participate in them. This enjoyment is enhanced by the fact that words have lost their power over us, because we have learned that words are not identical with the things they are tagged on.

The text speaks of 'individual (*gang-zag*) and 'the real' (*chos*). This is a reference to almost the whole history of Buddhist philosophical thought. 'Individual' is a word for what we call body and mind. It was assumed at the beginning of systematized Buddhist thought that 'individual' could claim only relative validity, while that which went into making the 'individual', the body and the mind in our example, were the 'real' stuff (*chos).*[19] In practical ways this meant that in dealing with others we could look for the 'real', without being taken in by 'names'. That is to say, we are able to appreciate a person regardless of whether we call him 'enemy' or 'friend'. This is no less than the recognition of values on which all cultural development depends, and in this recognition of values we ourselves grow, participating in a wider horizon of meaning and satisfaction. However, even the 'real' so conceived is still an imposed limitation, and as long as there is limitation, knowledge or Being-as-such and the absolute value it is is not present, or, at least, our knowledge of our being is warped.

We think of our being as this or that, judge it, evaluate it arbitrarily, and, in so doing, lose our being and fall a prey to either subjectivism or objectivism and their disruptive emotions. While appreciative-discriminative awareness born from listening enables us to realize the limitations of words which we naively tend to confuse with the thing they symbolize, and while this awareness born from thinking makes us realize our mistake of confusing two different categories and thereby leads us to scrutinize the inner processes responsible for our mistakes, it is through the appreciative-discriminative awareness born from attending to our being that we realize the futility of separating knowledge from the absolutely real.

In the unity of pristine cognitiveness and meaning (or meaningfulness), even the mystical level is transcended, and this is called the realization of Dharmakāya. As founding stratum and, hence, as an existential value, it is the *terminus a quo*. Its manifestation on all levels of human activity is the *terminus ad quem*, permanently grounded in the experience of the former. Vimalamitra declares:

> When the state into which no dichotomic thought enters is experienced, the yogi has, while in concentration, broken the stream of the fictions which are the outcome of his thoughts that move in the confines of 'memory'.[20] His staying (in this state) is Dharmakāya. When he stays there, (in the feeling

> of) radiancy with no (egocentric) apprehending (of this value), this is Sambhogakāya. When he comes out of this state of concentration and in his post-concentration state is carried into the varied world of playful manifestations, his continuing in the sphere of the latter's ease is Nirmāṇakāya.[21]

This passage makes it abundantly clear that Sambhogakāya is a participatory experience, through which we take delight in Dharmakāya. To the extent that this activity takes place, the Sambhogakāya 'lives' in the Dharmakāya and the Dharmakāya in the Sambhogakāya. This experience and delight, symbolized by Sambhogakāya, is not possible until and unless Dharmakāya has been experienced, but, Dharmakāya being there and being experienced, it may only be enjoyed through Sambhogakāya as having qualities which it is obviously impossible to describe without reference to a unique experience, which, in turn, is incommunicable to anyone. However, it is possible to cause another person to have an experience similar to the one that we have enjoyed. This is done through the Nirmāṇakāya, because it 'expresses' the experience of value in such a way as to communicate this expression to others. We need hardly remind ourselves that the three 'founding strata' or value-patterns (*sku, kāya*) are held together and are distinguished only philosophically, as moments or grades. Philosophically, we may speak of the continual and mutual enrichment of Dharmakāya by Rūpakāya (Sambhogakāya and Nirmāṇakāya) and of its 'expression' in Nirmānakāya. This philosophical appraisal of the three value-patterns is succinctly illustrated by Vimalamitra. He says

> If there were no Dharmakāya, we would not be able to distinguish between the real and the unreal.
>
> If there were no Sambhogakāya, we would not know what the five kings of pristine cognitiveness mean.
>
> If there were no Nirmāṇakāya it would not be possible to act on behalf of others.
>
> Therefore it is justifiable to speak of Dharmakāya as being in view of (life's inherent) meaningfulness.
>
> It is like speaking of the nobility, other individuals, and social groups being present when there is no uncertainty of their presence. It is justifiable to speak of the five kinds of pristine cognitions[22] as Sambhogakāya. It is like a universal ruler holding sway over four continents and enjoying them.
>
> It is justifiable to speak of Dharmakāya as acting on behalf of other sentient beings by manifesting itself for those who are to be made to develop. It is the Teacher, who is like a magician showing to others whatever they like, such as horses, elephants and so on. Therefore, Dharmakāya is, in view of (life's inherent) meaningfulness, real; it is Sambhogakāya because it serves as the basis of unending appreciative

> pristine cognitiveness; and since it is active incessantly as the activities of the Nirmāṇakāya, as Nirmāṇakāya it acts for and fulfills the needs of others.[23]

Vimalamitra also informs us what the five kinds of pristine cognitions are in themselves.

> The intrinsic nature of pristine cognitiveness is that it is irradiative, is not mixed with the categories (that between them define a postulate), and is forever open and self-sufficient.[24]

The important point here is the openness of the cognitive function, which can never be a merely 'empty' container or the 'voidness' of a blank mind, but must be thoroughly 'dynamic', because only in this way is it able to be appreciative and creative.[25] Consequently it, too, is not mixed with the categories that operate in nonappreciative awareness. Becuase of its openness if can assume any concrete form necessitated by a particular set of circumstances. This applies to Nirmāṇakāya as an active value-pattern in particular. It is in the true sense of the word *the* Teacher.

In our outward-directed thinking we always look for universal rules, mostly because they are the easiest way of shunning our own responsibilities and of avoiding 'growing up'. This also accounts for the fact that no amount of authoritarianism has ever been able to 'hold people in line' and to make them conform to its arbitrary demands. On the contrary, it has merely created rebellion which must be understood as a person's desperate attempt to regain his sense of dignity and worth. A person does not learn from what somebody professes, but from what somebody represents. To the extent that a person represents the immediate, deep and original perceptions and experiences of his Being, he is convincing, and can spur others to try to find those existential values which make his life more meaningful. The analogy makes it quite clear that the point is not that someone is acting upon someone else or that someone is passive and lets himself 'be carried away'. The magical show we witness is a symbol of the fact that there is more to life than we have as yet been willing to admit.

Inasmuch as the existential values, symbolized by Dharmakāya, Sambhogakāya, and Nirmāṇakāya, are not static entities located somewhere, but constitute and represent Being-as-such in a person's life, it would be a misconception if we were to assume that a person could or would have to 'give himself over' to them. One of the aspects of Being-as-such is cognitive responsiveness (*thugs-rje*) and to be responsive implies aliveness which, in turn, implies the capacity to change. Thus the embodiment of these existential values brings about a change in us that is felt as 'appearance'—which is not an appearance of something or a semblance, but an immediately felt *presence*. It is in this sense of 'appearance as a presence' that the three value-patterns appear to the person who makes them his way of development. Vimalamitra says:

> A person who makes (the value-patterns) the way knows that what comes as the external object is not something that can be ego-centrically apprehended and appropriated. The rising of non-dichotomic awareness is the dawning of the presence of Nirmāṇakāya. The rising of this presence in absolute bliss is the presence of Sambhogakāya.
>
> When mind as presence and (its origin) Dharmakāya have fused and when the streams of dichotomic fictions have ceased, this is the presence of the Dharmakāya.[26]

The 'presence' of these existential values as 'appearance, manifestation' is the way in which the person travels towards his goal. This, in turn, is the continual presence of these values in his life as real values which he experiences as being connected with the reality of his activity, and any verbal discussion or 'definition' is of secondary importance, if not wholly irrelevant. In a significant passage Vimalamitra speaks out about the ultimate presence of these existential values:

> The whole of appearance is pure in its own way. When appearance rises (in such a way that) the meaningfulness is no more (a content in mind), then it cannot be asserted propositionally that there is even so much as Dharmakāya. This is the absolute sphere of genuine presence. When in the climax of this experience the pristine cognition (born from) the intrinsic awareness (constituting Being-as-such) has reached its ultimate horizon, one cannot even speak of Sambhogakāya, because no further intensity is possible. This is the self-manifesting presence (of absolute Being), its self-irradiativeness, and its freedom from egocentric apprehension.
>
> When without resorting to the postualtes of body and speech, intrinsic awareness continuously stays with the immediately present, and when one is beyond the desire for instructive discussions and for meaningfulness (as some entity), then there is no such thing of which one could say 'Nirmāṇakāya'. This is ultimate non-activistic responsiveness.[27]

Apart from the fact that Dharmakāya is the presence of Being-as-such and cannot be reduced to anything else but itself, and that in its presence only silence reigns, two other points are noteworthy. Sambhogakāya is here described as a 'peak experience' in which the usual limits of egocentric consciousness have been transcended, so that we catch a view of, or experience something 'outside' our usual limited viewpoint as it were —although this 'outside' is our unlimited innermost Being. In this peak experience we are united with, actually participating in, Being-as-such, and it is from here that our actions and experiences on lower levels gain their distinct meaning. At this moment we create ourselves and become human beings. The other point, likely to cause some misconceptions, is that Nirmāṇakāya is said to be nonactivistic responsiveness. It has already been shown that responsiveness means to be alive, to be 'open'. How can aliveness be inactive? The answer lies in our error of confusing activity with activism, of assuming that to be active means to be a busybody and to meddle in other persons' affairs. If we are not inflicting suffering on others, euphemistically called 'doing good', we are not doing something, for our 'doing' means to ignore others as individuals and to brush aside whatever they may consider as values. Responsiveness, however, is a kind of aliveness which carries with it an appreciation of being and therefore enables a person to act whenever and wherever there is need, and, most important, according to the need. A responsive person is ready to act in knowledge of the need. He does not suffer from the compulsive neurosis of self-deception about his goodness as does the 'do-gooder' who in his market-orientation deliberately ignores the needs of others and sees in them only a means to gratify his cravings. Certainly, we do not help a person by making him conform to our over-evaluated ideas. But when we respect him as an individual our actions can only manifest themselves as infinite compassion[28] which is the opposite of any cheap sentimentality.

Although we may speak of value-patterns in the plural, they form a unit and interpenetrate one another. This idea of interpenetration has given rise to the idea of nine value-patterns instead of the customary three, each of the three being subdivided into three. Since through these value-patterns man also comprehends himself, his self-comprehension takes place in attending to these existential values. In giving attention to them, he seeks to give form not only to individual and collective experiences, but also to the activities of those values that constitute Being. In being given form they also must be 'localized', even if the place is no ordinary place whatsoever. In other words, Being-as-such or the absoluteness of value must 'take place', whereby it reveals all its possibilities. These are expressed in symbols which are a participation of ultimateness in its relativistically actual and veritable form. They also are a means of guaranteeing the presence of the value, so symbolized, to which man turns in worship. Vimalamitra says of the 'taking place':

> Dharmakāya's place is the sphere of the continuum (of experience); Sambhogakāya's place is the realm of the Akaniṣṭha-Ghanavyūha (heaven); Nirmāṇakāya's place is mount Gṛdhrakūṭa and elsewhere.[29]

By 'elsewhere' he means that, although the Gṛdhrakuṭa mountain near Rajgir was the spot where the Enlightened One was assumed to have taught the deeper message of Buddhism, any other place where true spirituality can be found can be considered the 'place' where we become awakened to our existential values.

We understand our existential values through images. The image is what it represents, and that which signifies *is* what it signifies, and among the symbols for absoluteness, ultimacy, and Being-as-such, the human image gains preference. This is never a matter of mere external resemblance to man, but something that is filled with what is emotionally moving and satisfying. This enables us to understand the interpenetration of the existential values and the symbolism involved, as well as to grasp their aliveness in viewing them in their existentiality (*sku*), communicativeness (*gsung*), and responsiveness (*thugs*). Thus Vimalamitra offers the following analysis:

Dharmakāya's Dharmakāya: Śrī-Samantabhadra,
Dharmakāya's Sambhogakāya: Śrī-Vajradhara,
Dharmakāya's Nirmāṇakāya: Vajrasattva.

Sambhogakāya's Dharmakāya: Vairocana–(rNam-par snang-byed gang(s)-chen mtsho),
Sambhogakāya's Sambhogakāya: The Buddhas of the five action-patterns (Vairocana, Ratnasaṃbhava, Amitābha, Amoghasiddhi, Akṣobhya),
Sambhogakāya's Nirmāṇakāya: Vajrapāṇi (or Amitābha).

Nirmāṇakāya's Dharmakāya: Vajrasattva,
Nirmāṇakāya's Sambhogakāya: The three Bodhisattvas of the three classes of beings (gods, men, demi-gods),
Nirmāṇakāya's Nirmāṇakāya: The six Buddhas of the six forms of life.

Dharmakāya's three communications: Atiyoga-, Anuyoga-, Mahāyoga-tantra,
Sambhogakāya's three communications: Kriyā-, Caryā-, Yogatantra,
Nirmāṇakāya's three communications: Vinaya, Sūtra, Abhidharma.

Dharmakāya's responsiveness: Having rejected nothing, absolutely perfect, unborn, without any propositions.
Sambhogakāya's responsiveness: just being-so (appearing in many forms without egocentricity), non-dual (irradiatively non-dichotomic), and irradiative and without egocentricity.
Nirmāṇakāya's responsiveness: Impartially encompassing all and everything in compassion.[30]

Another list of various kinds of responsiveness mentions a number of holistic feelings (*samādhis*), culminating in the experience of the indivisibility of radiance and openness, of 'appearance' and openness, and of intrinsic awareness and openness, and of the object and the mind (perceiving it), but does not explain them and merely lists their names.[31]

A few words may be said concerning the interrelationship of the value-patterns and their symbolic representations. In each of the six forms of life, into which traditionally the phenomenal world has been divided, there is the element of Buddhahood present, which has found its singular expression in the individual who was described as Buddha, "He who has become awakened and can awaken others." Constituting and representing the absoluteness of value and of Being-as-such; He is present in whatever limited form we may perceive ourselves. If, therefore, any situation is representative of (i.e., presents) Being-as-such, then the intricate value-presentation in the representative situation is properly termed Nirmāṇakāya's Nirmāṇakāya. Bodhisattvas can easily be understood as the form through which communion with the absoluteness of Being takes place, and this communion is variable in form. The existentiality of the situation constituting and presenting Being-as-such is termed Nirmāṇakāya's Dharmakāya, which is experienced and made intelligible through the symbol of Vajrasattva. Vajra is a term for absoluteness and Sattva for existence or existentiality. Because of this connotation Vajrasattva is both Nirmāṇakāya's Dharmakāya and Dharmakāya's Nirmāṇakāya.

While the bKa'-brgyud-pas[32] symbolize absoluteness by Vajradhara, "he who holds (to) absoluteness" in philosophical translation, and "he who holds a sceptre" in iconographic translation, the rNyingma-pas[33] see in his rich symbolism the wealth of an empathetic, and only indirectly ultimate, experience; hence they equate him with Dharmakāya's Sambhogakāya. For them the absoluteness of the absolute is Samantabhadra who in iconographic representations does not wear any ornaments—which are symbols of participation. Not only is Samantabhadra the symbol of the absoluteness of Being, but also, as the name implies, the symbol of the absolute goodness of Being. In the image of Samantabhadra, the life-affirming and positive character of Buddhism as relevant to the individual's growth and Being (Tantra) has found its most appealing expression.

Dharmakāya, as the absolute value-pattern, permeates and, as it were, makes possible Nirmāṇakāya, as the world of our lived existence, which is always permeated by values. Absoluteness is not something over and above or behind that which is relative; if it were it would be itself relative to something. The relativity of all that is is not itself relative to something;

this fact constitutes absoluteness. Hence, also, the world of lived existence is not a container in which man is locked up or into which he is 'thrown' meaninglessly (as Western existentialism claims), rather it is man's horizon of meaning. Man and world belong together and the one cannot be understood without the other. The world of our lived existence is the interpretation we give it. Therefore it is not a fixed 'expanse', but one that expands with our growing awareness. It includes all the persons, events, and things which we encounter and with which we communicate by feeling, thought, imagination and action; in this encounter we actually encounter ourselves. In brief, Nirmāṇakāya is the world of culture which emerges through our interpretation and which is grounded in our being responsive; without this responsiveness no human existence can be humanly lived. Responsiveness never refers to something lifeless, inert, but to something that challenges and is alive with potential meaning and value—to that which has something to tell us so that we may awaken to real being.

> Out of these reaches come various Nirmāṇakāyas such as man-made as well as natural monuments to existence, communication and responsiveness: Deities, paintings, script and so on; ponds and bridges, mansions and gardens, earth, water, fire, wind, flowers, trees, jewels, lamps, healing drugs and delicious food, clothes and ornaments and other amenities; paths to incidental and final happiness, and whatever appears as inert things that help the sentient beings to go where they want to go. This infinite wondrousness of Buddha-responsiveness is called 'the manifest indeterminate Nirmāṇakāya'.[34]

Indeterminate is said here because we never know beforehand what may become a challenge and an aid to growth, what may be our life-world. Although we may make a distinction between 'man-made' and 'natural', whatever there is in our life-world has value as constituting and lying at the very core of all that is. A painting is not just some canvas with colours put on it, having a certain shape and so forth, and being something that may be hung on the wall. We refer to a painting simply as a painting, which is not a neutral noun, but a value term. The same holds true for 'natural' phenomena like air and so forth. After all, it is the way in which we feel about being that acts as a guide as to how we shall create our life-world.

That the problem of being and, even more so, the experience of being ranked foremost in Buddhist thought is evident from the many discussions of the nature of Being, Dharmakāya sums up, or at least implies, the *fact* of Being, but its association with *dharma*, the universals and particulars by means of which we understand ourselves and the world we inhabit, leaves it too close to the conceptual realm which is *about* being—rather than the fact of being, pure and simple. It was in this context that the term *svābhāvikakāya* was coined, referring to the *fact* of Being, not to the concepts about it. Pure fact is that which is known by immediate apprehension alone, and strictly speaking, we can say nothing about it, since the moment we talk about it, we have *described* fact and have brought fact under concepts and propositions. Words can only point it out, but cannot convey it. This means that it must be experienced to be known. Its experience is pointed out by the term *mahāsukhakāya* 'absolute bliss', 'the ecstasy of Being.'[35]

The analysis of the various *kāyas* has shown that these terms refer to *ways of existing in a world horizon, not* to bodies of some hypothetical or concrete entity. Man is never an objective thing nor a set of things; as a living (existing) being he radiates into what may be called his vital field. The human being has his house and family, and also his homeland to which he becomes attached. His very life depends on the interaction between his existence conditioning his existence. This explains why the world he inhabits is called a Nirmāṇakāya just as he himself is a Nirmāṇakāya. Here, a further clarification becomes necessary. In speaking of ways of existing, we tacitly assume the distinction between the group and the individual, the public world, the differentiating styles of life, and the different horizons of meaning among the individuals. The public world is a vast continuum shared by a people or a nation and is a way of looking at things. However, this public world is quite distinct from the world of the responsible person who, in truth, is quite distinct from the mass individual, the group, the tribe, and even the nation. The group, its world, and their interaction belong, according to the interpretation given by Ch'eng Kuan to the Avataṃsaka-sūtra (Hua-yen-ching), to the 'impure' aspect of being.[36] 'Impure' is so called because it comprises the blind drives; the irresponsible actions due to 'ignorance' as when, for instance, we destroy our environment by sheer greed called 'progress'; or the introduction of divisions where there are none, as when we conceive of being as a plurality of chunks of being isolated in themselves. Contrasted with the group is the individual whose world is concerned with the clarification of being; and he, constantly dissatisfied with the fixed forms of existence, will strive to develop and to grow, to be *responsive* to life, to understand and not merely to accept and to live life blindly. The world of growth, of 'becoming enlightened', is different from the group world. Being 'pure', because appreciation and discrimination leading to an ever deepening understanding of the human situation come into play, the world of growth comprises not only the Śrāvakas, the Pratyekabuddhas, the Bodhisattvas, and the Buddha(s), but also the ways of being intrinsically aware and of what we are intrinsically aware. In being intrinsically aware we are not only aware of, for instance, a flower, but we also know what it means to *be* a flower. Overshadowing all, is the open dimension of Being–although not in the sense that Being as some sort of being holds together all that is, nor in the sense that being is additively the sum total of all that is. Being is present in and as what there is, and in so being present, it is, paradoxically, both something (what there is) and nothing (not being a presence or a representation *of* something); and since this is indivisible, it is termed 'non-dual'. The Avataṃsaka-sūtra mentions ten ways of existing: (i) the sentient beings, (ii) their environment, (iii) the karmic reaction responsible for the above ways, (iv) the Śrāvakas, (v) the Pratyekabuddhas, (vi) the Bodhisattvas, (vii) the Buddha(s), (viii) the way of being intrinsically aware, (ix) that of which we are intrinsically aware (*dharmakāya*), and (x) the open dimension of being (*śūnyatā*). Graphically the ten ways of being are as follows:

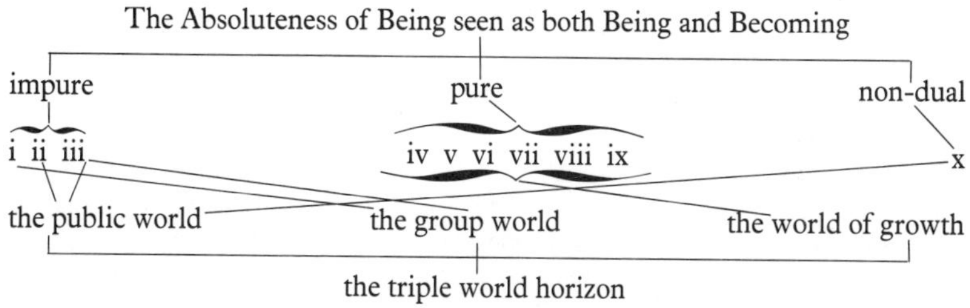

Ch'eng Kuan elaborates these ten patterns of being, or ways of existing, by pointing out that in 'the karmic reaction pattern' the emotional component has not been mentioned but is implied since it is the emotions that sustain our actions that are responsible for the plight of the world. The emotions, as the Buddhist texts unanimously declare, color our view and let us see reality only dimly and hence prompt us to frustrating actions which collectively keep us within a mass society and its regionalism. It is the individual that rises above the mass the the regionalism by widening his horizon. This process of growth reaches its climax in the Tathāgata who through his life exemplifies the embodiment of being and thereby rouses others to find their being. The Tathāgata way of existing, again can be seen, according to the *Avataṃsaka-sūtra*, in ten different existential patterns. These are taken from the 'history' of the Buddha and the influence he has had, as well as from the experience of being. These ten patterns are (i) the enlightenment, (ii) the resolve (to be born in the Tuṣita heaven as the preparatory step to enlightenment), (iii) the manifestation (including birth as apes and monkeys, deer, horse and so on, but in particular as a prince), (iv) the continuation (through his relics), (v) the major and minor characteristics, (vi) the awe inspiring nature, (vii) the way in which he is conceptually understood, (viii) the way of enriching life, (ix) the absoluteness of Being, and (x) the cognitive pattern which is all-creative in the sense that we create our world by understanding it, not by manufacturing it. An individual's lifeworld is never a dead 'thing' nor is it ever something moving inexorably in the direction of monotonously increasing entropy which at some time will reach the equilibrium state of death (physical and spiritual), but is a movement towards higher forms of organization. According to Ch'eng-Kuan,[37] i–iv are subsumed under Nirmāṇakāya, v is a Tathāgata's specific way of existing as the result (*vipāka*) of his development; vi is both Nirmānakāya and Vipākakāya, vii is both Nirmāṇakāya and Sambhogakāya; the remaining three are Dharmakāya.

The above makes it abundantly clear that the concept of 'three Kāyas' refers to the mystery of being in whose experience man finds his fulfillment. The mystery is the fact that Being-as-such is not some sort of being, since such a being would contrast with some other sort of being. As the Avataṃsaka-sūtra declares:

> The Tathāgatakāya pervades every place, every sentient being, every entity of reality, every country. It cannot be reached, but there is nothing it does not reach. Why? Because the Tathāgatakāya has no *kāya* (body). It is due to all sentient beings that it shows its *kāya* (king of being).[38]

And Ch'eng Kuan explains:

> Because it is without a *kāya*, it is nothing that can be reached, and because of its being nothing, there is nothing that it does not reach, just as *rūpa* (color-form) fuses with *śūnyatā* (the open dimension of Being). If *śūnyatā* had a *kāya*, its *kāya* would be an aggregate of matter which would resist *rūpa*. Iron may sink in water, but water does not enter (fuse with) iron.[39]

In our language this is to say, being (i.e., some being) does not constitute Being-as-such, but Being-as-such is manifest in all (sorts of) being.

Notes

1. Without exception, the historical person is referred to by the term Sakya thub-pa (Skt. Śākyamuni).

2. That *sangs-rgyas* was a descriptive term for an experience, if not for

experience *per se*, has always been in the mind of the Tibetan interpreters. *sangs* 'gone' was seen as the disappearance of opinionatedness, of the noetic-noematic complex termed 'Mind' ('sems), and *rgyas* 'unfolded', 'expanded' was seen as the taking-over by pristine cognitiveness (*ye-shes*).

3. This is technically known as *sku dang ye-shes 'du-bral med-pa* '(The fact that) 'founding stratum' and 'founded pristine cognitions' (are such) that they cannot be added to or subtracted (from each other'. See, for instance, *Chos-dbyings rin-po-che'i mdzod-kyi 'grel-pa Lung-gi gter-mdzod*, fol. 10b, 11a, 12a, 20b, 185a; *Theg-pa'i mchig rin-po-che'i mdzod*, 1:176, 606.

4. *Bi-ma snying-thig* (= *Snying-thig ya-bzhi*, vol. 7), p. 604. Vimalamitra, whose name is also given as Bye-ma-la-mu-tra, is closely connected with the rDzogs-chen (Absolute Completeness) teaching of the rNying-ma-pa (Followers of the Old Tradition). He is said to have revealed this teaching to Myang Ting-'dzin bzang-po and rMa Rin-chen-mchog who lived during the reign of Khri-srong lde(u)-btsan (755–797). He is further said to have been 300 years old when he came to Tibet. This obviously means that rDzogs-chen ideas existed long before the eighth century and that Vimalamitra was a very old man when he met the two influential Tibetans. Klong-chen rab-'byams-pa, in his *Zab-mo yang-tig* 2: 201, has preserved a tradition that Vimalamitra/Bye-ma-la-mu-tra came to Tibet in about 592 and that he promised to revitalize the rDzogs-chen teaching every hundred years. 'Gos lo-tsa-va in his *Deb-ther sngon-po* (George N. Roerich, *The Blue Annals*, The Asiatic Society of Bengal, [1949–1953]: Vol. 1, p. 191) distinguishes between two Vimalamitras. The whole problem of Vimalamitra/Bye-ma-la-mu-tra is still very much in the dark. Later Tibetan historical sources have given a very slanted account of the early period by perpetrating what today we would call 'political propaganda'. There is now sufficient evidence that there never was any 'bSam-yas debate' which alledgedly gave the victory to the Indian faction. See Yoshiro Imaeda, "Documents tibétains de Touen-houang concernant le Concile du Tibet" (= *Journal Asiatique*, Paris [1975], vol. 263, pp. 125–141).

5. Although literally translated, *lus* means 'body', it is always understood as 'the body as lived-in by me', never an an anatomical entity.

6. *Bi-ma snying-thig*, p. 602.

7. Ibid., p. 589.

8. Ibid.

9. sGam-po-pa, *Collected Works*, vol.Ba, fol.21b; vol.Khi, fol.30a.

10. Ibid., vol.Dza, fol.14a.

11. Ibid.

12. Ibid., vol.Cha, fol.8b; vol. Ha, fol.5b.

13. Ibid., vol.Tha, fol.40a.

14. *Theg-pa'i mchog rin-po-che'i mdzod* (Gangtok, n.d.): 1: 654.

15. Ibid.

16. Ibid.

17. *Chos-dbyings rin-po-che'i mdzod-kyi 'grel-pa Lung-gi gter-mdzod*, fol.195ab.

18. *Bi-ma snying-thig*, p. 598.

19. Herbert V. Guenther, *Buddhist Philosophy in Theory and Practice*, (Baltimore: Penguin Books, 1972), pp. 35ff.

20. On this term see Herbert V. Guenther, *The Royal Song of Saraha*, (Seattle: University of Washington Press, 1969, and Berkeley and London: Shambala, 1971), pp. 6 passim.

21. *Bi-ma snying-thig*, p. 599.

22. They are the traditional *ādarśajñāna, samatājñāna, pratyavekṣaṇājñāna, kṛtyānuṣṭhānajñāna*, and *dharmadhātujñāna*.

23. *Bi-ma snying-thig*, p. 596.

24. *Bi-ma snying-thig*, p. 616.

25. The lexical traslations of the technical term *stong-pa* (Skt. *śūnya*) by 'empty' or 'void' reveal the utter helplessness of the philologists in face of philosophical problems and also indicate the hold which a mechanical conception of the universe has exerted on their thinking—the 'empty container' with atomistic entities in it. The Buddhist term is easily understanable by a reference to quantum field theory, "in which every phenomenon that could happen in principle actually does happen occasionally in practice, on a statistically random basis" (Edward P. Tryon, "Is the Universe a Vacuum Fluctuation?" in *Nature*, vol. 246 December 14, 1973, pp. 396f.). This statement tallies with the remark in the *Theg-pa thams-cad-kyi mchog rab-gsang-ba bla-na-med-pa 'Od-gsal rdo-rje snying-po'i don ram-par bshad-pa nyi-ma'i 'od-zer*, rTse-le sna-tshogs rang-grol (born 1608), fol.5a and 6b, that sometimes there may occur what is termed 'sentient being' (*sems-can*) and sometimes what is termed 'Buddha' (*sangs-rgyas*). This idea itself goes back to the *bKra-shis mdzes-ldan chen-po'i rgyud* (= *rNying-ma rgyud-'bum*, 10: 672).

26. Ibid., p. 601.

27. Ibid., 601f.

28. The key-note of Buddhism as 'compassion' is thus grounded in its ontological Being-Awareness. This Being-Awareness is referred to by the familiar terms of *karuṇā* ('compassion') and *śūnyatā* ('the openness of Being'). In practical application, the *karuṇā*-facet of Being-as-such is indicated by and manifested through *upāya* (Tib. *thabs*), 'working out the existential problem of man', the *śūnyatā*-facet by *prajñā* (Tib. *shes-rab*), 'the awareness and appreciation of the problem that is to worked out'. *thabs* and *shes-rab* stand in a feed-back relationship. The more deeply I am aware of a problem the more intensely I am aroused to work out its solution, and the more capable I become of solving the problem, the more keenly I become aware of it.

29. Ibid., p. 590.

30. Ibid., p. 590ff.

31. To deal with the symbolism in all its ramifications would require the space of an encyclopedia. However, some of these symbols, particularly those commonly referred to by the term Dhyānibuddha (a term which is not found in any of the original texts, but is an invention of Western Sanskritist and descriptive

of the content of the visualization techniques) are known by their representations in painting and sculpture.

32. The bKa'-brgyud-pa ('Transmission of the Word') school of thought goes back to Mar-pa (1012–1096) who several times went to India and studied under Nāropa (1016–1100). The real founder of the school, however, is sGam-po-pa (1079–1153). Under his disciples the school branched off into several sub-schools.

33. The rNying-ma-pa ('The Old Tradition') tradition has remained philosophically most active throughout its history, to the present time. Its major teaching, the rDzogs-chen, is said to go back to dGa'-rab rdo-rje (ca. 52), Śrīsiṃha (ca. 345), Vimalamitra/Bye-ma-la-mu-tra (6th century?), Padmasambhava (8th century), and has continued through such illustrous persons as Klong-chen rab-'byams-pa (1308–1364), 'Jigs-med gling-pa (1729/30–1798), and Mi-pham rgya-mtsho (1846–1912). On Klong-chen rab-'byams-pa, see in particular Herbert V. Guenther, *Kindly Bent to Ease Us*, Emeryville, California: Dharma Publishing, 1975), vol. 1, pp. xiii–xxv.

34. *rDzogs-pa chen-po Chos-nyid rang-grol* (in Miscellaneous Writings (*gsung thor-bu*) of kun-mkhyen Klong-chen-pa Dri-med'od-zer, Delhi 1973), vol. 2, pp. 253f.

35. See Herbert V. Guenther, *The Royal Song of Saraha*, p. 91n.

36. *Hua-yen-ching Su-Ch'ao* (Taipei 1966), fasc.52, pp. 56f.

37. Ibid., pp. 61f. Ch'eng-kuan (760–820) is honoured as the fourth patriarch of the Hua-yen (Jap. Kegon) school of Chinese Buddhism. His exegesis must be considered as the most profound contribution to Chinese philosophical thought.

38. *Hua-yen-ching Su-Ch'ao*, fasc.62, p. 38.

39. Ibid., p. 39.

Insight and Paradox in Buddhist Thought

A.K.Chattarjee

I

One of the most important tasks in philosophy is to lay bare the conceptual framework of an area of discourse. One has to unearth and analyse the basic concepts of a particular segment of language and then map out the 'logical geography' of that system, i.e., show how the basic concepts are structured, and how they are situated in a total scheme. The problem gets infinitely complicated when we analyse, not the discourse that we are philosophising on, but the discourse of philosophy itself. A philosopher has then to perform the apparently impossible job of looking at himself from a distance, and somehow manage to occupy two incompatible positions at once, viz. that which is being analysed and the analysis itself. Yet if philosophy is to be any kind of conceptual analysis at all, it cannot avoid subjecting its own conceptual system to the same sort of scrutiny that it subjects others. Conceptual thinking has to include, not only thinking about concepts, but also thinking by means of concepts; and the problem is how these two activities are to be reconciled.

The conceptual framework within which a philosopher operates consists of certain core concepts which are intimately related in such a manner that the justification of one concept almost always depends on acceptance of a certain view on some other issue; the elucidation of a certain concept cannot be carried out in isolation from the entire framework. The notion of 'truth' easily stands out as one of the most basic concepts, if not *the* key concept in the entire range of a philosophical vocabulary. So long as philosophers were concerned with the problem of 'meaning', much prior to the admonition that they should rather look for something else ('use' for instance), most of their controversies stumbled on the question of the 'truth' of their statements.

What then does the adjective 'true' stand for? What is the sphere in which truth can significantly be affirmed? It is a commonplace truism to say that truth belongs only to indicative sentences. But what is a sentence? Truth does not pertain to a sentence when it is understood as consisting of a series of sounds or marks on paper, but only when it has what Frege calls, its 'sense'. "When we call a sentence true we really mean its sense is." The sense of a sentence is described by Frege as a 'thought'. "The thought, in itself immaterial, clothes itself in the material garment of a sentence and thereby becomes comprehensible to us. We say a sentence expresses a thought." Frege further observes that an indicative sentence contains not only a thought, but something else as well, viz. the assertion. Thought is a 'double fact' (*Doppeltatsache*) and two things must be sharply distinguished, viz. the content (the thought) which could be expressed without being laid down as true, and its assertion. The two are intimately connected and it is not easy to separate them. The difference stands out clearly in the case of a conditional sentence. When we assert Cpq, do we also assert p and q separately? The implication would hold whenever p is false, so that the assertion of p cannot form part of the total assertion of Cpq; p therefore remains unasserted and expresses only a thought, not its assertion.

To assert a thought is to go beyond the thought itself and to relate thought to the thinker. Assertion is not the thought but what we do to it or do about it, and the latter is irrelevant to the thought itself. Assertion is a mental act involving difficult psychological questions. Thought is something nonmental as Frege understands it, something independent of being asserted and thus independent of being related to a mind. A thought should be capable of standing on its own legs and does not require the prop of a person 'having' it. It is something impersonal and abstract, and though it forms part of the psychological casehistory of a thinking individual, the latter fact is not constitutive of it. Thought is thus what Hegel describes as 'objective thought' which he contrasts with 'subjective thought'. Thought in this sense is not to be equated with the act of being thought of, which is arbitrary and accidental to the nature of thought itself. "Freedom is obviously and intimately associated with thought, which as the action of the universal, puts us in relation only with a second self . . . Here we are at home with ourselves, yet there is no prominence allowed to any special aspect of the subject–mind . . . The mind as an ego, in a mere point of its being, as it were, shakes itself free of all the special limtations. . . ." Thought in this sense is universal and timeless, and 'needs no bearer to the contents of whose consciousness to belong'. A thought as Frege understands it is what is now termed a proposition.

If this objectivity and impersonality of thought be conceded, then it must be true that, to the extent that the thinker intrudes on his thought, the latter loses in its objectivity and thus ceases to be true. Otherwise the question of truth would be reduced to a psychological question. The thinker is the bearer of his thinking but not of thought. Truth of a thought is timeless, and is completely independent of the person who happens to think it. In considering the truth of a thought, we have to abstract it from the personality of the thinker and his way of thinking. What matters in the final analysis is the thought that is accomplished, and not the banner under which that is done. If cheating is wicked, it would still remain so even if the person propounding it were himself a cheat. The wickedness of the person does not make the thought wicked or untrue. Stated in this banal form, the truth of the distinction between thought and thinker seems too obvious to be labored and any confusion between them would straightway be indicted as some sort of *ad hominem* reasoning.

II

Let us then try to apply this distinction to Buddhist thought and see how far thought in that context is separable from the thinker, viz. Buddha himself. To the extent that Buddhist thought can be considered in isolation from its founder, it can aspire to objectivity; while if it is inextricably bound up with a person, its insights and discoveries would take on an appearance of intolerable paradoxes.

Buddha is generally hailed as the initiator of the rationalist trend in Indian philosophy, rationalism being understood as contrasted with dogmatism and authoritarianism. Orthodox systems of Indian philosophy are presumed to have arisen out of a corpus of revealed truths, either in a unilinear manner out of the Vedas, including the Upaniṣads, or in a multilinear manner out of mutually independent and sometimes conflicting traditions like the Vedas and Āgamas. The basis of an orthodox system is always alleged to be a body of revealed truths, and the role of reason in the further elaboration of the system is severely restricted to exegetical problems. The Nyāya-Vaiśeṣika comes nearest to the paradigm of an independent rationalist system, although it never explicitly puts forward the claim to be so. Tradition, too, has accorded it a place in the so-called *āstika* systems of thought. A first look at the Sāṅkhya system would make it appear as if its basic tenets were arrived at as the result of pure metaphysical reasoning, not tied to any revelation. But had it been really so, the Vedāntic criticism of the Sāṇkhya as *aśabda*, as not conforming to what has been revealed, would be pointless, as irrelevant as saying to a Hindu that his activities are unIslamic. Being tied, directly or deviously, to the revealed Word, every orthodox system is seriously engaged in elucidating and vindicating the role of *śabda* as an independent source of knowledge. Revelation gives access to a kind of knowledge which we could not have gained otherwise. Other *pramāṇas* give us knowledge of the empirical and the sensuous; from the very nature of the case they could tell us nothing about the nonempirical or the transcendent. The basic metaphysical insights are attained not as the result of any empirical investigation—if they were, the disputes could be settled by empirical means—they are necessarily of a nonempirical nature and revelation or *śabda* remains our only access to them. Hence *śruti* occupies a very critical position in all the orthodox systems. Enumeration of *śabda* as one *pramāṇa* coordinate with others does not bring out the full force of this source of knowledge; it provides the theoretical basis and framework within which alone the *pramāṇas* are allowed to function. We can have perception or inference only when the metaphysical perspective has already been laid down, and this is the work of *śabda*.

III

It is against this background of a tradition-oriented metaphysics that the putative revolt initiated by Buddha is to be understood. Buddha is supposed to have reacted against an unhealthy dependence on revealed authority, which he construed, rightly or wrongly, as degenerating into an empty ritualism (*śīlavrataparāmarśa*). Thought gets subjugated to the letter and the spirit of free inquiry is curbed. In order, therefore, to rediscover the metaphysical insight and its significance, one has to depend not on any external authority, but on one's unaided and unfettered reason. In a famous and oft-quoted passage Buddha is said to have exhorted: "Be ye lamps unto yourselves; be ye a refuge to yourselves; betake yourselves to no external refuge; hold fast to the truth as a lamp; hold fast as a refuge to the truth; look not for refuge to anyone besides yourselves."

If this passage represents the point of departure of Buddhist thought, we have to ask ourselves how far the thought expressed in it can be viewed as pure thought in Frege's sense, and not as the thought *of* a Buddha. Let us see how far we can go in the direction of clarifying the issues involved. Buddha is in effect recommending to us a criterion of acceptability of a metaphysical statement. The statement in question is not to be accepted on the strength of *śabdapramāṇa* or any revealed authority, but only when it commends itself to one's unbiased reason. This criterion as to which propositions to accept and which not to accept is a purely formal criterion, in the sense that it lacks any content; it does not tell us which propositions in particular are to be accepted. That such a criterion needs formulation at all implies that the criterion is not trivial or intuitively obvious, since in that case everybody would accept only what is reasonable and there would be no occasion for advising somebody as to how to accept. The advice "Don't accept anything on authority" is an expression of the fear that an untutored mind might do precisely that and thus be led astray. The criterion therefore is not immediately patent to the uninitiated and has to be taught, i.e. to be accepted on authority.

The contours of a paradox now begin to emerge. Buddha is teaching something which is not immediately obvious to one's unaided reason, viz. the criterion of acceptability itself. The teaching that one should accept only what appeals to one's reason has itself not been left to be worked out by means of an appeal to reason, but rather has to be taught or be revealed. An imperative has to be proclaimed to correct its factual absence. If a situation S already obtains in fact, there would be no point in articulating the imperative, "Do S." One does not say "Shut the door" when as a matter of fact the door is already shut. Similarly the imperative "Accept a thought only by means of reason" implies the fear that acceptance is ordinarily based on other considerations, and the imperative comes as a corrective. The paradox therefore is that a certain criterion of acceptability is being offered which cannot however be formulated except by violating the criterion itself. One is being asked to accept propositions on a certain basis, but the proposition "propositions should be accepted on a certain basis" does not itself have that basis. And if an exception is made for this proposition in particular as being based on some other criterion, then the teaching to the effect that there is no other valid criterion of acceptability is rendered infractuous. The paradox here is not peculiar to Buddhist thought but arises in other philosophical traditions as well. When Locke, for example, declares that nothing comes into the mind except through the senses, this knowledge itself is not sense-given but could only be *a priori*. The criterion of knowledge according to empiricist philosophy is itself not empiricistically founded, but appears paradoxically to be an insight of reason. It is a theory which does not seem to conform to its own criterion as to what constitutes a valid theory; it has itself not been shown to have been obtained as a generalization from observed empirical data.

If the criterion Buddha offers is not itself based on reason, we should have to seek some other basis for it. Why should we be guided by reason alone and not take things on trust? The only plausible answer would be that this is so because it has been so taught by the Buddha. It is accepted because it is *the word of the Buddha*. If we could have discovered it for ourselves we would not have gone to a Buddha for whom therefore there would have been nothing left to teach. That any person other than the Buddha can independently discover the truth for himself is a possibility that is flatly rejected by the Ābhidharmika. Buddha alone has discovered it by himself; for all others it must remain something that has been revealed. Even a full realization of the truth therefore makes those persons only *arhats*; they cannot claim complete Buddhahood (*samyaksaṃbuddha*) since they cannot strike a virgin path for themselves. A thought thus is being appraised in terms of the credibility of the thinker, and to that extent the thought is not impersonal or objective insofar as it is not being dissociated from the thinker. The thinker in the person of Buddha looms large behind the criterion of acceptability. Once such a criterion is somehow given we could proceed on our own but we cannot dispense with its initial giveness. We are being directed in a certain way, and the direction itself is given to us, presumably not discoverable otherwise.

IV

A possible way out of the paradox is to hold that the criterion of acceptability does not apply to itself, is not self-referring. The paradox arises only when the criterion comes under its own scope, and can be avoided therefore by stipulating that this sort of vicious self-reference is not to be permitted. The stipulation in question is only a variation of Russell's rule: "Whatever involves all of a collection must not be one of the collection." Take the sentence "The sentence I am going to utter is false" and name that sentence S. If allowed to be self-referring S says about itself that it is false, and is therefore false only when it is true, and true when it is false. The stipulation is that S is about some other sentence S′ which comes under its scope, and S says in effect that S′ is false. In case I utter S and stop there, there is no other sentence S′ which S is about, and S becomes vacuous and therefore meaningless. In the same way Buddha's criterion that a sentence is acceptable only when it is reasonable does not amount to saying that the criterion itself is acceptable because it is reasonable. It is, as already seen, revealed, and we start applying the criterion of reasonableness only when the criterion is already available to us by other means. But this sort of defense will not do, since the core of the paradox still persists. Now we are saying that 'reasonableness' itself is not reasonable and I do not know how we can make any sense out of this. We are being advised to accept sentences on the basis of their reasonableness. But when we ask why should we be doing that we are told that we should do so because it is the word of the Buddha!

Buddha, however, does not stop with formulating a criterion of acceptability. He goes on to tell us what assertions he has found by means of his own enlightenment, i.e. his own unaided reason, and recommends these assertions to us. Buddha gives us not only a criterion but also certain definite sentences which presumably conform to that criterion. The simultaneous assertion of these two, viz. the criterion and what conforms to it, has a certain incompatibility about it. Since the criterion demands a rejection of all authority and asks one to depend on one's resources, it is distinctly odd to recommend something more to be externally added on. The theory Buddha seeks to recommend is the theory of *dharma* and its several classifications into *dhātus, āyatanas* etc. There are two separate strands in Buddha's teachings which might roughly be described as rationalism and criticism. Rationalism seeks to discard all tradition and authority as being externally imposed on thought; it seeks to transcend all belief based on mere faith unsupported by the light of reason, and appeals for accepting only what is justified by one's reason. Criticism is the rejection of the naive belief in a world of enduring things. Nothing endures, everything perishes. An ultimate element of existence or a *dharma* is something evanescent, devoid of internal complexity and persistence in time, indeed not a 'thing' at all in any ordinary sense of the term.

It must be confessed at once that criticism or *nairātmyavāda* is not entailed by rationalism itself, but is something grafted on to it. Rationalism is not a particular doctrine but only a method of formulating a doctrine; no particular philosophy as such can be based on pure reason. The exhortation to base everything on reason is empty since it does not by itself tell us which things to accept. The constraint exercised by reason on acceptability can essentially mean nothing more than acceptance of the formal laws of logic, but laws of logic, though necessary, can never be a sufficient basis for a particular metaphysical construction. So long as any two propositions are simultaneously satisfiable, the philosopher, in asserting two such propositions, does not violate any canon of reason. Let p and q be two such propositions. But both the sets 'p and q' as well as 'p and not-q' are equally simultaneously satisfiable. Lack of satisfiability arises only in the conjunction of both the sets, i.e. KKpqKpNq. Barring that no inconsistency results either in accepting the set 'p and q' or the set 'p and not-q'. There might well be two different philsophies, each containing one of these sets, so that both the philosophies are individually consistent, and reason by itself cannot guide us in making our choice. Any metaphysical system therefore is, from a logical point of view, equally justified or rather equally free from the necessity of being justified. As Quine observes: "One who regards a statement on this subject (metaphysics) as true at all must regard it as trivially true. One's ontology is basic to the conceptual scheme by which he interprets all experiences, even the most commonplace ones. Judged within some particular conceptual scheme . . . and ontological statement goes without saying, standing in need of no separate justification at all." There is thus no special merit in *nairātmyavāda* as against *ātmavāda* so that it could be said to be more reasonable than the other.

A theory of *dharma* does not follow from Buddha's criterion of acceptability. Though there is no logical inconsistency between the theory and the criterion, it is distinctly odd to say: "Accept A or B as appeals to your reason. Accept A." The second part of the imperative seems to neutralize the logical force of the first part. But this is precisely what Buddha does. The oddity lies in the attempt both to let the issue remain open and at the same time also to persuade us to accept one scheme of viewing things rather than another. On the one hand, we are to learn from ourselves and from nobody else, but on the other hand, we do learn something from Buddha, and that too, not merely a formal criterion, but a particular metaphysical doctrine.

There is thus a tension in Buddhist philosophy, viz. a tension between rationalism and authority, between reason and revelation. This tension has a dual aspect. First, there is the paradox of rationalism in the sense that nothing is given to us and the giveness of this criterion itself. Secondly, we have the paradox of rationalism in the sense of openness to all philosophy and at the same time acceptance of a particular metaphysics by denying its opposite.

V

It is plausible to argue that Buddha himself was not unaware of this tension, and this awareness might be one explanation of his celebrated 'silence'. Though his silence was originally associated with the so-called unanswerable questions (*avyākṛta*) later Mahāyānists exaggerated it so as to extend it to all his teachings, including the theory of *dharma* itself. There is a characteristic Mahāyāna dogma that "Between that night during which the Tathāgata attained to enlightenment and the night during which he will be completely extinguished, in that time not one syllable was spoken by the Tathāgata, and he will not speak a single syllable: the Buddha word is a non-word." Be that as it may, Buddha seems to have been aware that if one were to be motivated by pure rationalism then particular answers to metaphysical questions would seem to be pointless. His silence may be construed as a reminder to his followers not to take his word, i.e. the *dharma* theory, too seriously and that there is a deeper facet to his philosophy.

The other tension however, viz. one between reason and revelation, is recalcitrant to this way of explaining things away. If we are to analyze things by ourselves, why should we require a Buddha to tell us that this is what we should do? It is at this point that the objective and impersonal character of Buddha's thought is no longer capable of being safeguarded, and the personality of Buddha necessarily supervenes as the source of this revelation. The personality in question is nevertheless not individual, since individual traits and idiosyncrasies in Buddha's personality are not, in this context, relevant. What sort of person Buddha was is beside the issue. It is something universal that is involved here, some source of revelation.

Mahāyāna, therefore, no longer keeps the two, viz. the teaching (*dharma*) and the universal personality that reveals the teaching (Buddha), separate and distinguishable. The two are identical. This is a confession that thought here can no longer be dissociated from the thinker and, as such, is not objective. Mahāyāna seems to be built around the personality of Buddha. It is not mere idolatry, deification of its founder as a mark of awe and respect, but has deeper roots. Buddhism cannot make room for Buddha, the source of revelation of its basic insights, in its metaphysical conspectus of things, which latter therefore seems inexorably in need of being transcended. If a metaphysical perspective is to be discovered for oneself, and if that is the essence of Buddhism, then there can be only one Buddhist, viz. Buddha himself. For others, the teaching is *not* worked out by oneself but is given as revealed. Alternatively, the teaching should be apprehended afresh and independently by each individual, so that for him it is as though such a person as Buddha never existed and never taught anything. For Mahāyāna the latter alternative, viz. that each individual is a Buddha in the making (*tathāgatagarbha*) is itself to be revealed by Buddha! This transcendental source of *dharma* is *dharmakāya*, which is also the ultimate reality (*dharmatā*) going beyond the *dharmas*. What proclaims the *dharmas* cannot be counted as one more *dharma*.

This internal strain in Buddhist thought was felt, to a greater or lesser extent, by all the schools of Buddhism. The Mādhyamika seems to be a paradigm case of rationalism. For him every view is essentially void (*śūnya*) and this is sought to be established, not by an appeal to some revealed text, but purely by logical means. Every view (*dṛṣṭi*) stands self-refuted. That this is the nature of any metaphysical construction cannot however be taken to be intuitively obvious or self-evident since, had this been the case, the views would not have arisen in the first instance. Once the essential voidness (*svabhāvaśūnyatā*) of views, is made explicit, this might become obvious and clear as broad daylight, but this *śunyatā* has initially to be made explicit, *has to be revealed*, and this is precisely what Buddha did. Reason thus is not autonomous even in the Mādhyamika, but is set going by a revelation.

Take again the case of the later Sautrāntika school in which we have fresh indications that things are not quite all right in Buddhism. The Sautrāntika accepts the traditional Ābhidharmika distinction between what is (*paramārtha*) and what appears to be (*saṃvṛti*). The *paramārtha* is *svalakṣaṇa*, the unique and discrete point-instant. On this is imposed thinghood, permanence and substantiality by constructive imagination (*kalpanā*) which is thus the principle of falsification. These two orders of existence are mutually exclusive, since reality and appearance can have nothing to do with each other. Their modes of knowing are also correspondingly two which again are mutually exclusive and do not overlap in their respective ranges. They are perception (*pratyakṣa*) and inference (*anumāna*) and the content of one is the opposite of that of the other. This theory is known as *pramāṇaviplava* or *pramāṇavyavasthā*. The two *pramāṇas* are not merely disparate, as is indeed trivially entailed by their twoness, but are incommensurable. We have in the Sautrāntika situation all the essential ingredients of an ugly paradox inherent. Any theory that claims to subsume all possible knowledge under either of two different categories has at the same time to make room for the theory itself. The theory of *pramāṇaviplava* cannot however itself be brought under either perception of inference as the Sautrāntika understands them. It is a general theory and not an ultimate point-instant (*svalakṣaṇa*) which could be perceived) even if, per impossible, it were to be perceived it would have to be excluded from the *sāmānyalakṣaṇa*, and so could not inform us about the latter. At the same time it is not an inferrable free floating universal, since it is also a theory about the particular and its mode of being known. How is then the theory itself known at all? It seems to transcend both the accepted modes of knowing, and thus to constitute a third kind of knowledge, transcending perception and inference both; but this possibility is ruled out by the very formulation of the theory. *Pramāṇavyavasthā* seems to be a metalogical discovery, not amenable to the usual *pramāṇas*. It can only be *revealed*, and that too, by somebody who somehow sees both *svalakṣaṇa* and *sāmānyalaksaṇa* side by side, as it were– an impossible feat indeed.

In other systems, too, the fundamentals are not discovered empirically, but must in some sense be given or revealed. How does a metaphysician know that there are seven *padārthas* or two *tattvas*–neither more nor less? But in the case of the Sautrāntika the situation worsens because of the complication introduced by *pramāṇaviplava*. A knowledge somehow obtained from one source would not be applicable in another domain forbidden to it, as it is possible in the case of the Nyāya or the Sāṇkhya philosopher.

VI

In all these respects the basic tension in Buddhism is between the particular doctrines of a school and the source of these doctrines, a source which transcends the doctrines themselves. Extreme emphasis on rationalism by attempting to bypass its source of revelation leads to a cul-de-sac, with the result that, in the end, all the doctrines seem spurious, hanging in thin air because unable to produce their credentials, and the only teaching seems to be the teaching of silence (*tūṣṇīmbhāva*). Revelation is at the very core of a metaphysical construction, and no amount of rationalism could explain revelation away. Buddhist is no exception; it starts on a militant note, claiming to discard all revelation, authority and tradition, but paradoxically this claim itself is seen as what it really is, viz. a fresh revelation. The paradox arises because thought here is not an ordinary kind of thought, but a thought to the effect that no external imposition on it would be tolerated! The Buddhist accepts this thought as taught by the Master. Buddhist thought cannot therefore be dissociated from Buddha, the thinker.

Saṃskāra-duḥkhatā and the Jaina Concept of Suffering

Padmanabh S. Jaini

IN *Chapter Six* of the *Abhidharmakośa-Bhāṣya* Vasubandhu engages in a lengthy discussion of the meaning of suffering, or *duḥkha*, the first noble truth of Buddhism. This discussion revolves around the following interesting question: if feeling (*vedanā*) is defined as threefold—pleasant (*sukhā*), unpleasant (*duḥkhā*) and neither pleasant nor unpleasant (*aduḥkhāsukhā*), why is it that all *sāsrava*, or defiled, dharmas are held to be *duḥkha*? To answer this question Vasubandhu distinguishes three kinds of *duḥkha*: the suffering of pain (*duḥkha-duḥkhatā*), the suffering of change (*vipariṇāma-duḥkhatā*) and the suffering of conditionedness (*saṃskāra-duḥkhatā*). The suffering of pain is associated with painful feeling (*duḥkhā-vedanā*); the suffering of change, with pleasant feeling (*sukhā-vedanā*), because the loss of what is pleasant is suffering; the suffering of conditionedness is associated specifically with neutral feeling (*aduḥkhāsukhā-vedanā*) but more generally with all *saṃskṛta* dharmas, because they are produced by conditions (*pratyayābhisaṃskāra*) and are impermanent (*anitya*).

It is sometimes maintained that in the first noble truth the Buddhists, by emphasizing suffering, take a one-sided view of life and fail to do justice to the pleasant aspects of man's experience. But Vasubandhu argues strongly for the reality of pleasure, despite the fact that on another and more profound level it represents a form of suffering. The notion of 'level' here is a critical one; for in effect Vasubandhu is distinguishing between two quite different levels of *duḥkha*; suffering as a conditioned feeling of pain (*duḥkha-d.*), and suffering as the awareness of conditionlity itself (*samskāra-d.*). The former might be called mundane, or *a posteriori*, suffering—a psycho-physical state brought about by what is unpleasnat (*amanāpa*) and opposed to the feeling of pleasure (*sukha*); the latter represents a transcendental, or *a priori*, a kind of suffering—the metaphysical condition for both pleasure and pain, opposed only to *nirodha*, the unconditioned (*asaṃskṛta*) state free from all feelings. As a painful feeling *duḥkha-d.* is a *vipāka*—that is, an experience brought about by past karma (in this case bad karma). *Saṃskāra-d.*, on the other hand, is not a feeling as we ordinarily understand it, nor is it the product of any specific past action; rather it is an expression of ignorance (*avidyā*) and its attendant craving (*tṛṣṇā*). Thus, the cause of *saṃskāra-d.* lies at the very root of *saṃsāra* itself; and it is for this reason that it is said to be recognized only by the *āryas*, those who have had an insight into the nature of man's existence. It is this kind of suffering in particular which is intended by the first noble truth.

The distinction between mundane and transcendental suffering allows us to understand how Buddhism, and other Indian systems, while proclaiming the unsatisfactoriness of man's basic condition, can yet recognize the validity of his search for pleasure. Good karma will produce the fruit of pleasure; and this fruit is not to be eschewed, for without it we should be condemned to an existence of unrelieved pain in some dark corner of hell. Still, no amount of good karma will free us from the conditioned state in which we are forever striving to gain pleasure and avoid pain; the suffering of this conditionedness can be extinguished only through the elimination of ignorance, which is the very condition for karma. This two fold structure of *duḥkha*, with its distinction between suffering as painful feeling and suffering as the state of conditionedness and ignorance is characteristic, not only of Buddhism, but of other Indian religious systems as well. It is probably nowhere more clearly expressed than in the teachings of the Jainas; and it is these teachings which I should like to discuss here.

The Jaina religion has been referred to by Renou as "Buddhism's darker reflection." Yet for all its austerity and other-worldliness the Jainas, too, recognize that this life is not only suffering but is a mixture of pleasure and pain. In its embodied state the soul (*jīva*) experiences—and, indeed, must experience—both pleasant and unpleasant feelings (*veda*). The former are referred to by the Jainas as *sātā*, and are understood as both the mental and the physical states of ease, happiness, pleasure, etc. Their opposite is *asātā*. Like the *sukha* and *duḥkhā-vedanā* of the Buddhists, both *sātā* and *asātā* are the fruit (*vipāka*) of karma: good karma (*puṇya*) produces sātā, bad karma (*pāpa*) produces *asātā*. Unlike the Buddhists, however, the Jainas distinguish different kinds of karma which effect the soul differently. Thus, the karma productive of good (*śubha*) and evil (*aśubha*) bodies (in the human heavenly, animal and infernal existences) is known as *nāma-karma*. The *nāma* and the *vedanīya* karmas are always present to the *jīva* as long as it is bound to a body; hence, the embodied soul is never free from pleasant and unpleasant feelings. Consequently, the Jainas recognize that in our ordinary life we have no choice but to act in such a way as to bring about the production of *sātā* and avoid the production of *asātā*. Since these two arise in accordance with our own actions (such as compassion, charity, asceticism and their opposites), it is possible for us to follow a moral course which will maximize our happiness and reduce our suffering. Yet it is not possible for us, so long as we remain in this body, to free ourselves entirely from unpleasant feelings.

Like the Buddhists the Jainas believe that an existence characterized by the incessant fluctuation of pleasant and unpleasant feelings is basically unsatisfactory and an expression of man's karmic bondage. The *vedanīya-karma* which binds man to a life of feeling is, like all types of karma, not inherent in the soul. According to the Jainas the *jīva* in its pure isolated state (*kaivalya*) is characterized by the qualities (*guṇa*) of infinite knowledge (*jñāna*), perception (*darśana*), vigour (*vīrya*) and bliss (*sukha*). These qualities are obstructed or defiled by the influx (*āsrava*) of the various kinds of karmic matter, whose association with the soul represents the bondage (*bandha*) from which the Jaina path seeks to free man. Once freed from this bondage, the *jīva* perfectly manifests its inherent qualities.

The discrimination of karma into various types is based on the qualities of the soul: for each *guṇa* there is a corresponding karma which adversely effects it. The four major *guṇas*—knowledge, perception, vigour and bliss—are described by the Jainas as 'positive qualities' (*anujīvi-guṇa*)—that is, qualities of which we are partially aware in the state of bondage and which can be brought to perfection when the soul attains isolation from karmic matter. Interestingly enough, the Jainas reserve a special kind of 'negative quality' (*pratijīvi-guṇa*) to describe the *jīva*'s freedom from *vedanīya-karma*. This quality is known as *avyābādha*, the absence of restlessness or hurt; it represents the freedom from all feelings, whether pleasant or unpleasant. It would appear to be negative, not only in the sense that it is characterized by an absence of feeling, but because it is never experienced during the state of bondage. In the notion of *avyābādha* the Jainas seem to be emphasizing, perhaps even more than the Buddhists, that the restlessness associated with the presence of feeling—even pleasant feeling—is at some level alien and painful to man. Vasubandhu understands both *sukha* and *duḥkha* as suffering because they are conditioned and impermanent; in this respect feelings (*vedanā*) are suffering—in the same sense, and for the same reason that all *saṃskrta* dharmas are ultimately suffering. Thus he specifically says that *vedanā* is to be seen as *duḥkha* in the same way that the other four *skandhas* are *duḥkha*. The Jainas, however, by positing a special negative quality of the soul specifically representing the absence of feeling (*veda*) would appear to give particular significance to the suffering associated with *vedanīya* karma.

As in Buddhism and other Indian religious systems the root cause of man's bondage is ignorance and the passions, called by the Jainas '*moha*' and '*kaṣāya*' respectively. The influx of *vedanīya* and other forms of karmic matter ultimately depends on the existence of *moha*, which is itself the expression of another kind of karma known as *mohanīya*, or delusion-producing. *Mohanīya* karma is understood as two-fold: *darśana-mohanīya*, or that which deludes one's insight (into the nature of reality); and *cāritra-mohanīya*, or that which deludes one's actions. The former is associated with ignorance proper; the latter,with its attendant passions (*kaṣāya*). As long as *mohanīya-karma* operates the soul remains embodied, and the *vedanīya* and other kinds of karma continue. Once *mohanīya* has been destroyed, the jīva will automatically (and within that life-time) be liberated from all karmic matter, return to its proper state of isolation (at the moment of death), and perfectly manifest its inherent qualities.

Like other kinds of karma, *mohanīya* effects a specific quality of the soul. Yet surprisingly, the Jainas tell us that the *guṇa* effected by mohanīya is bliss (*sukha*). Here the term *sukha* is not to be confused with the Buddhist notion of *sukhā-vedanā*, which we have been translating as 'pleasant feeling' and which corresponds to the Jaina *sātā*. Unlike these latter notions, *sukha* is not a feeling—i.e., it is neither a physical nor a mental event; for the mind (*manas*), it will be remembered, is for the Jainas itself a form of matter, and as such is as alien to the *jīva* as the body. Rather, like the other *guṇas* which qualify the soul, *sukha* emerges precisely when the *jīva*, by attaining omniscient cognition, frees itself from dependence on the senses and the mind. It is, then, an absolute state of bliss which, like knowledge (*jñāna*), is inherent in the soul's very existence.

Sukha differs from knowledge, however, in one important respect. Knowledge in the presence of karma is not itself altered by that karma. The karma which effects knowledge is known as *jñānāvaraṇa*, or knowledge-obstructing. It is so called because it represents an obstruction (*āvaraṇa*) to knowledge much as an object may obstruct a light. In the case of *sukha*, however, the presence of *mohanīya-karma* brings about an actual transformation in the *guṇa* itself. This transformation, known as *vibhāva-pariṇāma*, represents the defilement of *sukha* and constitutes a change of state, much as a liquid may change its state into a solid. The defiled state of *sukha* is *moha*.

The fact that, unlike other types of karma, *mohanīya* brings about a real transformation of the soul—or rather, of its *sukha* quality—suggests its centrality in the system, and allows us to understand in what sense it represents suffering. The Jainas do not specifically describe the state of *moha* as *duḥkha*. Indeed, the term *duḥkha* is conspicuously absent from their technical lexicon. Nevertheless, the function of *moha* in the Jaina system is clearly parallel to the Buddhist notion of *saṃskāra-duḥkhatā*. Like the latter it represents the *a priori* condition for all our ordinary experience, and, hence, for our experience of pleasure and pain. It stands, then, in opposition, not to pleasure as we ordinarily understand it, but to an absolute state of bliss, which is realized precisely in the absence of both pleasure and pain. This state of bliss is, as it were, our birthright, the very nature of our souls. But through the agency of karma it has undergone *vibhāva-pariṇāma*, and has been transformed or perverted into *moha*. In this sense *moha* might be called a metaphysical kind of suffering—the instability and internal contradiction of a being whose actual state is a denial of his true nature. Conversely, *sukha* may be understood as the peace and the completeness of the *jīva* existing in a state of perfect accord with its own being (*svabhāva-sthita*).

If we are correct in identifying *moha* with suffering it is clear that it shares with the Buddhist *saṃskāra-duḥkhatā* a somewhat paradoxical character. For in both Buddhism and Jainism suffering, because it is transcendental, is not recognized by the ordinary man. In a sense we suffer without realizing it. Both systems teach that only one with insight into the basic structure of our existence is really aware that such an existence is unsatisfactory. In Buddhism only one who is free from *avidyā* can clearly recognize the universality of *anitya*; in Jainism only one who is free from *moha* can understand that the true quality of the soul is *sukha*.

I should like to acknowledge the assistance of Carl Bielefeldt in the preparation of this paper.

Nietzsche and Nāgārjuna
The Origins and Issue of Scepticism

Mervyn Sprung

Ever since it occurred to me that the traditionally denigrated *ataraxia*—'untroubledness of soul' as Sextus Empiricus calls it—of the Greek sceptic Pyrrho might be a Greek attempt to comprehend the *nirvāṇa* of the Indian Buddhists, or, at least (historical influence aside) was to be understood as raising the same problems for philosophy, scepticism has fascinated me. Most of those referred to as sceptics—and some not commonly so named—were, I found, nisally concerned with the human situation as a predicament demanding investigation and some form of resolution; concerned, hence, with the function of knowledge, of philosophy if you like, within the horizon of predicament and resolution. The thinkers I have in mind do not understand knowing, including philosophical knowing, as a privileged way to a resolution of the human predicament; they expose, rather, the uncertainty, the unfoundedness, the embarrassing unintelligibility of what elsewhere passes for knowledge. Whatever their criticism of knowledge—and there is a notable similarity in the divergent arguments of Indian, Greek and European—they all set its capacity and function well within the total human scene. They all see knowledge exhausting itself well before any resolution of the human predicament is reached; they all repudiate the notion of metaphysical truth; they all hold that knowing is not the model on which to understand how human beings relate to the way things really are. It is this nisal concern of the sceptics that lures one to circle, curious, around the bait they hold out . . . just at the limits of our faculties.

So the scepticism of the academics–Greek or European–is not my interest. The subtleties of perceptual illusion, the frailties of inductive inference, the indecencies of deductive arguments, the conundrums of negation, in short the ten *tropoi* of Sextus Empiricus, though invariably the scene of a sceptic performance and nourishment for the enterprise, are not my concern. Presupposing all this, I want to consider what sceptics–the people I call sceptics–have thought about the relationship between knowing, or what outside of scepticism passes for knowing, and the possible ways of coping with the predicament they found themselves in as humans. This can be put into two questions: 1. Knowing what, does the sceptic repudiate knowing? Or, certain of what, does he deny certainty to knowledge? Or, and this broadens the question, out of what resource does the sceptic repudiate–as do the exemplars I shall work with–the entire human enterprise in its conventional form? 2. How is this unspoken basis, in virtue of which the sceptic pursues his seemingly perverse *via negativa* of repudiation, related to a way of resolving the human predicament? Or, how is the unspoken basis of scepticism related to the trans-sceptical belief into which scepticism so often issues?

Now the rubric 'scepticism' has, of course, an ample variety of uses. It may mean a negative dogmatism which brings striking reasons for rejecting reason (the Greek 'academic' sceptics). It may mean that suspension of judgment (the Greek Pyrrhonists who introduced the term *epochē* into philosophy). It has been used by and for those (exclusively Europeans) who hold that the propositions of science fail to be certain but that the propositions of faith, being ultra-rational, are certain (Montaigne, Pascal). And then there are those who undertake to discredit the human enterprise in its entire conventional expression: knowledge, ethical norms, social institutions. Cynics or nihilists they may be called, but when, as in the case of Nietzsche, (who speaks strongly for scepticism but scornfully of sceptics) and the Indian Buddhist, Nāgārjuna, (who didn't know the word) this sweeping condemnation is accompanied by a no less confident resolution of the sceptical predicament, they are not cynics or nihilists but, in my book, surpassing sceptics.

In pursuit of the two imprecise questions I have sketched I shall give some consideration to the thought of three men: Pyrrho, a Greek who very probably knew India, Nietzsche, a European who knew what he could of India but misunderstood most of it and Nāgārjuna, an Indian Buddhist who probably knew nothing of either Greece or Europe. It is not the comparison of three quixotically chosen thinkers which interests me; it is to see what each of these can say about scepticism and its issue.

Pyrrho

It is striking that Pyrrho, in an age of science, subordinated philosophical inquiry to the end of human happiness. Sextus Empiricus, in his account of Pyrrho,[1] does not refer to Pyrrho's doctrines but to his *agōgē*, his way or his method—which was to suspend judgment about particular claims to truth or falsehood—the *epochē* reinvoked in a limited sense by Husserl. A consistent refusal to affirm or deny claims to particular truth led to an untroubledness of soul which Pyrrho called *ataraxia*. *Epochē*, it appears, was not a series of acts but a stable disposition for which the question of truth or falsehood did not arise.

This disposition is founded on the view that all things are by nature indeterminable (*adiaphora*). Each thing no more is than it is not, than it both is and is not, than it neither is nor is not. The distinction between truth and falsehood is vacuous; opinions and beliefs, as claims to knowledge, are illusory and to be eschewed. Sextus Empiricus explains (incautiously?) that untroubledness of soul was the *telos* of the sceptical way and that *epochē* was the means to it. Abjuring truth, Pyrrho used argument, as a physician would medicine, to cure specific ills.

Pyrrho bequeaths us a classical model of scepticism against which we can measure other sceptics, especially Nietzsche and Nāgārjuna. For later reference we may note: 1. The work of the intellect serves the purposes of a non-intellectual end: 2. In two respects his scepticism is compromised. Suspension of judgement does not extend to the arguments in favour of the suspension of judgement—they are like the ladder which may be kicked away after one has climbed up it. The immediately given (*phainomena*) *is* what it is given *as*, and so breaks the sceptical circle.

Nietzsche

When we take up Nietzsche we sense at once how well he knew the Greek sceptics yet how far beyond them he could go with the intervening millenia of European philosophy to support him. Nietzsche's scepticism is no longer a matter of epistemology or of personal happiness. He offers a metaphysics of scepticism, indispensable to his understanding of the human adventure, which is a critique of ontology. He speaks scornfully of sceptics, does not think of himself as a sceptic, yet praises what he calls 'scepsis' as the only intellectually honest way of philosophical enquiry. He accepts a scepticism which admits of testing, urges unconditional scepsis toward all traditional concepts, and holds the ultimate scepticism to be the view that truth is merely irrefutable error. In the face of this radical scepsis, or rather *because* of it I will argue, Nietzsche emerges as the greatest of romantics: celebrating the promise of the creative will. With a flourish he suspends Pyrrho's suspension of judgement at the crucial moments.

Nietzsche's scepticism works its way into many areas: He finds a deceptiveness in the heart of all things; he sees concepts and all the creations of language as fictions; he holds that truth is a delusion; and he sees human motives and valuations as subject to fraudulent influences.

Nietzsche's life and thinking pendled between *Leiden*, suffering, and *Erlösung*, release from it. The pervasive erring of things–the debilitating effect of error (*Irrtum*), deception (*Taüschung*) and falsehood (*Lüge*)–is close to the root of the matter. "There is a treacherous principle in the very heart of things."[2] There is a conspiracy to deceive in language as such, as well as in any attempt at self-understanding, and even in the simplest things of the everyday. "The mistakeness or deceptive character of the world in which we believe we live is the most certain and most unshakeable thing our understanding can fasten on."[3]

One of the preferred targets of his criticism is the reifying influence of language. This, Nietzsche thought, was impelled by the omnivorous need of humans to secure themselves in a stable and reassuring world of familiar objects and ideas. The notion of a thing, for example, and with it that of substance, was a mere word inflated by fear and the creative urge, and projected onto a restless, temporal flux which was, in itself, wholly insubstantial and un-thing-like. If the concepts 'thing' and 'substance' stand for human need and are errors, deceptions, and lies, if taken as true, no less so are cause, effect, motion, space, matter, spirit, will, reason, thinking, self and so on. These are all fictions, 'unusable' as Nietzsche says. They spring up precisely at the point where knowledge ceases. Even the notions of subject and object are errors, fictions concealing the absence of what they purport.

On this understanding of language we can hardly expect the notion of truth to extricate Nietzsche from his scepticism. His aphorism "truth is merely a species of error" is well known.[4] Nietzsche understood what is commonly called 'knowing' as an aspect of the struggle of the human species to secure a world in which it could create and, creating, survive.

Knowing, indeed, is an aspect of the constituting of such a world. "The will to have things knowable creates the illusion that things really exist," Nietzsche says.[5] Truth, which at one level is "the will to become master of the manifold of sensations" (a new version of the deduction of the categories of the understanding) is, at another level, the expression of what must be if humans are to fulfill their potential. In neither case is truth an epistemological term and in both it functions as an unavoidable falsehood which only scepsis can disclose. At best, truth can be an *honest* lie.

Nietzsche's scepsis worked its way into the ethical realm as well. The wellspring of human motivation is poisoned by our inability to accept our present predicament, whatever it may be, as our *own*. Unaware of this impotence and of the need for revenge which is based on it, we live into the future rancourously, without innocence. The motives we admit for our acts conceal their real origins. Our conventional sense of what is good and what is bad is treacherous. We are capable of unconsciously transmuting positive values into something to be rejected if an enfeebled life-situation requires this, and we are capable of transmuting disvalue into something good for the same reason. Vigilant scepsis is the only protection we have against such unconscious value-inversions. If the immediately given, even of the inner sense, is suspect, one must wonder what basis remains for a grounding of existence.

Nietzsche's scepticism is almost universal yet not quite. He destructs the possibility of knowledge, he rejects the certainty of the given and yet he founds his own views on an intuitive sense that flux in time is truer than timeless substance and that *Wille zur Macht*—creative power as the last truth—is truer than the laws of mechanics. Holding such views he, it appears, undermines his own critique of metaphysics. His scepticism is not self-referring. We are here at a point of radical ambiguity, perhaps ambivalence, in Nietzsche's work.

Is he the metaphysically irresponsible artist? Or did he know that he was leaping into a medium other than knowledge when he took his stand on the 'truth' of the eternal return, *Übermensch* and *Wille zur Macht*? Perhaps both, but I proceed on the second assumption. When Nietzsche leaves scepsis for his own doctrines he is no longer on the ladder of knowledge but is in a dimension where the authority of the farthest future, creatively thought, is primary. And, as I think, he knew this.

Eternal return and the other notions of Nietzsche's personal metaphysical treasury are most interesting if we take them, not as terms of metaphysical explanation, but as an attempt (heroic? futile?) to draw the horizon within which future metaphysics would have the power of explanation. Nietzsche says he wants to *teach* the idea of eternal return as a *doctrine* to replace traditional metaphysics and religion.[6] That does not sound like one more metaphysical theory. It is a principle of discipline and of selection of those capable of creating in the new wasteland. Nietzsche held that it is the ancient and proper function of the philosopher to create new values for his age. Knowing, thus, transmutes into creative will; and this makes the new wasteland bearable: one must become an amphibian, at home both in meaninglessness and in the affirmation of new values.

Nietzsche is a symbiosis of contradictories: out of a passion for knowing he destructs knowledge; and out of the depths of this scepsis arises his faith in the human adventure. His horizontal terms—*Wille zur macht, Übermensch, Ewige Wiederkunft*—do not serve a gnoseological intent, they serve a transformational intent. Hatred of time can and should become affirmation of each perishable moment in its eternity; *ressentiment* can and should become innocence; the suffering of scepsis can and should issue in the release of joy. This is the art of human existence. This is not a theory, it is a way, a way out of human *Leiden*.

Nāgārjuna

Any consideration of sceptism in the thought of Nāgārjuna, indeed of any Buddhist, would recall the fourteen *avyākrta* topics of the early *sūtras*. Buddha is said to have distinguished clearly between matters on which one could take a stand—for example that one knows if a fire is blazing in front of one or not—and matters on which one could not take a stand—for example whether body and soul are one or different. The first lie within possible experience. The second, the *avyākrta* topics, are said to be *nopeti*, not apposite, not intelligible, not true questions, presumably because they are beyond any means of determination by human faculties. Thus, the Buddhist is, in questions of metaphysics, a natural sceptic. Not all schools, however, were sceptics in the more radical sense of Pyrrhonic epochism, nor resolute destructors of the concept of knowledge as Nietzsche was. Nāgārjuna and the Mādhyamika school are both.

Nāgārjuna and his commentator Candrakīrti are orthodox Buddhists in understanding the human predicament to be an affliction deriving from the spontaneous appropriativeness, aversion, and illusoriness of unenlightened existence. No human activity, however remote from the instinctive level, is free of these afflictions: they are the basic determinants of all human experience, so far as it is unenlightened, including the noblest of deeds and the most sophisticated of philosophies. There is no autonomous faculty of reasoning in the human which could be free of the distortions of the afflictions (*kleśas*) of appropriativeness or desire, aversion, and misconception or illusion. There can be no Greek *nous* in Mādhyamika nor any Christian *intellectus*; the divine is not present in the human world in the form of reason. *Buddhi*, the ratiocinative faculty, is as subject to the *kleśas* as character and motives (*saṃskāras*) are. The Mādhyamikas' attack on all theories, all ways of looking at things, all perspectives, as the key to removing the *kleśas*, follows from this. The Pyrrhonic eschewal of *doxa*, opinion, comes to mind here. Nietzsche's attack on what he called the 'little reason' (the merely rational, the faculty of philosophers) as inherently ego-driven and hence distorted, is interestingly parallel to the Mādhyamika attack on *buddhi*. Śāntideva says quite simply *buddhiḥ saṃvṛtiḥ*. The intellect is the faculty of appearances, not of the way things are.

Language, in its turn, arises from and serves the needs of 'kleshic', i.e. afflicted, existence as interpreted by intellect. The world of everyday objects is inseparable from naming and being named. Thing and name arise together: there is no unnamed thing and no name without its objective correlate. Language appears to be semiotic and to refer to entities but, in fact, names are a handy means of dealing with practical situations which arise within unregenerate existence. For the enlightened this appearance of naming is dissipated and language becomes transparent to the intention of the speaker. Unenlightened language, however, is as incapable of expressing the truth of things as *buddhi* is of grasping it. Language is a natural phenomenon, not the cryptic voice of *Brahman* or being or Buddha: it is the voice of the afflictions.

On this basis Mādhyamika sets out, as is well known, to undermine not only all philosophies and all ideologies but every last category and concept constituting the everyday world on which the philosophies and ideologies are founded. In this ruthless march through the everyday world all our familiar friends are slaughtered: people, things, cosmos, causality, time, knowledge, heaven and hell, and for the Buddhists ignorance and enlightenment, even Buddha himself. Events have no purpose; conventional existence is denied any meaning. Total scepticism and with it nihilism seem imminent.

But, one wonders, is this omnivorous repudiation of the everyday world not as dogmatic as the realism it attempts to invalidate? Often one is inclined to think so: the attack is directed at shaking everyday naive faith in a real world. Yet it is not so. Mādhyamika picks its way clearly around the pitfalls of negative dogmatism. Realism is to be uprooted because that happens to be the block which Mādhyamika finds in the way of a more adequate understanding of the nature of things. The aim is not, as it was for Nietzsche, to establish that everyday things are *un*real, for that would be nihilistic dogmatism, but to clear the mind to be free to take things as neither real as commonly supposed, nor as unreal, as the dogmatic nihilist (the illusionist) would have them. Nāgārjuna's aim is to undermine both realism and nihilism; the mind is to be freed by eschewing all possible forms of ontological assertion, whether affirmative or negative. (This is the Buddhist *catuṣkoṭi* which has precisely the same formulation as that given earlier for Pyrrho). Nāgārjuna emerges in this light as an epochist, i.e., as one for whom the question of truth of falsehood does not arise. He is more radical than Pyrrho who held immediate impressions, *phainomena*, to be as they appear, because he withholds ontological determination even from the immediately given. He is more consistent, and perhaps more courageous than Nietzsche, who, though he gave good reasons for not trusting the given, in the end knew no other way out of the helplessness of scepticism than to invoke his own intuitive sense. Nietzsche did not exercise and could not have exercised the Pyrrhonic *epochē;* Nāgārjuna does so, and more radically than Pyrrho.

These few remarks about Nāgārjuna raise the same two questions we began with. Out of what authority does Nāgārjuna presume to demolish knowledge and the world it sustains? And, how is this authority related to what replaces the demolished world?

It is relevant to the first question to remember that Nāgārjuna is the most relentless rationalist of whom we have a record in any tradition. His procedure as a philosopher is shockingly simple: if an idea or a theory is not intelligible, does not make sense (*na yuktam, nopapadyate*), than what it asserts cannot exist. As no idea or theory can be found which is intelligible through and through it follows that nothing exists as conceived and the presumption is that nothing we can conceive of exists. Some unspoken criterion is clearly at work in this high-handed procedure. Some inkling of what *would* make sense seems to be implied.

Indeed, underlying Nāgārjuna's scepticism is an unspoken, perhaps even an unaware, conviction that the truth of things *does* make sense; that, as opposed to the everyday, it is the mark of *tattvam* to make sense.[7] It seems that the philosopher's rationality is a failed attempt to make sense out of existence, that it is a faulty version of a more adequate sense. Nāgārjuna formulates drastically "all things make sense for him for whom *śūnyatā*—the absence of being in things—makes sense; nothing makes sense for him for whom *śūnyatā* does not make sense."[8] Even as he exposes the helplessness of the little reason, *buddhi*, in the face of existence he works out of an unannounced conviction that all things do hold together in sense if one can find the way to realize this. That way is clearly not on the raft of conceptual dogmatisms. Yet what the underlying presupposition presupposes is not graspable until the traditional faith in rational dogmas is effectively broken. What that unspoken conviction is, is a problem in itself, but it appears that it is capable of making sense of everything.

Nāgārjuna proceeds on the further, less tangible assumption that the way things truly are is other than the realist's naive everyday world. Implicit in every turn of thought is his Buddhist faith in the plane of the 'unborn', faith in the transformability of existence, in the omnipresence of the Buddhanature. This faith, though clearly distinct from it, is not separable from his belief in the underlying sense of all things, though it might be difficult to trace this.

And now a word about the second question: How is the source of the Mādhyamika sceptical devastation related to what issues from it? How is the initial, inexplicit conviction related to the explicit conviction which arises from the ashes of scepsis? Well, what does issue from Mādhyamika scepsis? It is, as I think, the middle way. How is that? The Mādhyamika scepsis dissipates the possibility of holding to being or non-being as categories of truth, as means of entering into the way things really are—*tattvam*. In the way things really are, nothing arises in time in its own right as an entity (*pratītyasamutpāda*). This is *śūnyatā*, the way things really are.[9] The truth of things—if being and nonbeing are put aside—can no longer be conceptually given but becomes a way of taking things, a way in which things neither are in being nor are not in being—the middle way. This is beyond the field of theory without being mere practice. It fuses the two. It appears that to comprehend *śūnyatā*, which is still close to theory, is to be already in the middle way. To be in the middle way, which resembles practice, is to persist in a vision of the truth which seems to be close to theory—but perhaps is not.

So an implicit and initially unfounded supposition that things make sense in the end and that men can realize that sense, issues in an explicit faith that the middle way embodies that realization. How is implicit related to explicit? How can the relatively sober assumption that there is a sense in things metamorphose into the conviction that a way has been established? What is the function of scepsis in this process? Scepsis is the expression of the unaware conviction that in the rejection of proferred knowledge, a criterion is being applied which overrides all other criteria. Mādhyamika proceeds in the faith that *tattvam* is available implicitly as the overriding criterion to judge the worth of the manifold of named things (*prapañca*) and all views concerning it. *Tattvam* is the immanent whole of sense which condemns *prapañca* as unintelligible and hence devoid of being. The truth of things was guiding the sceptical process throughout. The criterion: "Does this make sense?" transmutes into the way of enlightenment; and indeed *tattvam* is often given as a synonym of *śūnyatā*.

Now to pause and ask where we have emerged. Pyrrho must stand by, at this point, as a silent model of the sceptic, because we know much less about him than we do about Nietzsche and Nāgārjuna. Both Nietzsche and Nāgārjuna destruct the everyday world; they share the view that no everyday world is available except as already constituted by language; and they both hold that language embodies distortions and ignorances which deprive the world of its claim to be available as fact. We might expect this to be the end of language and the triumph of radical scepticism. But it is neither: in both cases language takes wing into new fields and scepticism transmutes into existential doctrine. Language, made self-aware by the purge of scepsis, becomes the means of moving beyond the everyday. Nietzsche becomes the legislator of values, using language noncognitively; Nāgārjuna becomes the wise physician prescribing therapies. Nietzsche's new 'truth'—eternal return and creative power—are true only for the one who is no longer living in the rancour of the everyday world, but is innocent of vengefulness; Nāgārjuna's truth—that the way of things is not given in terms of being or nonbeing—can be realized only by an enlightened person. Both are close to Chuang Tzu's view that truth is what a true man holds. So scepticism may have something to say about the limits of language and the nature of metaphysics.

Nietzsche was impelled by a tormenting passion for knowledge, which drove him into his sceptical repudiation of traditional knowledge. Nāgārjuna was impelled to his rejection of all preferred theories and categories—because they failed to make sense—by an implicit criterion of what *would* make sense. The irony common to both undertakings is that the implicit criterion, the implicit promise if you will, is never realized in its own terms: it turn out to be, in principle, unrealizable. Nietzsche's passion for knowledge does not, after its tour through scepsis, yield knowledge: it transmutes into the courage of the *Übermensch* to live by the doctrines of creative power and the eternal return. Nāgārjuna's implicit whole of sense does not, after uncovering a world of nonsense, yield explicit sense: it transmutes into the way of *śūnyatā*, the middle way. Nietzsche's doctrines are not what his scepsis was in search of, namely, knowledge; Nāgārjuna's way is not any kind of sense, at least it is not what was absent in the nonsense of everyday beliefs. In both cases the implicit criterion seems to have functioned something like a provisional, half-aware version of what its resolute application yielded: passion for knowledge becomes creative affirmation, the knowledge of passion; the search for a whole of sense becomes a way of taking things. It is as if the initial sceptical concern were itself a deception, perhaps an analogical version of what it was, unknowingly, in search of; a version shaped to the understanding of one who had not yet been through the sceptical process.

The questions with which I began are still with us. Perhaps they have served the purpose of luring us into a field where we can see that the categories epistemology, axiology, ontology are not final; where we can see that the questions raised by scepticism invite another vocabulary.

Notes

1. *Sextus Empiricus*, Loeb Classical Library (trans. R. G. Bury) 1:1-25.
2. Friederich Nietzsche, *Werke in Drei Bänden*, vol. 2, *Jenseits von Gut und Böse*, 34. Herausgegeben von Karl Schlechta, München: Carl Hauser Verlag.
3. Ibid.
4. Friederich Nietzsche, *Der Wille zur Macht*. 493, Kröner Verlag, 1930.
5. Ibid., 517.
6. Ibid., 462.
7. *Mūlamadhyamakakārikās de Nāgārjuna*, Publiée par Louis de la Vallée Poussin. (St. Petersbourg, 1913): p. 67, line 12 to p. 68, lines 1 and 2.
8. Ibid., Chapter 24, *Kārikā 14*.
9. Ibid., Chapter 24, *Kārikā 18*.

The Unspeakable in Metaphysics

R. K. Tripathi

THE UNSPEAKABLE, *prima facie*, should have no place in philosophy. After all, philosophy is not just mute experience but a system of thought and discourse, and as such it should have nothing to do with the unspeakable; the unspeakable is its own condemnation. There is a patent contradiction in speaking about the unspeakable—the unspeakable introduces mysticism in philosophy, and mysticism and philosophy should not be confused. For philosophy, whatever is knowable must be speakable and again the speakable must also be knowable. If one speaks of something unknowable, one is obviously contradicting oneself. "Whereof one cannot speak, thereof one must be silent" (Wittgenstein).

In spite of the above *prima facie* case against the unspeakable, for many reasons it seems worthwhile discussing this question. For one thing, a dominant school of contemporary thought seems to be primarily concerned with language and what can be expressed in language, and so it seems necessary to go into the question whether everything is speakable or there is something which is beyond language. One cannot tacitly take it for granted that everything must be speakable. Secondly, not only the mystics but also great critical philosophers such as Plato, Kant, Nāgārjuna, Śaṇkara, etc. allow a place for the unspeakable in their systems. Unless we reject them outright as pseudo-philosophers (and that is not a small responsibility) it is necessary to make an attempt to understand the circumstances which force the acceptance of the unspeakable. Wittgenstein's advice to remain silent about the unspeakable seems to be rather platitudinous. Of that which one cannot speak, one has got to remain silent; and it does not require a prophet to ask us to remain silent about that which one cannot speak. The real question is not whether one should or should not speak about the unspeakable but whether there is or is not something whereof one cannot speak. The question is how one comes to admit the unspeakable; one has to be silent only after recognizing or noticing the unspeakable. Then alone one can say whether the unspeakable is dispensable or indispensable. There is still another reason why the question regarding the unspeakable must be discussed. The acceptance or the nonacceptance of the unspeakable seems to be closely related to a certain conception of philosophy—the question is not so innocent or so simple as it might appear on the face of it. If we deny the unspeakable we should know what we are denying and whether it is legitimate and necessary to deny it.

I

Let us first of all try to bring out the precise meaning of the unspeakable in philosophy. This is necessary, because the term 'unspeakable' is used in different ways which should be clearly distinguished. The unspeakable is partly like and partly unlike the invisible. The term 'invisible' is used for both what is not and also what *cannot* be seen: for instance, sound. But the expression unspeakable is used in philosophy not for what is not spoken but for what cannot be spoken in any language. The expression 'cannot be' itself is understood in different ways. To begin with, in literature when we intend to express something of the highest or superlative degree, we say that it is indescribable. Here the object is tangible and something within experience and imagination, and the difference between the speakable and the unspeakable is a matter of degree and not of kind. Then, there is the psychological meaning of 'cannot be spoken.' When we have an experience which is unanalyzable or incommunicable in terms of something else, we say that it is unspeakable. This is so in the case of most intense or most complex or most simple experiences. There is nothing intangible or unknowable here; the difficulty is only regarding analysis which is necessary for communication. Finally, there are the logical and metaphysical meanings of the unspeakable. Although the logical and metaphysical meanings are connected, they should be nonetheless distinguished.

Logically the unspeakable is that which involves some kind of incompatibility. This is illustrated by the Jaina concept of *avaktavya* (unspeakable) and the Advaitin's concept of *anirvacanīya* (unspeakable). The Jainas accept the *avaktavya* because logically the *asti* (is) and the *nāsti* (is not) cannot be simultaneously (*sahārpaṇa*) posited or spoken. It is a different matter whether there is or is not something which requires the positing or speaking of *asti* and *nāsti* simultaneously at the empirical level. The Jaina metaphysics which requires the concept of *avaktavya* may be questioned, but it cannot be questioned that the *avaktavya* refers to the logical difficulty of simultaneous affirmation and negation.[1] The Advaitin's seem to introduce the concept of *anirvacanīya* for a different reason; it is as a protest against the law of excluded middle, a protest against the view that the *sat* (real) and *asat* (unreal) are not only exclusive but also exhaustive categories and as such a thing must be either *sat* or *asat*. The Advaitin points out that it is not possible to speak of the false (rope-snake) either as *sat* (as it is cancelled) or as *asat* (as it appears) or as both because that would be contradictory. Hence the false is *anirvacanīya* or unspeakable.[2] The difficulty here again is just logical; the concept of *anirvaccanīya* or *sadasad vilakṣaṇa* (different from both *sat* and *asat*) is not metaphysical but only epistemological or logical. There is no question of transcendence either in the case of the *avaktavya* or the *anirvacanīya*.

The unspeakable in the metaphysical sense refers to the transcendent or the Unconditioned such as the *Brahman* of the Advaitins or the *Śūnya* of the Mādhyamikas or the Absolute of Plotinus or the thing-in-itself of Kant. The peculiar feature of the unspeakable in the metaphysical sense is that it is based on a distinction of two levels of reality, the empirical and the transcendent. The transcendent is unspeakable because it transcends all empirical categories or is arrived at by a negation of all empirical forms of speech. The transcendent is not one more reality beside the empirical but something which supersedes or dethrones the empirical. The difference between the absolute and the empirical is not merely of degree but of levels or kind. The transcendent is unspeakable because speech is awakened to its futility in regard to it. It is in this metaphysical sense that we are here going to consider the question of the unspeakable.

II

It would appear that even in metaphysics such entities are admitted that are unspeakable but quite different from the transcendent or the Absolute. There are, for instance, the *viśeṣas* of the Vaiśeṣikas and the *svalakṣaṇas* of the Buddhists. They too seem to be inherently unspeakable metaphysical entities. Neither the *viśeṣas* nor the *svalakṣaṇas* can be described as A is B; they are so particular and so simple that they can be neither analysed nor classified. The *viśeṣas* are *svatovyāvartaka* or self–distinguishing; they are not distinguised in terms of predicates, and so are the *svalakṣaṇas* with the added characteristic that they are momentary. The question is: how far is it legitimate to accent such metaphysical unspeakables. The Vaiśeṣika argument for the *viśeṣas* is rather tenuous. If something self-distinguishing is to be admitted why not accepted as self-distinguishing the substances themselves which the *viśeṣas* are supposed to distinguish? The concept of *viśeṣa* is wholly *a priori*, there is nothing in experience to warrant its supposition. No wonder that later Naiyāyikas find this doctrine redundant. But apart from metaphysical superfluity, there is also a logical difficulty. The question is whether the *viśeṣas* are related or unrelated to each other. If they are related then they cease to be *svatovyāvartaka* or self-distinguishing. If they are not related, then is there not a patent contradiction in admitting a plurality of absolutes or independent entities? The very concept of self–distinction is riddled with difficulties. If A is self-distinguished, then it would be distinct from B, C, D, etc.; all the distinctions would be inherent in it with the result that it would bulge into an infinitely complex entity and cease to be self-distinguished and simple.

The *svalakṣaṇas* of the Buddhists, though similar in many respects to the *viśeṣas*, stand on a different footing. The Buddhists make a distinction between the empirical (*saṃvṛti*) and the transcendent (*pāramārthika*), a distinction not made by the Vaiśeṣika. The *svalakṣaṇa* is the thing-in-itself as Stcherbatsky puts it. So the *svalakṣaṇa* is unspeakable for two reasons. Firstly, it is absolutely particular or unique and irrepeatable like the *viśeṣas* and secondly, it is transcendent like *Brahman* or *Śūnya* and not an object of empirical knowledge. *Brahman* or *Śūnya* is also unique and irrepeatable and can be regarded as *svalakṣaṇa* or being its own *lakṣaṇa* that is, known only in terms of itself and not in terms of any thing else.

Like *Brahman* or *Śūnya*, the *svalakṣaṇa* too is beyond all determination of *kalpanā* (conception), but while the former is beyond number, the *svalakṣaṇas* must be many. So the question is whether number and distinction can be introduced in the sphere of the transcendent. A plurality of the unconditioned seems to be a contradiction in terms. Rightly, therefore, the Mādhyamikas criticise the pluralism of the realist Buddhist even as the Advaitins object to Sāṅkhya doctrine of the plurality of *puruṣas*. The unspeakable or the unconditioned cannot be many; plurality is possible only in the realm of the conditioned. The *viśeṣas* and *svalakṣaṇas* are no doubt unspeakable as they are conceived, but they are metaphysically illegitimate.

If the transcendent cannot be many; much less can it be complex or made up of parts. It should be something like the self-conceived and self-existent substance of Spinoza, but not like the Absolute of Hegel or Bradley. The absolute of both Hegel and Bradley is an infinite whole free from incompleteness and inconsistency. But is it really transcendent or unspeakable? Probably not. The reason is that the absolute in both these systems is a synthesis or harmony of finite parts shorn of their incongruity; it is a totality, though not a mere totality but a harmonious one. It has therefore parts and cannot be called unspeakable in the proper sense. There is no real transcendence in the sense that there is no independent whole; the whole depends on parts which are not transcended or rejected but only transformed. This conception of the absolute does not bring out the true nature of the absolute as transcendent and unrelated. The unspeakable in the proper sense refers to the unrelated transcendent.

III

It is obvious that in order to understand the nature of the unspeakable, it is necessary to understand the nature of the transcendent–metaphysically the unspeakable means the transcendent and the transcendent must be unspeakable, for the transcendent is neither many nor complex. Speech such as A is B means either that A and B are related or that B is the predicate of A. The transcendent, being beyond all duality, cannot be expressed in the form of any proposition; it is unspeakable. The *viśeṣas* are not transcendent; the *svalakṣaṇas* of the Buddhists, though supposedly transcendent, cannot be so because they are many; the absolute of Hegel and Bradley though numerically one is made up of parts.

If the transcendent is absolutely beyond the empirical, it may be asked whether it has any thing to do with the empirical or the conditioned. In answer, we may mention three typical views of which only one seems to be satisfactory. To begin with, there is the view of Hegel and Bradley. Here the absolute is constituted by the finite and the many; it is their harmonious integration or unity. So here the absolute is really not absolute but dependent on its constitutent parts. There is too much of immanence. Real independence can be had only by emphasizing the transcendence of the

Absolute, that is, by stressing that the Absolute is not *necessarily* related to the finite and the conditioned; it is free. This is a point not well appreciated in either Hegel or Bradley.

If there is too much stress on immanence in Hegel and Bradley, Nāgārjuna seems to err on the side of transcendence. The *Śūnya* of Nāgārjuna is so transcendent that it seems to have nothing to do with the conditioned. This is the second approach to the problem of the relation between the absolute and the relative. Nāgārjuna takes such an extreme view that he is not prepared to say, at least not explicitly, that the *Śūnya* is the ground or *adhiṣṭhāna* of the relative; he is afraid of succumbing to a *dṛṣṭi* (point of view) which he abhors and criticizes. The trouble in this view is that the *Śūnya* is so removed from the relative, and there is such a wide gulf, that it does not touch our life and experience at any point and seems to be no better than mere nothing.

Midway between these two extremes is the view represented by Advaitism. The absolute is neither constituted by the relative nor is it completely cut off from it; it is the very ground of the relative; it is what lends reality to the relative; it is what makes the relative appear as absolute or real. The relation between the two is neither mutual nor non-existent but one-sided; the relative depends on the absolute but the absolute does not in any way depend on the relative. Depending on the absolute the relative is parasitical—the relative gets its nourishment and sustenance from the absolute and thereby succeeds in concealing it. It thus becomes necessary to reject and negate the relative which covers the very ground where the absolute grows. Transcendence therefore does not mean merely adding something at the top; it means rejection of the relative. The unconditioned can be had only by negating the conditioned; the two cannot be had side by side or sinultaneously. When the conditioned is taken as real, the absolute is out of sight. When the absolute is known, the conditioned is emptied and its reality drained off, because it is the unconditioned that gives reality to the conditioned. To get at the unconditioned only means to be deconditioned and not to be in possession of another reality over and above the conditioned. Advaitism therefore emphasizes both the immanence and transcendence of *Brahman* equally. As the ground of the universe *Brahman* is immanent; it is our very self, our true self, as it is completely free from all duality. *Brahman* is equally transcendent. But for immanence we could have no contact with *Brahman* and but for trasndendence, *Brahman* could not be absolute or free from all imperfections; it could not be our goal. In one case we could not realize *Brahman* and in the other case, we would not care to realize it. *Brahman* as transcendent is unspeakable and even utterly unspeakable. But *Brahman* is, for that reason, not unknowable—since *Brahman* as immanent, is our very self which is present in all states and which cannot be denied in any way what-so-ever.

IV

Although the Advaitic conception of the Unconditioned seems to be most appropriate, it does not follow that there is only one way of arriving at it. There is the Kantian way which consists in showing that all our knowledge is conditioned by forms of intuition and categories of understanding. The unconditioned or the thing-in-itself is beyond these conditions of knowledge. Kant has been criticized for talking about the thing-in-itself which is supposedly beyond all knowledge. The Hegelians point out that the admission of an unknown and unknowable thing-in-itself is on the one hand a patent self-contradiction and on the other leads to agnosticism. In order to get rid of the difficulty, it is suggested that the thing-in-itself be regarded as a mere concept or category and not as something beyond all categories. It may be pointed out, however, that Hegel seems to have missed the whole point of the Kantian analysis. He fails to see that if the thing-in-itself were just a category, it would cease to be the ground of knowledge and thus cease to be the thing-in-itself. If it be argued that there is no need of accepting something as the ground of knowledge, our answer would be that if no ground of knowledge is admitted, then no distinction can be made between perception and thought, or knowledge and imagination. It is the thing-in-itself that prevents thought from being empty and also gives content to thought. No wonder that Hegel is not able to distinguish between the form (thought) and the matter (intuition) of knowledge. For Hegel, mere consistency is truth, because there is nothing else except thought. For the same reason, Hegel is not able to make a distinction between cancellation and mere contradiction. Thought is formal and is governed by the formal law of contradiction; it gives only validity or consistency. Immediate experience or intuition gives content to thought and enables us to distinguish between knowledge and imagination. The falsity of the snake depends not on any contradiction, but on immediate experience. The thing-in-itself is accepted just to make intuition possible; it is not to be taken as a dark hurdle to the omniscience of thought. But for the thing-in-itself, thought itself would become the thing and there would be no scope for falsity. When Kant says that the thing-in-itself is unknowable, what he means is that it cannot be known in the manner in which a particular thing or the conditioned is known; it can certainly be known as the ground of the conditioned. It is known as unknown and so it is speakable as unspeakable, and not literally speakable.

The phrase 'speakable as unspeakable' reminds us of a certain error which contemporary positivists seem to share with Hegel. It is implicitly assumed that all speech as well as all thought is literal. Speech and thought concerning empirical objects are no doubt literal, but just as speech is sometimes not literal, so also, thought is sometimes only symbolic and not literal. The reason is that ordinary speech-forms and thought-forms correspond to empirical objects; when the same speech-forms and thought-forms are employed in the context of the non-empirical or the transcendent, they become necessarily symbolic; the form is empirical, but the content is non-empirical. This is what deceives the positivists who expect even metaphysical propositions to have the same kind of meaning which empirical propositions have. So it is really the positivist who is deceived by the form of metaphysical propositions—not the metaphysicians. When the unspeakable is spoken, the positivists, such as Hegel, sees a contradiction, because he does not see the distinction between the literally spoken and merely spoken.

The phrase 'known as unknown' like the phrase 'speakable as unspeakable' must be explained in order to show that there is no contradiction in Kant's thesis that the thing-in-itself is unknown. The idea that something can be known as unknown is not very common, especially in the parlance of western thought. An analysis of perceptual experience reveals that all percpetion implies the paradox of known unknownness. When I see a table, do I believe that the table comes into existence along with my perception of it? Perception and its object cannot be simultaneous, otherwise they cannot be distinguished; the object must be prior. Even a Berkeley would not say that seeing brings things into existence. Berkeley said only that the essence of a thing and not its existence consists in being perceived—that is, there is nothing hidden like an inner core; all that is in a thing is there on the surface; there is no depth. So when a thing is perceived, it must be—as we naturally believe—already there in order to be perceived. If so, the question arises: how do we come to know or believe even before perceiving that a thing is there? One must admit there is some kind of known unknownness of a thing; before an object is known, it must be known as unknown. This point is better brought out if we refer to our experience of illusion and its cancellation. We first see a snake; when light is brought in, we find a rope there. When we see the snake, we do not know about the rope, but is not the rope there even before it is seen? Do we not realize that even when we saw only a snake, the rope was already there—or rather, that it was the rope itself that appeared as a snake? That is to say, we admit the existence of the rope even when it was not known; the rope is known as unknown. The thing-in-itself of Kant can in the same manner, without any anomaly or contradiction, be said to be known as unknown.

Another way of discovering the transcendent or the unspeakable is given by the Mādhyamika. This method does not consist in establishing the conditioned nature of all knowledge; it establishes the contradictory nature of all thought or so-called knowledge. The *tattva* (absolute) cannot be contradictory. It therefore must be transcendent to thought, which is inherently and necessarily contradictory. The antinomical nature of thought was accepted also by Hegel, but Hegel dogmatically imagined that thought could somehow heal itself or its contradictions in the Absolute, and therefore that it was not necessary to go beyond thought. There is thus no real transcendence in Hegel. Bradley seems to have a better insight when he suggests that it is only in some kind of immediacy that the essential duality of thought could be overcome; but the trouble with Bradley, as with Hegel, is that the world or appearance is too much with him; he thinks that the Absolute will be shorn of content without appearances.[3] But the Mādhyamika deliberately calls the *tattva*, *śūnya* or devoid of appearance, only to emphasize that though the absolute is beyond the relative, it is not nothing. To be beyond speech, which is fraught with contradiction, is not to be nothing. Silence itself is a state of speech; silence is not dumbness.

A third way of getting at the unspeakable or the unconditioned is found in Advaitism. The method adopted here is the method of negating all duality (*advaita*). The *tattva* (absolute) being beyond all duality is for that very reason beyond all speech as well; there can be no speech in the realm of pure identity. The subject-object duality is the most basic and primordial; all other dualities are derivative. Speech, like love, seems to presuppose duality—but the very purpose of speech as also of love is defeated if there is real duality; communication requires communion too. The greater the communion or identity, the greater the success of speech. The point is that what is completely different or other cannot be known, much less communicated. Only the self can be truly known; all objective knowledge, i.e. empirical knowledge, is pseudo-knowledge, and therefore speech based on duality does not give real knowledge. Speech is truly communicative when it transcends its duality and refers to pure identity or self; and there speech attains silence; we reach the unspeakable. *Brahman* is unspeakable not because it is unknown or because it is nothing, but because it is transcendent, beyond all duality. The unspeakable in Advaitism refers to the pure identity implicit in all duality. This brings us to another feature of the unspeakable in Advaitism. *Brahman* is unspeakable not only because it is transcendent but also because it is the light of all light; it is self-evident. Speech reveals or makes evident what is not evident by itself. But language itself, not being self-luminous, requires some other light to illumine it, and that light is the light of *Brahman*. That which illumines language cannot itself be the object of language.[4] Speech is evident but *Brahman* is self-evident (*svayamprakāśa*) and unspeakable. As self-evident, *Brahman* is immanent in all that is evident. We can thus say that *Brahman* is unspeakable not only because it is transcendent, but because it is immanent as well. If at all, speech can be relevant to *Brahman* only negatively; even the so-called *svarūpalakṣaṇas* (terms indicating the intrinsic nature of *Brahman*) are understood only negatively. *Brahman* can be spoken of only as unspeakable.

V

The short review given above of the three ways of arriving at the unspeakable is meant to bring out and emphasize one point, namely, that the unspeakable or the transcendent cannot be reached (and is even meaningless) without negation or rejection. It is this feature, the feature of negating appearance or the conditioned, that is common to all the different ways of reaching the unconditioned. Kant rejects all empirical knowledge as mediated by forms of intuition and understanding; the Mādhyamika rejects all thought as full of contradiction; the Advaitin rejects all duality as derivative or dependent and hence false. In order to be able to appreciate the nature and significance of the unconditioned or the unspeakable, it is necessary to understand the role of negation in philosophy. The emergence of philosophic consciousness, which means an earnest *jijñāsā* (desire to know) or search for truth, implies an incipient negation of what we already know as true. So long as we hold empirical knowledge and experience as true, there is no earthly reason why we should go in search of truth. Philosophy is not a mere extension of knowledge in the sense that science is. It does not extend our existing knowledge of things; it rather rejects and replaces our knowledge for the simple reason that our present knowledge is found useless not for our day to day life but also for the purpose of enabling us to attain the highest goal of life, namely, eternal and infinite happiness. The positivists therefore are quite right when they say—though they say it with a different motive—that philosophy does not extend the boundaries of our knowledge of the world. Philosophy does not and even cannot extend our empirical knowledge because it starts by rejecting that knowlege. In fact, if philosophy did not reject empirical knowledge, there would be no justification for philosophy to appear on the scene. Either philosophy is utterly useless—as it does not serve enpirical purpose and even confuses the empirical issues—or there is a non-empirical purpose for which philosophy is relevant. To be able to adhere to the non-empirical goal, philosophy must negate the empirical. Philosophy is negation. Even the positivist negates; he negates the transcendent. But how does he get the idea of the transcendent? He gets it by negating the empirical. So the basic or primary negation is the negation of the empirical. Either the empirical is not even questioned or it is reaffirmed. In one case one is at the level of the unreflective animal; in the other case one is a positivist. But in both cases, one takes the empirical itself as absolute. So the absolute is never to be got rid of; the only question is whether we choose to accept the empirical itself as absolute, or choose to go forward to seek the real absolute. Since the empirical is full of relativity and contradiction, it cannot be taken as unconditioned or absolute. Metaphysics must reject the empirical and those who hug the empirical must reject metaphysics.

Negation as a necessary feature of all metaphysics enables us to distinguish the unspeakable of the metaphysician from the unspeakable of the mystic. For the mystic, the unspeakable is mute experience, an experience which cannot be either translated in terms of another experience or be literally described. The mystic has to take recourse to superlatives, paradoxes, and symbolism, as devices to speak of the unspeakable. But in the metaphysician's approach, as it is critical from the outset, the unspeakable is discovered after negating the speakable or the empirical. For the positivist it is not only that the empirical is speakable but also that the speakable is empirical. The unspeakable being non-empirical is for him pure nonsense. For the metaphysician the unspeakable is significant because the empirical cannot be ultimate.

Our emphasis on negation distinguishes our position from that of some brother metaphysicians. When we say that metaphysics is concerned with the transcendent and that the transcendent is unspeakable, we are aware that there are metaphysicians who are either not absolutists or who so conceive the absolute that it cannot be really regarded as unspeakable. Realists as pluralists are generally not absolutists. Rāmānuja tries to synthesize realism with absolutism, but his absolute is not really absolute or transcendent. In fact, he seems to waver between the absolute as a totality and the absolute as the 'self' of the universe. Realists cannot be absolutists. Metaphysicians who accept some kind of determinate (*saguṇa*) absolute do not see the force of the argument that all determination is negation. In either case, metaphysics is not well-conceived. The logic of negation, with which metaphysics starts, must go the whole hog and cannot rest until it reaches the pure transcendent, the indeterminate, or the unspeakable. It is interesting to note that Rāmānuja agrees that *Brahman* is unspeakable—yet he takes the expression unspeakable in a literary sense rather than in the really metaphysical sense; it means for him only something of the superlative order.

Saṇkara in his commentary on the *Brahma Sūtra* 1.1.4, raises the question whether *śruti* (scripture) is not self-contradictory when it says that *Brahman* is unspeakable and yet speaks of *Brahman*. His answer is that *śruti* does not speak of *Brahman* as an object (*idamtayā*); by negation it only removes our ignorance of *Brahman*.

Conclusion

In this short paper on the unspeakable, our aim has been threefold. To begin with, we want to insist that the very emergence of metaphysics is rooted in some kind of negation. In fact, metaphysics may be considered as reflection on negation, and not as a positive speculation concerning reality. Metaphysics so conceived is necessarily concerned with the Unconditioned, with that which cannot be negated, or with the unspeakable. Secondly, it has been shown that the unspeakable in metaphysics does not refer to anything mysterious but only to the transcendent. There is no contradiction in talking about the transcendent as the unspeakable, because what the term suggests is not that we are forbidden to say anything, but that there is a mode of knowing the Transcendent different from that of knowing the empirical. Finally, we claim that this view of metaphysics, and hence of the absolute, disarms the positivist whose range is only within the speakable or rather the literally speakable. The unspeakable or the transcendent is beyond the purview of the positivst, and metaphysics as concerned with the transcendent, remains unaffected by the onslaughts of the positivists' criticism. The positivist, on account of his empiricistic obsessions, is simply out of court. There neither is, nor can there be, any communication between the positivist and the metaphysician; they talk two languages—or rather, they make two very different uses of language. The metaphysician uses language to go beyond language while the positivist uses language to tie himself to the empirical.

Notes

1. See the author's article on *Avaktavya* in *Philosophy East and West*, July 1968.

2. C. F. Bradley, *Appearance and Reality*, p. 164: "We cannot, on the one hand, accept anything between non-existence and reality, while, on the other hand, error obstinately refuses to be either."

3. Ibid., p. 433: "The Absolute, we may say in general, has no assets beyond appearances."

4. *Yasya bhāsā sarvamidam vibhāti. Kathopaniṣad* 2,15.

Movements of Religious Life and Thought and Religious Diversity

Robert Lawson Slater

IN RECENT YEARS an approach to the study of religions has been developed, which is a notable departure from that of many of the Western pioneers of modern studies of this subject. This new approach has meant a greater regard for religious diversity *within* the religious traditions of mankind, which may mean a greater regard for significant *movements* of religious life and thought than has been the case in the past. I propose, with illustrative reference to Shin Buddhism, to consider how this new approach may mean new answers to questions raised by students in this field.

While pioneers such as Max Müller may be seen as having themselves encouraged new movements of religious life and thought, most such writers paid little or no attention to movements which were indicated by religious debates and conflicts within the various religious traditions that were studied. On the contrary, in calling attention to comparable statements of belief in the various scriptures and texts which they had before them, they presented the religions of mankind as 'baskets' of statements of belief which were passed on, without significant change, from one generation to another. The various religions might be distinguished from interpretative systems of thought, but Western scholars were disposed to identify religions with such interpretative systems, which might be labelled monistic, or dualistic, theistic, deistic and so on. As for the people who might 'adhere' to these statements of belief and systems of thought —they were placed very much in the background.

As time passed, with the entry of psychologists, sociologists, and others to this field who viewed it from particular standpoints, and with historians at most of their elbows, there were new approaches to the study of religions. By and large these new approaches have meant increasing regard not only for varieties of religious experience but also for varieties of religious expression. People are brought more and more into the foreground—religious people who may not only differ from one another while having much in common, but people who may change.

I am not, however, saying that the particular new approach to which I here refer has not been anticipated by others in the past, although it is in sharp contrast to earlier approaches. Nor do I claim that it is the only new approach of our day, nor, again, that it is being followed in all the respects I shall name.

The new approach to which I refer may be distinguished from other approaches by:

1. regard for what may come into view if we study the particular *histories* of the different religious traditions of mankind;
2. regard for the religious diversity *within* each of these traditions;[1]
3. regard for *central symbols* or clusters of symbols 'giving rise to thought'—and the tensions associated with thought[2]—which may lead us to look for such internal diversity; and
4. consequent regard for movements of religious life and thought which may be signified by such diversity—a regard which may mean new answers to some of the old questions raised by students of religion.

What may bring this approach into view is a lively contemporary discussion as to the use of the term 'religion', or 'religions'. It has been forcibly argued that we should be done with this term.[3] The term 'religion', it is maintained, has become so wedded to the mistaken concept of religion as some kind of 'entity', that its use has meant turning a blind eye to the personal faith—which should be distinguished from belief—of the millions of people we should have in view, as well as a blind eye to "the richness, the radical diversity, the unceasing shift and change"[4] in the various religious traditions.

To this it might be replied that some who have deliberately used the term 'religions', including Rudolf Otto, have been anything but blind to the personal faith of religious people or to the diversity and shift and change in religious traditions, specifically in the Hindu and Christian traditions. Otto was among the first to challenge a narrow identification of India's 'Way of Faith' with what was presented in any one of the various Indian schools of thought. But Otto saw equal need to observe differences between one religion and another (a need which some who emphasize religious diversity today are disposed to question or discount). It was in this particular regard that Otto deliberately used the term 'religions'.

Otto, indeed, might be described as one of the heralds of the new approach. When we have regard for particular historical settings and follow the course of a particular stream of religious history, comparing what happened in one with what happened in another, as did Otto, we are more likely to observe how religious differences may signify movements of religious life and thought. For here we have, as Mahatma Gandhi observed,[5] people held together by what they have in common—a particular spiritual heritage passed on from one generation to another—however differently they may respond to this heritage. The more people value this heritage, the more earnestly they may think about it. As they seek to discover its meaning for their own generation and their own lives, the more they may experience the tensions of such thinking out. They may listen to others, being challenged by what they hear, and especially challenged, perhaps, when they hear conclusions or interpretations which they themselves may have considered and rejected. Their opposition to what is said may be the more vehement for this very reason.[6]

It might be said that here we have hidden tensions—existing only in the mind of the believer—coming into the open, coming on stage from behind the scenes. They spell out, in public, tense religious differences made manifest by passionate debates and conflicts which are deplorable in many respects, but not entirely deplorable to those who may see and accept them as signifying healthy movements of religious life and thought. Thus did a Christian divine affirm: "God hath a hand in these divisions to bring forth further light."[7]

And here it is that regard for central symbols in the religious traditions may be relevant and illuminating. For of religious symbols it may be said that they not only 'give rise to thought' but they express or 'spell out' paradoxical situations,[8] since they may be rich with a meaning which remains partly hidden and unknowable. If we had merely a reference to propositional premises leading to logical conclusions, as some have maintained or implied, then religious differences might be more easily resolved by appeal to reason. If it is accepted that all such propositional premises come second, part of the 'thinking' to which the initial symbols 'give rise', these symbols being the governing reference, then paradoxical tensions may be expected and accepted. Thus, those who hold to such a view, pursuing their study of religions with regard for paradoxical central symbols, may very well look for and expect to find tense religious differences signifying movements of religious life and thought.

It remains to be seen how such an approach may spell answers to questions which have been raised with regard to what is observed in this field.

One such question has to do with Pure Land Buddhism and Shinran's teaching in particular. Here we have a 'religion of grace' presented in terms so out of keeping with other Buddhist teachings that some have dismissed it as not Buddhist at all and others have attributed it to Buddhists meeting with Christian teachers.[9] I recall the bewilderment of some of my Burmese friends as they looked around them in Tokyo and Kyoto and listened to expositions of Buddhist faith and practice by Japanese scholars at the Ninth International Congress for the History of Religions. "This," they exclaimed, "is not Buddhism!"

I can understand their bewilderment and verdict, especially if they were referring to Shin teaching and practice. For the Buddhist teaching they had learned in Burma was of the Theravada school, emphasizing what has been called the doctrine of Self-help which was equated with the original Buddhist teaching as expounded by Gotama the Buddha. As the scholarly Burmese *bhikkhu*, U Thittila, has put it,

> The Buddha teaches men to rely upon themselves in order to achieve their own deliverance, not to look for any external savior. . . . The Buddha says, "By oneself, indeed, is evil done; by oneself is one defiled; by oneself is evil left undone; by oneself, indeed, is one purified." (*Dhammapada*)[10]

In sharp contrast to such exposition, there is the doctrine of Other-help emphasized by Shinran and others—Other-help available to all who turn to Amida Buddha, seeking to attain his Pure Land where they will be free from all the hindrances which now beset them. Shinran exclaims: ". . . In this befouled age, gone is Self-power."[11]

The contrast between these two teachings may also be stated with reference to what has been called 'faith through understanding' (understanding of the Path made known by the Buddha, and dependence on his teaching), as distinguished from 'faith through person' (response and devotion to a teacher), which a Japanese Buddhist scholar has compared with the faith of the disciples who responded to the call of Jesus, "Follow me."[12]

The same Japanese scholar allows that the "original type of Buddhist faith" is faith through understanding, but he is swift to add that examples of faith through person may also be found in earlier, original Buddhism. He quotes a passage from the *Sutta-nipata* about an old *bhikkhu* who expressed his devotion to the Buddha: "I do not stay away from him even for a moment . . . I see him in my mind and with my eye, vigilant night and day," while in the same breath he emphasizes what the Buddha taught and "faith through understanding."[13]

This may lead us to turn back the pages of Buddhist history and observe how in even the earlier Theravada tradition, with all its emphasis of Self-help, there are what may be called anticipations of the doctrine of Other-help—as the Buddha is regarded not only as the Enlightened One but also as the Compassionate One. And while some have regarded his enlightened presentation of the Path as a sufficient evidence of his compassion, others may have been the more persuaded of this compassion by some of the *Jataka-tales* of what the Buddha not only said and taught, but of what he did—of the Buddha who was the good physician of the scriptures, concerned with removing poisoned arrows from afflicted sentient beings, rather than with answering all their questions.

Thus, it may be concluded that there is some evidence of a movement of religious life and thought—throughout Buddhist history—leading up to Shinran's gospel of Other-help. A fuller account of this movement might show more clearly that throughout Buddhist history there has been tension between the Buddhist regard for Self-help and the growing regard for Other-help. Even in the more positive Shin Buddhist presentation of this Other-help, the tension continues. This, indeed, is what might be expected by those who regard the Buddha, who is both the Enlightened One and the Compassionate One, as the central symbol of the whole Buddhist tradition.

All told, we have here a new and different answer to the question regarding the origin of Shin Buddhism than might be given by those who compare statements of belief and take little or no account of the religious differences which may signify movements of religious life and thought.

Notes

1. E.g., Wilfred Cantwell Smith, *The Meaning and End of Religion*. New York, 1962, p. 144.
2. Paul Ricoeur, *The Symbolism of Evil*. Boston, 1967, pp. 347ff. Charles Davis, *Christ and the World Religions*. London, 1970.
3. Smith, op. cit.
4. Ibid., p. 144.

5. M. K. Gandhi, "Hinduism," in *Young India*, October 6, 1921.

6. Cf. Paul Tillich, *Christianity and the Encounter of the World Religions.* New York, 1963, p. 57.

7. Jeremiah Burroughes, *Irenicum*. London, 1646, pp. 242–45.

8. Mircia Eliade, "The Structure of Religious Symbolism," in the *Proceedings of the 9th International Congress for the History of Religions*. Tokyo, 1960, p. 508.

9. Eg., Arthur Lloyd, *Shinran and his Work*. Tokyo, 1910.

10. U. Thittila, "The Fundamental Principles of Theravada Buddhism," in *The Path of the Buddha* ed. Kenneth W. Morgan. New York, 1956, p. 72.

11. *Shinshu Seiten* Hawaii, 1955, p. 238.

12. Fumio Masutani, *A Comparative Study of Buddhism and Christianity.* Tokyo, 1957, p. 81.

13. *Sutta-nipata* p. 201 *S.B.E.* Vol. 10 quoted by Fumio Masutami, op. cit., pp. 81–82.

Complete Bibliography of the Writings of Professor T. R. V. Murti

Books

Ajñāna: Co-author with G. R. Malkani with R. Das (Murti's Contribution pp. 115 to 226). London: Luzac and Co., 1933.

The Central Philosophy of Buddhism. London: George Allen and Unwin Ltd. 1st Edn. 1955, 2nd Edn. 1960; Reprinted 1966, 1970, 1974.

Papers and Articles

"The Rational Basis of Advaitism," *The Philosophical Quarterly* (shortened henceforward as *P.Q.*), Indian Institute of Philosophy, Amalner, India, 1930.

"The Neutral Monism of Bertrand Russell," *Banaras Hindu University Magazine*, 1931.

"Logic and Internal Relations," *P.Q.*, 1931.

"George Santayana's Doctrine of Essence," (2 Articles), *B.H.U. Magazine*, (Two Issues), 1932.

"Are Difference and Identity Relations?," *P.Q.*, 1932.

"Nāgārjuna's Refutation of Motion and Rest," *P.Q.*, October, 1933.

"The Theory of Judgment in the Indian Systems" (1), *P.Q.*, 1933.

"*The Vibhrama Viveka of Maṇḍana Miśra*," (A Review), *P.Q.*, 1933.
"*The Six Ways of Knowing*" of Dr. D. M. Datta (Review Article), *P.Q.*, 1933.
"The Universal and the Particular," *P.Q.*, 1933.
"Knowing, Feeling and Willing as Functions of Consciousness," *P.Q.*, January 1934.
"Perception and its Object," *P.Q.*, vol. 5. 1, April, 1934.
"Types of Indian Realism" (1), *P.Q.*, 1934.
"Types of Indian Realism" (2), *P.Q.*, 1935.
"Illusion as Confusion of Subjective Functions," *P.Q.*, 1935.
"The Development of the Philosophy of Spinoza," (Review Article), *P.Q.*, vol. 11. 1, July, 1935.
"The Concept of Philosophy," *P.Q.*, April, 1936.
"The Place of Feeling in Conduct in the Vedānta," *P.Q.*, 1937.
"The Gita Conception of Philosophy and Religion," in the *Journal of the Banaras Hindu University*, July, 1938.
"The Conception of Body," *P.Q.*, vol. 15. 1, April, 1939.
"*Indian Realism* of Dr. Jadunath Sinha," (Review Article), *P.Q.*, 1940.
"The Nature and Value of Metaphysics," *P.Q.*, 1942.
"*A Study of Hindu Doctrines* of Rene Guénon," (Review Article) in the *Journal of the Banaras Hindu University*, Vol. 9, October, 1943.
"The Two Traditions in Indian Philosophy," in *The University of Ceylon Review*, vol. 10. 3, July, 1952.
"The Metaphysical Schools of Buddhism," in *The History of Philosophy, Eastern and Western*, vol. 1, London: George Allen and Unwin Ltd., 1952.
"Radhakrishnan and Buddhism," in *The Philosophy of Sarvepalli Radhakrishnan* (Library of Living Philosophers), New York: Tudor Publishing Company, 1952.
"The Philosophy of Spirit," in *The Contemporary Indian Philosophy*, 2nd Edn., (Library of Philosophy). London: George Allen and Unwin Ltd., 1952.
"The Rise of the Philosophical Schools" in the *Cultural Heritage of India*, vol. 3, Calcutta: Ramakrishna Mission, 1953.
"Buddhism and Contemporary Indian Thought," *Revue Internatinale de Philosophie*, No. 37, Fasc. 3, 1956.
"The Contribution of Buddhism to Philosophy," in the *Symposium on Buddhism's Contribution to Art, Letters and Philosophy*, 2500 Buddha Jayanti Celebrations, Govt. of India, 1956.

"Hinduism and Buddhism," in *The Traditional Cultures of South-East Asia* (pp. 210–271). Sponsored by the UNESCO, Madras: Orient and Longmans, 1958.

"The Two Definitions of Brahman in the Advaita," in the *K. C. Bhattacharyya Memorial Volume*, Indian Institute of Philosophy, Amalner, India, 1958.

"Some Thoughts on the Indian Philosophy of Language," Presidential Address, Indian Philosophical Congress, 37th Session, Chandigarh, 1963.

"The Concept of Philosophy," in *The Concept of Philosophy*, (Seminar Papers), The Centre of Advanced Study in Philosophy, B.H.U., Varanasi, 1968.

"Vedanta and Buddhism," (Seminar Papers), The Centre of Advanced Study in Philosophy, B.H.U., 1968.

"The World and the Individual in Indian Religious Thought," in *The Status of the Individual in East and West*, University of Hawaii, Honolulu, 1968, p. 199–216.

"The Concept of Freedom as Redemption," in the *Types of Redemption*, *Numen*, Suppl. 18, Amsterdam: E.J. Brill, 1970.

"Nature and Function of Reason" (Inaugural Address), A Summary in the *Anviksiki* Centre of Advanced Study in Philosophy, B.H.U., Varanasi, 1973.

"Saṃvṛti and Paramartha in Mādhyamika and Advaita Vedānta," in the *Two Truths of Buddhism and Vedānta*, Holland, Dodrecht: Reidel Publishing Company, 1973.

"Some Comments on the Philosophy of Language in the Indian Context," in the *Journal of Indian Philosophy*, No. 2, Dodrecht: Reidel Publishing Company, 1974.

"Knowledge and Truth," Presidential Address, Golden Jubilee Session of the Indian Philosophical Congress, Delhi, 1975. Pd. in *Knowledge, Culture and Value*, Part 1. Delhi: Motilal Banarasidass.